Frommer's

PORTABLE

London

by Darwin Porter & Danforth Prince

IDG Books Worldwide, Inc.
An International Data Group Company

Foster City, CA • Chicago, IL • Indianapolis, IN • New York, NY • Southlake, TX

ABOUT THE AUTHORS

Veteran travel writers **Darwin Porter** and **Danforth Prince** share their love of their favorite European city in this guide. Darwin, a bureau chief for *The Miami Herald* at the age of 21 who later worked in television advertising, wrote the first-ever guide to London for Frommer's. He's joined by Danforth, formerly of the Paris bureau of the *New York Times*. Together, they're the authors of several best-selling Frommer's guides, notably to England, France, the Carribean, Italy, and Germany.

IDG BOOKS WORLDWIDE, INC.

An International Data Group Company
919 E. Hillsdale Blvd.
Suite 400
Foster City, CA 94404

Find us online at **www.frommers.com.**

ISBN 0-02-863072-6
ISSN 1094-7663

Editor: Alice Fellows
Production Editor: Donna Wright
Photo Editor: Richard Fox
Design by Michele Laseau
Staff Cartographers: John Decamillis, Roberta Stockwell
Page Creation by Marie Kristine Parial-Leonardo, Julie Tripetti

SPECIAL SALES

For general information on IDG Books Worldwide's books in the U.S., please call our Consumer Customer Service department at 1-800-762-2974. For reseller information, including discounts, bulk sales, customized editions, and premium sales, please call our Reseller Customer Service department at 1-800-434-3422.

Manufactured in the United States of America.

5   4   3   2   1

Contents

Index   224

List of Maps

AN INVITATION TO THE READER

In researching this book, we discovered many wonderful places—hotels, restaurants, shops, and more. We're sure you'll find others. Please tell us about them, so we can share the information with your fellow travelers in upcoming editions. If you were disappointed with a recommendation, we'd love to know that, too. Please write to:

Frommer's Portable London
IDG Travel
1633 Broadway
New York, NY 10019

AN ADDITIONAL NOTE

Please be advised that travel information is subject to change at any time—and this is especially true of prices. We therefore suggest that you write or call ahead for confirmation when making your travel plans. The authors, editors, and publisher cannot be held responsible for the experiences of readers while traveling. Your safety is important to us, however, so we encourage you to stay alert and be aware of your surroundings. Keep a close eye on cameras, purses, and wallets, all favorite targets of thieves and pickpockets.

WHAT THE SYMBOLS MEAN
✪ Frommer's Favorites

Our favorite places and experiences—outstanding for quality, value, or both.

The following abbreviations are used for credit cards:

AE	American Express	EURO	Eurocard
CB	Carte Blanche	JCB	Japan Credit Bank
DC	Diners Club	MC	MasterCard
ER	enRoute	V	Visa

FIND FROMMER'S ONLINE

Arthur Frommer's Budget Travel Online (**www.frommers.com**) offers more than 6,000 pages of up-to-the-minute travel information—including the latest bargains and candid, personal articles updated daily by Arthur Frommer himself. No other Web site offers such comprehensive and timely coverage of the world of travel.

The Best of London

*A*s London prepares to welcome some 30 million visitors at the millennium, the city on the Thames is dusting off its monuments and unveiling new attractions. The Dome at Greenwich is the centerpiece of the millennium celebrations. This is the most ambitious project ever undertaken for visitors, highlighting Britain's past achievements and its surprises for the future in the way of products and developments. But with or without a Millennium Dome, London is called the Futura 2000 of cities. Its giddy energy and cutting-edge style have made it the new-wave capital of trendsetting chic. Many view the year 2000 and beyond as the point where the past of Britain will meet the future.

The British Airways London Eye in the heart of the capital is a giant Millennium Ferris Wheel to open in December 1999 on the South Bank. The world's largest observation wheel, it will give you a perspective of the British capital and a sweeping view of a skyline usually reserved for planes or birds.

But wait—there's more. The Tate Gallery of Modern Art is establishing a new national gallery. The British Museum's Great Court is being turned into a dramatic new public space. Construction is proceeding rapidly on the Millennium Bridge at Southwark, along the banks of the Thames, the first pedestrian-only bridge to be built across the Thames in the 20th century, linking St. Paul's Cathedral with the new Tate when it eventually opens.

The British capital is more eclectic and electric than it's been in years. There's almost a feeding frenzy setting out to prove that London is the most pulsating, vibrant city on the planet, even rivaling New York for sheer energy, outrageous art, trendy restaurants, and a nightlife equal to none. *Newsweek* hailed London as a "hip compromise between the nonstop newness of Los Angeles and the aspic-preserved beauty of Paris—sharpened to New York's edge." *Wine Spectator* proclaims more modestly that "The sun is shining brighter in London these days."

If you just don't give a hoot about the new London—if this sea of change worries you more than it appeals—rest assured:

Traditional London still lives, basically intact under the veneer of hip. This ancient city has survived a thousand years of invasion, from the Normans to the Blitz, so a few scenesters moving in isn't going to change anything fundamental. From high tea at Brown's to the changing of the guard at Buckingham Palace, the city abounds with the culture and charm of days gone by.

1   Frommer's Favorite London Experiences

- **Watching the Sunset at Waterloo Bridge:** Waterloo Bridge is the ideal place for watching the sun set over Westminster, to the west. From here, you can see the last rays of light bounce off the dome of St. Paul's and the city spires in the East End, too.
- **Enjoying a Traditional Afternoon Tea:** Nothing is more typically British. Try the Hotel Goring, dating from 1910. From the lounge, you'll look out on a small garden as you enjoy finger sandwiches (often watercress or cucumber), the hotel's special Ceylon-blend tea, scones and clotted cream, and the chef's famous light fruitcake offered from a trolley.
- **Cruising the Thames:** A trip up or down the river will give you an entirely different view of London. You'll see exactly how the city grew along and around the Thames and how many of its landmarks turn their faces toward the water. See "Sightseeing & Boat Tours Along the Thames" in chapter 6.
- **Spending Sunday Morning at Speakers' Corner:** At the northeastern corner of Hyde Park, near Marble Arch, a 19th-century British tradition carries on. Speakers sound off on any subject they wish, and "in-your-face" hecklers are part of the fun. Anyone can get up and speak. The only rules: You can't blaspheme, be obscene, or incite a riot. The tradition began in 1855—before the legal right to assembly was guaranteed in 1872—when a mob of 150,000 gathered to attack a proposed Sunday Trading Bill. Orators from all over Britain have been taking advantage of this spot ever since.
- **Studying the Turners at the Tate:** Upon his death in 1851, J.M.W. Turner bequeathed his personal collection of 19,000 watercolors and some 300 paintings to the people of Britain. He wanted his finished works, some 100 paintings, displayed under one roof. Today at the Tate, you see not only Turner, but also glimpses of the Thames through the museum's windows. How appropriate—the artist lived and died on its banks in Chelsea and painted the river in its many changing moods.

- **Strolling Through Covent Garden:** George Bernard Shaw got his inspiration for *Pygmalion* here, where the character Eliza Doolittle sold violets to wealthy opera-goers and became a household name around the world. The old fruit and vegetable market, with its Cockney peddlers, is long gone. What's left today is just as interesting: Covent Garden is one of its hippest shopping districts. You can wander about and discover colorful street stalls, boutiques, and shops selling one-of-a-kind merchandise, and all the while enjoy the city's best sidewalk entertainment. There's an antiques market in the piazza on Monday and a crafts market Tuesday through Saturday. When you're parched, plenty of pubs in the area will quench your thirst.

- **Treasure-Hunting for Antiques:** Some 2,000 antiquarians live within the city limits of London. Check with the tourist office to see if a major antiques fair is on at the time of your visit; the Dorchester Fair and Grosvenor House Fair take place in June. If a fair isn't being held while you're in London, head for one of the following antiques centers; they sell everything from plain old junk (mugs with Prince Philip's face on them) to rare bric-a-brac. The best ones are **Gray's and Gray's** in the Mews, 58 Davies St. (Tube: Bond Street), and **Alfie's Antique Market,** 13–25 Church St. (Tube: Edgware Road).

- **Shopping Harrods:** Regardless of how many times you visit London, it's hard to resist a visit to this vast Knightsbridge emporium. Spread across 15 acres, Harrods proclaims as its motto *Omnia Omnibus Ubique* or "everything for everyone, everywhere." They mean it, too: Someone didn't believe the claim, and in 1975 called Harrods at midnight and ordered that a baby elephant be delivered to the home of the governor of California and his first lady—Mr. and Mrs. Ronald Reagan in Sacramento. The animal arrived safely, albeit a bit bewildered. (Nancy even sent a "thank you" note.) The food halls are our favorite section, with some 500 different cheeses and some 163 brands of whiskey among zillions of other goodies. It's estimated that at Christmas, Harrods sells 100 tons of Christmas puddings. You can even arrange your funeral at the store.

- **Rowing on the Serpentine:** When the weather's right, we always like to head to this 41-acre artificial lake in Hyde Park. In 1730, a stream was dammed to create the artificial lake. Its name derives from its winding, snakelike shape. At the Boathouse, you can rent (they call it "hire") a boat by the hour. With the right companion, it's one of the most idyllic ways to spend a sunny London afternoon. Renoir must have agreed; he depicted the custom on canvas.

- **Making a Brass Rubbing:** Re-create all those costumed ladies and knights in armor from England's age of chivalry. One good place to make your very own brass rubbing is the crypt of St. Martin-in-the-Fields in Trafalgar Square; the staff there will be happy to show you how.

- **Spending a Night at West End Theater:** London is the theatrical capital of the world. The live stage offers a unique combination of variety, accessibility, and economy—and perhaps a look at next year's Broadway hit.

- **Crawling the London Pubs:** Americans bar hop; Londoners do a pub crawl—there are some 5,000 pubs within the city limits. Traditional ones remain, especially in central London, making it worthwhile to go on a pub crawl. While making the rounds, you can partake of that peculiarly British fare known as "pub grub," which might include everything from a ploughman's lunch (a hunk of bread, cheese, and a pickle) to a plate of shepherd's pie. However, if you go to the right places, some of that pub grub today has been turned into gourmet fare, better than in many restaurants.

  Here's our favorite crawl, which gives you a chance to see several of London's districts: Begin at **Dickens Inn** by the tower on St. Katharine's Way (E1), and then go on to **Ye Olde Cheshire Cheese,** Wine Office Court, 145 Fleet St. (EC4), before making your way to **Cittie of Yorke** at 22–23 High Holborn (WC1). Then it's off to **Old Coffee House** at 49 Beak St. (W1) in Soho, before descending on **Red Lion,** 2 Duke of York St. (SW1). If you're still standing, rush to **Shepherd's Tavern,** 50 Hertford St. (W1) in Mayfair, before the publican rings the bell for "final call."

2　Best Hotel Bets

- **Best Historic Hotel:** Founded by the former manservant to Lord Byron, stylish **Brown's Hotel,** 29–34 Albemarle St., W1 (☎ 0207/493-6020), dates back to Victorian times. It's one of London's most genteel hotels, from its legendary afternoon tea to its centenary *Times* clock in the reception area.

- **Best for Business Travelers:** For wheeling and dealing, head to the **Langham Hilton,** 1 Portland Place, W1 (☎ 0207/636-1000), Hilton's flagship hotel in Europe. At times it seems that all the world's business is conducted from this nerve center. It can sound like the Tower of Babel, but it's humming along just fine.

- **Best for a Romantic Getaway: The Gore,** 189 Queen's Gate, SW7 (☎ **800/637-7200**), has been sheltering lovers both on and off the record since 1892. The place is eccentric and a lot of fun, and the staff doesn't bother you unless you need something. For nostalgia-accented romance, request the Venus Room—its bed was once owned by Judy Garland.

- **Best Trendy Hotel: The Lanesborough,** 1 Lanesborough Place, Hyde Park Corner, SW1 (☎ **800/999-1828**), is a sumptuous temple of luxury—$1.7 million was spent on each guest room. Not surprisingly, it attracts glitterati galore.

- **Best Lobby for Pretending That You're Rich: The Dorchester,** 53 Park Lane, W1 (☎ **800/727-9820**), has a long Promenade with London's largest floral display and rows of faux-marble columns with ornate gilt capitals. Even if you can't afford to stay at this citadel of luxury, come by for the traditional afternoon tea.

- **Best Newcomer of the Year:** You don't normally think of Smithfield as a hotel district of London, but **The Rookery**, 12 Peter's Lane, Cowcross St., EC1 (☎ **0207/336-0931**), is luring some of London's most discerning visitors. It's quirky and fun, and loaded with atmosphere in its individually decorated bedrooms of great charm and comfort. Even the bathrooms still retain their Victorian cast-iron fittings.

- **Best for Thoroughly British Ambience:** In a gaslit courtyard in back of St. James's Palace, **Dukes Hotel,** 35 St. James's Place, SW1 (☎ **800/381-4702**), has a nearly unsurpassed dignity. From the bread-and-butter pudding served in the clubby dining room to the impeccable service, it's the epitome of what Britain used to be.

- **Best Re-creation of an English Country House:** Tim and Kit Kemp are hoteliers of charm, taste, and sophistication. They were in top form when they combined two Georgian town houses into the **Dorset Square Hotel,** 39–40 Dorset Sq., NW1 (☎ **0207/723-7874**). They've made an English country house right in the heart of the city: Gilt-framed paintings, antiques, tapestry cushions, and mahogany bathrooms make you feel warm, cozy, and elegantly refined.

- **Best Service: 22 Jermyn Street,** SW1 (☎ **800/682-7808**), does more for its guests than any other hotel in London. The owner, a technology buff, even offers Internet services to his guests. He also diligently informs you of the hottest and newest restaurants, along with old favorites, the best shopping buys, and even what's hot in theater. The staff doesn't deny any reasonable request—they even grant some unreasonable ones.

- **Best Location:** Creaky, quirky **Fielding Hotel,** 4 Broad Court, Bow Street, WC2 (☎ **0207/836-8305**), is hardly London's finest hotel, but oh, the location! It's in an alleyway in the dead center of Covent Garden. You're in the heart of the real excitement of London, almost opposite the Royal Opera House, and with pubs, shops, markets, and restaurants, even street entertainment, just outside your door. Stay here, and London is yours.

- **Best Health Club & Pool: The Savoy,** The Strand, WC2 (☎ **800/263-SAVOY**), has a unique health club and large swimming pool, built atop the historic Savoy Theatre, overlooking the heart of London. For guests looking to tone up or wind down, it's the best gym in Central London; the views make it extra special. There is also a massage room, plus state-of-the-heart health and beauty treatments.

- **Best Moderately Priced Hotel:** Housed in three historic homes on Soho Square, **Hazlitt's 1718**, 6 Frith St., W1 (☎ **0207/434-1771**), was a fashionable address two centuries ago—and so it is again today. One of London's best small hotels, it's a favorite with artists, actors, media people, and models. Many bedrooms have four-posters.

- **Best B&B: Vicarage Private Hotel,** 10 Vicarage Gate, W8 (☎ **0207/229-4030**), fits the bill if you want old-fashioned English charm and hospitality—all at affordable prices. Close to Kensington High Street, the family-run B&B charges only a modest price for a cozy nest in Kensington—that is if you can forego a private bath.

- **Best Value:** Savvy hotel shoppers seek out **Aston's Budget Studios,** 39 Rosary Gardens, SW7 (☎ **0207/590-6000**). The accommodations here range widely in price, and well they should: They vary from basic lodgings to designer suites.

3 Best Restaurant Bets

- **Best for Romance: Mirabelle**, 56 Cruzon St., W1 (☎ **0207/499-4636**), is the place to go. The waitstaff is very discreet. When Jeremy Irons wanted to have a private moment alone with the late Princess Di, and with all of London as their choice, he chose Mirabelle. London's most outstanding chef, Marco Pierre White, now runs this elegant retreat, and when you can take your eyes off your partner you can concentrate on his wildly creative dishes.

- **Best Place for a Business Lunch:** Instead of some noisy City tavern serving up bangers and mash, impress your clients by taking them to **Poons in the City,** 2 Minster Pavement, Minster Court, Mincing Lane, EC3 (☎ **0207/626-0126**). This fabled Chinese restaurant is elegantly outfitted with furniture and accessories from China, and the menu is wide ranging enough to please most clients. After a taste of the finely chopped wind-dried meats or the crispy aromatic duck, it'll be a snap to seal the deal.

- **Best Spot for a Celebration:** There's no spot in all of London that's more fun than **Quaglino's,** 16 Bury St., SW1 (☎ **0207/930-6767**). On some nights, as many as 800 diners show up at Sir Terence Conran's gargantuan Mayfair eatery to dine, laugh, and gossip. It's the best place in London to celebrate almost any occasion—and the food's good, too. There's live jazz on Friday and Saturday nights.

- **Best Newcomer of the Year:** One of London's most talked about new restaurants, **Rhodes in the Square**, Dolphin Square, Chichester St., SW1 (☎ **0207/798-6767**), is the domain of celebrated chef Gary Rhodes. In a discreet residential district, this chef—a media darling—continues to win new friends and please old palates with his take on giving a new twist to staid British cuisine. He's always innovative, always filled with good surprises.

- **Best Value:** Cheap and cheerful **Simply Nico,** 48A Rochester Row, SW1 (☎ **0207/630-8061**), grand Chef Nico Ladenis' "moment of whimsy," offers some of the best value fixed-price meals in London. This isn't the fabled haute cuisine Nico serves on Park Lane, but quality ingredients are beautifully prepared into some of the best French food in central London. Breast of guinea fowl with lentils and other specialties will keep you coming back for more.

- **Best Traditional British Cuisine:** No restaurant, not even Simpson's-in-the-Strand, is quite as British as **Wiltons,** 55 Jermyn St., SW1 (☎ **0207/629-9955**). As other British restaurants loosen up, Wiltons remains fiercely entrenched in tradition. It serves the same menu it did to the 18th-century nobs of St. James's. We're talking grilled plaice, steaks, chops, kidneys, whitebait (a Victorian favorite), and game dishes such as roast widgeon (a wild fish-eating river duck).

- **Best Pub Grub:** Tom Conran, son of Sir Terence Conran, is attracting all of London to **The Cow,** 89 Westbourne Park Rd., W2 (☎ **0207/221-0021**) even people who haven't been in a pub for years. Leading the revolution in upgrading pub cuisine, The Cow somehow manages to secure the biggest and juiciest oysters in town. Proof that the London pub scene has changed radically: The hip young staff even serves finger bowls to its even hipper clientele.

- **Best Indian Cuisine:** London's finest Indian food is served at **Café Spice Namaste,** in a landmark Victorian hall near Tower Bridge, 16 Prescot St., E1 (☎ **0207/488-9242**). You'll be tantalized with a bewildering array of spicy southern and northern Indian dishes. What we especially like about this place is its strong Portuguese influence; the chef, Cyrus Todiwala, is a former resident of Goa (a Portuguese territory absorbed by India long ago), where he learned many of his culinary secrets.

- **Best Desserts: Nico Central,** 35 Great Portland St., W1 (☎ **0207/436-8846**), is the place to satisfy your sweet tooth. The "puddings" menu is extremely limited, but is it ever choice: The caramelized lemon tart is the best we've ever had in London. The nougat ice cream with a strongly flavored blackberry coulis was worth a return visit, as was the walnut and Armagnac parfait. Other unforgettable desserts accompanying memorable meals here have included a velvety smooth warm chocolate mousse with pear sorbet, and a poached pear sablé made even more delectable with a caramel ginger sauce.

- **Best People-Watching:** In Karl Marx's former apartment house, **Quo Vadis,** 26–29 Dean St., W1 (☎ **0207/437-9585**), is a joint venture of London's *enfant terrible* chef, Marco Pierre White, and Damien Hirst, the artist who wowed the London art world with his cow carcasses in formaldehyde. With a pedigree like this, it's no wonder this is the hottest see-and-be-seen circuit in town. If Goldie Hawn should come to London, this is where you'd find her. And the food's not bad, either.

- **Best Afternoon Tea:** While everyone else is donning their fancy hats and heading for the Ritz (where, chances are, they won't be able to get a table), you should retreat to the **Palm Court at the Waldorf Meridien,** Aldwych, WC2 (☎ **0207/836-2400**), in the grand 1908 Waldorf Hotel. The Sunday tea dances here are legendary: Originating with the famous "Tango Teas" of the 1920s and 1930s, they've been going strong ever since, interrupted only by war and a few other inconveniences.

- **Best Pre-Theater Menu:** Opposite the Ambassador Theatre, **The Ivy,** 1–5 West St., WC2 (☎ 0207/836-4751), is popular for both pre- and *après*-theater dining. The brasserie-style food reflects both traditional English and modern continental influences. You can try longtime favorites such as potted shrimp or tripe and onions, or more imaginative dishes such as butternut pumpkin salad or a wild mushroom risotto.

- **Best For Kids:** After you and the kids have visited the Tower of London, take them to **Dickens Inn by the Tower,** St. Katharine's Way, E1 (☎ 0207/488-2208), an old spice warehouse turned three-floor restaurant with sweeping views of the Thames and Tower Bridge. Dickens Inn serves tasty well-stuffed sandwiches, platters of lasagna, and steaming bowls of chili. One whole floor is devoted to serving pizza.

- **Best Fish 'n' Chips:** The best place to introduce yourself to this trad British dish is **North Sea Fish Restaurant,** 7–8 Leigh St., WC1 (☎ 0207/387-5892). Unlike the overcooked frozen fish served at those joints around Leicester Square, North Sea's fresh cod comes perfectly prepared: crisp batter on the outside, moist and tender fish inside. The haddock is equally delectable—and what a big platter it is.

2

Planning a Trip to London

*T*his chapter tackles the hows of your trip to London—all those things needed to get your trip together and take it on the road, whether you're a frequent traveler or a first-timer.

1 Visitor Information

Before you go, you can get information from the following **British Tourist Authority** offices: 551 Fifth Ave., Suite 701, New York, NY 10176-0799 (☎ **800/462-2748** or 212/986-2200); 111 Avenue Rd., Suite 450, Toronto M5R 3J8, Canada (☎ **888/VISIT-UK** or 905/405-1840); Level 16, Gateway, 1 Macquarie Place, Sydney, NSW 2000, Australia (☎ **02/9377-4400**); and Suite 305, Dilworth Bldg., at Customs and Queen Streets, Auckland 1, New Zealand (☎ **09/303-1446**). The British Tourist Authority maintains a Web page at **www.visitbritain.com**.

For a full information pack on London, write to the **London Tourist Board,** Glenn House, Stag Place, London SN1E 5LT (☎ **020/7932-2000**). You can also call the recorded-message service, **Visitorcall** (☎ **01839/123456**), 24 hours a day. This number cannot be dialed outside Britain. Various topics are listed; calls cost 50p (85¢) per minute.

Time Out, the most up-to-date source for what's happening in London, has joined the Net, so you can also log on for current information; you'll find the weekly magazine at **www.timeout.co.uk**. You can also pick up a copy at any international newsstand.

London Guide (www.cs.ucl.ac.uk/misc/uk/london.html) is run by London's University College and has practical information on cheap dining and accommodations in the Bloomsbury area close to the university. There are also travelogues and tips for theatergoers.

To book accommodations by credit card (MasterCard or Visa), call the **London Tourist Board Booking Office** at ☎ **020/732-2020,** or fax them at 0171/932-2021. They're available to make bookings Monday to Friday from 9:30am to 5:30pm (London time). There is a £5 ($8.25) fee for booking.

2   Entry Requirements & Customs

DOCUMENTS   Citizens of the United States, Canada, Australia, New Zealand, and South Africa require a passport to enter the United Kingdom, but no visa. Irish citizens and other members of European Union countries need only an identity card. The maximum allowable stay for visitors is 6 months. Some Customs officials will request proof that you have the means to eventually leave the country (usually a round-trip ticket) and visible means of support while you're in Britain. If you're planning to fly on from the United Kingdom to a country that requires a visa, it's wise to secure the necessary visa before your arrival in Britain.

Your valid driver's license and at least one year's driving experience is required to drive personal or rented cars.

Residents of the **United States** applying for a first-time passport, you need to go in person to one of 13 passport offices throughout the U.S., a major post office (call the number below to find out which ones accept applications), or a federal, state, or probate court. You must bring along a certified birth certificate as proof of citizenship, and two identical passport-sized photos (2 in. by 2 in.). For people over 15, a passport is valid for 10 years and costs $60 ($45 plus a $15 handling fee); for those 15 and under, it's valid for 5 years and costs $40. If you have a valid passport issued within the past 12 years, you can renew it by mail and bypass the $15 handling fee. Processing normally takes 3 weeks. For general information, call the **National Passport Agency** (☎ 202/647-0518). To find your regional passport office, call the **National Passport Information Center** (☎ 900/225-5674; http://travel.state.gov).

Residents of **Canada** can pick up a passport application at one of 28 regional passport offices or most travel agencies. The passport is valid for 5 years and costs $60. Children under 16 may be included on a parent's passport, but need their own to travel unaccompanied by the parent. Applications must be accompanied by proof of Canadian citizenship and two identical passport-sized photographs. For information, contact the central **Passport Office, Department of Foreign Affairs and International Trade,** Ottawa K1A 0G3 (☎ 800/567-6868; www.dfait-maeci.gc.ca/passport). Processing takes 5 to 10 days if you apply in person, or about 3 weeks by mail.

Residents of **Australia** can apply at their local post office or passport office or search the government Web site at **www.dfat.gov.au/passports/**. Passports for adults are A$126 and for those under 18

No Pets, Please

Sorry, but you can't bring your pet to England. Six months' quarantine is required before a pet is allowed into the country. An illegally imported animal is liable to be destroyed.

A\$63. Residents of **New Zealand** can pick up a passport application at any travel agency or Link Centre. For more info, contact the **Passport Office,** P.O. Box 805, Wellington (☎ **0800/225-050**). Passports for adults are NZ\$80 and for those under 16 NZ\$40.

WHAT YOU CAN BRING INTO THE U.K. Visitors (17 and older) coming to England from a non-European Union (EU) country or bringing in goods bought tax-free within the EU may bring in 200 cigarettes (or 50 cigars or 250 grams of loose tobacco), 2 liters of still table wine, 1 liter of liquor (over 22% alcohol content) or 2 liters of liquor (under 22%), and 2 fluid ounces of perfume. Visitors entering England from an EU country may bring in goods bought tax-paid in the EU as follows: 800 cigarettes, 200 cigars, and 1 kilogram of loose tobacco; 90 liters of wine, 10 liters of alcohol (over 22%), and 110 liters of beer; plus unlimited amounts of perfume.

WHAT YOU CAN BRING HOME Returning **U.S. citizens** who have been away for 48 hours or more may bring back, once every 30 days, \$400 worth of merchandise duty free. You'll be charged a flat rate of 10% duty on the next \$1,000 worth of purchases. Be sure to have your receipts handy. On gifts, the duty-free limit is \$100. You cannot bring fresh foodstuffs into the United States. For more information, contact the **U.S. Customs Service,** 1301 Constitution Ave. (P.O. Box 7407), Washington, D.C. 20044 (☎ **202/927-6724**) and request the free pamphlet *Know Before You Go.* It's also available on the Web at www.customs.ustreas.gov/travel/kbygo.htm.

For a summary of **Canadian** rules, write for the booklet *I Declare,* issued by **Revenue Canada,** 2265 St. Laurent Blvd., Ottawa K1G 4KE (☎ **613/993-0534**). Canadian citizens can use their Can\$500 exemption once a year and after an absence of 7 days, and can bring back duty free 200 cigarettes, 2.2 pounds of tobacco, 40 imperial ounces of liquor, and 50 cigars. In addition, you may mail gifts to Canada at the rate of Can\$60 a day (write on the package "Unsolicited gift, under \$60 value"). All valuables you have with you should be declared on the Y-38 form before departure from Canada.

The duty-free allowance in **Australia** is A$400 or, for those under 18, A$200. Personal property mailed back from England should be marked "Australian goods returned" to avoid payment of duty. Australian citizens can bring in 250 cigarettes or 250 grams of loose tobacco, and 1.125 liters of alcohol. If you're returning with valuable goods you already own, you should file form B263. A helpful brochure, available from Australian consulates or Customs offices, is *Know Before You Go.* For more information, contact **Australian Customs Services,** GPO Box 8, Sydney, NSW 2001 (☎ **02/9213-2000**).

The duty-free allowance for **New Zealand** is NZ$700. Citizens over 17 can bring in 200 cigarettes, or 50 cigars, or 250 grams of tobacco, plus 4.5 liters of wine and beer, or 1.125 liters of liquor. Fill out a certificate of export, listing the valuables you are taking with you. Most questions are answered in a free pamphlet available at New Zealand consulates and Customs offices: *New Zealand Customs Guide for Travellers*, Notice no. 4. For more information, contact **New Zealand Customs,** 50 Anzac Ave., P.O. Box 29, Auckland (☎ **09/359-6655**).

3 Money

CURRENCY

POUNDS & PENCE Britain's decimal monetary system is based on the pound sterling (£), which is made up of 100 pence (written as "p"). There are now £1 coins (called "quid" by Britons), plus coins of 50p, 20p, 10p, 5p, 2p, and 1p. Even though the 0.5p coin has been officially discontinued, it will be around for a while. Banknotes come in denominations of £5, £10, £20, and £50.

As a general guideline, the price conversions in this book have been computed at the rate of £1 = $1.65 (U.S.). Bear in mind, however, that exchange rates fluctuate daily.

GETTING CASH & EXCHANGING MONEY

EXCHANGING MONEY It's a good idea to exchange enough money before you go to get from the airport to your hotel.

London banks generally offer the best rates of exchange. Your hotel will usually offer the worst rate. You're likely to obtain a better rate for traveler's checks than for cash. Banks are usually open Monday to Friday from 9:30am to 3:30pm. Many of the "high street" branches are now open until 5pm; a handful of central London branches are open until noon on Saturday, including **Barclays,** 208 Kensington High St., W8 (☎ **020/7441-3200**).

Money exchange is now also available at competitive rates at major London post offices, with a 1% service charge.

American Express is at 6 Haymarket, SW1 (☎ **800/221-7282** or 0171/930-4411) and other locations throughout the city. They charge no commission when cashing traveler's checks. However, a flat rate of £2 ($3.30) is charged when exchanging the dollar to the pound. Most other agencies tend to charge a percentage rate commission (usually 2%) with a £2 to £3 ($3.30 to $4.95) minimum charge. Other reputable firms are **Thomas Cook,** 45 Berkeley St., W1A 1EB (☎ **800/223-7373** or 0171/408-4218), branches of which can also be found at Victoria Station, Marble Arch, and other city locations; and, for 24-hour foreign exchange, **Chequepoint,** at 548 Oxford St., W1N 9HJ (☎ **020/7723-1005**) and other locations throughout London (hours will vary). Try not to change money at your hotel; the rates they offer tend to be horrendous.

ATMs   Check with your bank to find out if you need a new personal ID number (PIN) to use in automatic teller machines (ATMs) overseas. ATM networks are **Cirrus** (☎ **800/424-7787;** www. mastercard.com/atm/) and **Plus** (☎ **800/843-7587;** www.visa.com/ atms); check the back of your ATM card to see which network your bank belongs to. Note that many banks impose a fee every time a card is used at an ATM from a different city or bank.

CREDIT CARDS   Credit cards are a safe way to carry money and provide a convenient record of all your expenses. You can also withdraw cash advances from your credit cards at any bank (though you'll start paying hefty interest the moment you receive the cash, and you won't receive frequent-flyer miles on an airline credit card). At most banks you can get a cash advance at the ATM with your PIN number. If you don't know your PIN number, call the phone number on the back of your credit card and ask the bank to send it to you. It usually takes 5 to 7 business days, though some banks will provide the number over the phone if you pass a security clearance.

TRAVELER'S CHECKS   Traveler's checks are as reliable as currency, unlike personal checks, and can be replaced if lost or stolen. Be sure to keep a record of your traveler's checks' serial numbers, separate from the checks themselves, so that you're assured of a refund in an emergency.

You can get traveler's checks at almost any bank. **American Express** offers denominations of $10, $20, $50, $100, $500, and $1,000. You'll pay a service charge ranging from 1 to 4%. You can also get American Express traveler's checks over the phone by calling ☎ **800/221-7282;** by using this number, Amex gold and platinum cardholders are exempt from the 1% fee. AAA members can obtain checks without a fee at most AAA offices.

Visa offers traveler's checks at Citibank locations nationwide, as well as several other banks. The service charge ranges between 1.5 and 2%; checks come in denominations of $20, $50, $100, $500, and $1,000. **MasterCard** also offers traveler's checks. Call ☎ **800/223-9920** for a location near you.

THEFT   Almost every credit card company has a toll-free number that you can call if your wallet or purse is stolen. They may be able to wire you a cash advance off your credit card immediately, and in many places, can deliver an emergency credit card in a day or two. The toll-free directory will provide the number. Visa's emergency number is ☎ **800/336-8472** in the U.S., or ☎ **410/581-9994** outside the U.S. American Express cardholders and traveler's check holders should call ☎ **800/221-7282** for all money emergencies. MasterCard holders should call ☎ **800/307-7309** in the U.S. or call **collect** ☎ **525/326-2566** outside the U.S. Odds are that if your wallet is gone, the police won't be able to recover it. However, your credit card company or insurer may require a police report number.

4 When to Go

CLIMATE

A typical London-area weather forecast for a summer day predicts "scattered clouds with sunny periods and showers, possibly heavy at times." Summer temperatures seldom rise above 78°F, nor do they drop below 35°F in winter. London, being in one of the mildest parts of the country, can be very pleasant in the spring and fall. Yes, it rains, but you'll rarely get a true downpour. It's heaviest in November, when it reaches $2^1/_2$ inches on average.

The British consider chilliness wholesome and usually try to keep room temperatures about 10°F below the American comfort level.

CURRENT WEATHER CONDITIONS   In the United States, you can dial ☎ **1/900-WEATHER,** and then press the first four letters of the desired foreign city—in this case, LOND for London—for the time of day in that city, plus current temperatures, weather conditions, and forecasts. The cost is 95¢ per minute. Another good way to check conditions before you go is on the Weather Channel's Web site: **www.weather.com**.

HOLIDAYS

In England, public holidays include New Year's Day, Good Friday, Easter Monday, May Day (first Monday in May), spring and summer bank holidays (last Monday in May and August, respectively), Christmas Day, and Boxing Day (December 26).

LONDON CALENDAR OF EVENTS

January

- **London Parade,** from Parliament Square to Berkeley Square in Mayfair. Bands, floats, and carriages. January 1. Procession starts around 2:45pm.
- **January sales.** Most shops offer good reductions. Many sales now start as early as late December to perk up the post-Christmas slump. The most voracious shoppers camp overnight outside Harrods to get in first.
- **Charles I Commemoration.** Anniversary of the execution of King Charles I "in the name of freedom and democracy." Hundreds of cavaliers march through central London in 17th-century dress, and prayers are said at the Banqueting House in Whitehall. Free. Last Sunday in January.

February

- **Chinese New Year.** The famous Lion Dancers in Soho. Free. Either in late January or early February (based on the lunar calendar).
- **Great Spitalfields Pancake Race.** Teams of four run in relays, tossing their pancakes. At noon on Shrove Tuesday (last day before Lent) at Old Spitalfields Market, Brushfield Street, E1. To join in, call ☎ **020/7375-0441.**

March

- **St. David's Day.** A member of the Royal Family usually presents the Welsh Guards with the principality's national emblem, a leek; call ☎ **020/7414-3291** for location and further information. March 1 (or nearest Sunday).
- **Chelsea Antiques Fair,** a twice-yearly gathering of England's best dealers, held at Old Town Hall, King's Road, SW3 (☎ **01444/482-514**). Mid-March (and again in mid-September).

April

- **Harness Horse Parade,** a morning parade of heavy working horses in superb gleaming brass harnesses and plumes, at Battersea Park. Call ☎ **01733/234-451.** April 5.

- **The Queen's Birthday** is celebrated with 21-gun salutes in Hyde Park and on Tower Hill at noon by troops in parade dress. April 21.

May

- **Shakespeare Under the Stars.** If you want to see *Macbeth, Hamlet,* or *Romeo and Juliet* (or any other Shakespeare play), our advice is to bring a blanket and a bottle of wine to watch the Bard's works performed at the Open Air Theatre, Inner Circle, Regent's Park, NW1. Take the Tube to Regent's Park or Baker Street. Previews begin in late May and last throughout the summer. Performances are Monday to Saturday at 8pm, Wednesday, Thursday, and Saturday also at 2:30pm. Call ☎ 020/7935-5756 for more information.
- **May Fayre and Puppet Festival,** Covent Garden. Procession at 10am, service at St. Paul's at 11:30am, then Punch and Judy shows until 6pm at the site where Pepys watched England's first show in 1662; call ☎ 020/7375-0441. Second Sunday in May.
- **The Royal Windsor Horse Show** is held at Home Park, Windsor Castle (☎ 01753-860633); you might even spot a royal. Mid-May.
- **Chelsea Flower Show,** Chelsea Royal Hospital. The best of British gardening, with displays of plants and flowers of all seasons. Tickets are available through Ticketmaster (☎ 020/7344-4343). The show runs from 8am to 8pm on May 20; tickets are £25 ($40). On May 28, the show runs from 8am to 5:30pm, and tickets are £24 ($39.60). Call ☎ 020/7630-7422 for more information. Ticket sales must be made in advance.

June

- **Kenwood Lakeside Concerts,** ☎ 020/8348-1286. Annual concerts on the north side of Hampstead Heath. Fireworks displays and laser shows enliven the premier musical performances staged here. Music drifts to the fans from a performance shell across the lake every Saturday in summer from early July to early September.
- **Royal Academy's Summer Exhibition.** This institution, founded in 1768 with Sir Joshua Reynolds as president and Thomas Gainsborough as a member, has sponsored summer exhibitions of living painters for some 2 centuries. Visitors can both browse and make art purchases, many of them quite reasonable in price. Exhibitions are presented daily at Burlington House, Piccadilly Circus, W1. Call ☎ 020/7439-7438 for details. From early June to mid-August.

- **Royal Ascot Week.** Ascot Racecourse is open year-round for guided tours, events, exhibitions, and conferences. There are 24 race days throughout the year with the feature race meetings being the Royal Meeting in June, Diamond Day in late July, and the Festival at Ascot in late September. For further information, contact **Ascot Racecourse,** Ascot, Berkshire SL5 7JN (☎ **01344/622211**).

- ✪ **Trooping the Colour,** Horse Guards Parade, Whitehall. The official birthday of the queen. Seated in a carriage (no longer on horseback), the royal monarch inspects her regiments and takes their salute as they parade their colors before her. A quintessential British event religiously watched by the populace on TV. Held on a designated day in June (not the queen's actual birthday). Tickets for the parade and two reviews, held on preceding Saturdays, are allocated by ballot. Those interested in attending must write to apply for tickets between January 1 and the end of February, enclosing a stamped, self-addressed envelope, or International Reply Coupon—exact dates and ticket prices will be supplied later. The ballot is held in mid-March, and successful applicants *only* are informed in April. For details, write to **HQ Household Division,** Horse Guards, Whitehall, London SW1X 6AA, enclosing a self-addressed envelope with an International Reply Coupon.

- ✪ **Lawn Tennis Championships,** Wimbledon, Southwest London. Ever since the players in flannels and bonnets took to the grass courts at Wimbledon in 1877, this tournament has drawn a socially prominent crowd. Although the courts are now crowded with all kinds of tennis fans, there's still an excited hush at Centre Court and a certain thrill in being here. Late June to early July. Tickets for Centre and Number One courts are handed out through a lottery; write to **All England Lawn Tennis Club,** P.O. Box 98, Church Road, Wimbledon, London SW19 5AE (☎ **020/8946-2244**), between August and December. A certain number of tickets are set aside for visitors from abroad, so you may be able to purchase some in spring for this year's games; call to inquire. Outside court tickets are available daily, but be prepared to wait in line.

- **City of London Festival,** annual arts festival throughout the city. Call ☎ **020/7377-0540** for information about the various programs and venues. Held in June and July.

July

- **City of London Festival.** Classical concerts at various venues throughout the City, including St. Paul's Cathedral; for details, call ☎ **020/7377-0540.** Early July.
- **Hampton Court Palace Flower Show,** East Molesey, Surrey. This widely acclaimed 5-day international is eclipsing its sister show in Chelsea; here, you can actually purchase the exhibits. Call ☎ **020/7834-4333** for exact dates and details. Early July.
- **Royal Tournament,** Earl's Court Exhibition Centre, Warwick Road. British armed forces put on dazzling displays of athletic and military skills, which have been called "military pomp, show biz, and outright jingoism." For information and details about performance times and tickets, call ☎ **020/7244-0244.** Ticket prices range from £6 to £26 ($9.90 to $42.90). July 21 to August 2.
- **The Proms.** "The Proms"—the annual Henry Wood Promenade Concerts at Royal Albert Hall—attract music aficionados from around the world. Staged almost daily (except for a few Sundays), these traditional concerts were launched in 1895 and are the principal summer venue for the BBC Symphony Orchestra. Cheering, clapping, Union Jacks on parade, banners, and balloons create summer fun. Mid-July to mid-September.

August

- **Notting Hill Carnival,** Notting Hill. One of the largest street festivals in Europe, attracting more than a half-million people annually. Live reggae and soul music combine with great Caribbean food. Free. Two days in late August (usually the last Sunday and Monday). Call ☎ **020/8964-0544** for information.

September

- **Chelsea Antiques Fair,** Chelsea Old Town Hall, King's Road, SW3. Mid-September (see March, above, for details).
- **Raising of the Thames Barrier,** Unity Way, SE18. Once a year, a full test is done on this miracle of modern engineering; all 10 of the massive steel gates are raised against the high tide. Call ☎ **020/8854-1373** for exact date and time.

October

- ✪ **Opening of Parliament,** House of Lords, Westminster. Ever since the 17th century, when the English cut off the head of Charles I, the British monarch has had no right to enter the House of Commons. Instead, the monarch opens Parliament in the House of Lords, reading an official speech that is written by the government of the day. The monarch rides from Buckingham Palace to Westminster in a royal coach accompanied by the Yeoman of the Guard and the Household Cavalry. The Strangers' Gallery is open to spectators on a first-come, first-served basis. First Monday in October.

- **Judges Service,** Westminster Abbey. The judiciary attends a service in Westminster Abbey to mark the opening of the law term. Afterward, in full regalia—wigs and all—they form a procession and walk to the House of Lords for their "Annual Breakfast." You'll have a great view of the procession from behind the Abbey. First Monday in October.

- **Quit Rents Ceremony,** Royal Courts of Justice, WC2. An official receives token rents on behalf of the queen; the ceremony includes splitting sticks and counting horseshoes. Call ☎ **020/ 7936-6131** for free tickets. Late October.

November

- **Guy Fawkes Night.** Commemorating the anniversary of the Gunpowder Plot, an attempt to blow up King James I and his Parliament. Huge organized bonfires are lit throughout the city, and Guy Fawkes, the plot's most famous conspirator, is burned in effigy. Free. Check *Time Out* for locations. Early November.

- ✪ **Lord Mayor's Procession and Show,** from the Guildhall to the Royal Courts of Justice, in the City of London. This impressive annual event marks the inauguration of the new lord mayor of the City of London. The queen must ask permission to enter the City's square mile—a right that has been jealously guarded by London merchants from the 17th century to this very day. You can watch the procession from the street; the banquet is by invitation only. Second week in November.

December

- **Caroling Under the Norwegian Christmas Tree.** There's caroling most evenings beneath the tree in Trafalgar Square. Early December.

5   Tips for Travelers with Special Needs

FOR TRAVELERS WITH DISABILITIES

Many London hotels, museums, restaurants, and sightseeing attractions have wheelchair ramps. Persons with disabilities are often granted special discounts at attractions and, in some cases, nightclubs.

These are called "concessions" in Britain. It always pays to ask. Free information and advice is available from **Holiday Care Service,** Imperial Building, 2nd Floor, Victoria Road, Horley, Surrey RH6 7PZ (☎ **01293/774535;** fax 01293/784647).

Bookstores in London often carry **Access in London** £8 ($13.20), a helpful publication listing facilities for persons with disabilities, among other things.

The transport system, cinemas, and theaters are still pretty much off-limits, but **London Transport** does publish a leaflet called *Access to the Underground,* which gives details of elevators and ramps at individual Underground stations; call ☎ **020/7918-3312.** And the **London black cab** is perfectly suited for those in wheelchairs; the roomy interiors have plenty of room for maneuvering.

Artsline, 54 Chalton St., London NW1 1HS (☎ **020/ 7388-2227;** fax 0171/383-2653), offers free information about wheelchair access to theaters (also theaters with hearing aids), museums, cinemas, and other attractions. Artsline will mail information to North America, but it's even more helpful to contact Artsline once you arrive in London; the line is staffed Monday to Friday from 9:30am to 5:30pm.

An organization that cooperates closely with Artsline is **Tripscope,** The Courtyard, 4 Evelyn Rd., London W4 5JL (☎ **020/8994-9294;** fax 0181/994-3618), which offers advice on travel in Britain and elsewhere for persons with disabilities.

A World of Options, a 658-page book of resources for travelers with disabilities, covers everything, even biking trips. It costs $35 ($30 for members) and is available from **Mobility International USA,** P.O. Box 10767, Eugene, OR 97440 (☎ **541/ 343-1284,** voice and TDD; www.miusa.org). Annual membership for Mobility International is $35, which includes their quarterly newsletter, *Over the Rainbow.* In addition, **Twin Peaks Press,** P.O. Box 129, Vancouver, WA 98666 (☎ **360/694-2462**), publishes travel-related books for people with disabilities.

The Moss Rehab Hospital (☎ **215/456-9600**) has been providing friendly and helpful phone advice and referrals to disabled travelers for years through its **Travel Information Service** (☎ **215/456-9603;** www.mossresourcenet.org).

You can join **The Society for the Advancement of Travel for the Handicapped (SATH),** 347 Fifth Ave. Suite 610, New York, NY 10016 (☎ **212/447-7284;** fax 212-725-8253; www.sath.org) for $45 annually, $30 for seniors and students, to gain access to their vast network of connections in the travel industry. They provide information sheets on travel destinations, and referrals to tour operators that specialize in traveling with disabilities. Their quarterly magazine, *Open World for Disability and Mature Travel,* is full of good information and resources. A year's subscription is $13.00 ($21 outside the U.S.).

Travelers with disabilities may also want to consider joining a tour that caters specifically to them. One of the best operators is **Flying Wheels Travel,** 143 West Bridge (P.O. Box 382), Owatonna, MN 55060 (☎ **800/535-6790**). They offer various escorted tours, with an emphasis on sports, as well as private tours in minivans with lifts. Other reputable specialized tour operators include **Access Adventures** (☎ **716/889-9096**), which offers sports-related vacations; **Accessible Journeys** (☎ **800/TINGLES** or 610/521-0339), and **Directions Unlimited** (☎ **800/533-5343**).

Vision-impaired travelers should contact the **American Foundation for the Blind,** 11 Penn Plaza, Suite 300, New York, NY 10001 (☎ **800/232-5463**), for information on traveling with seeing-eye dogs.

FOR GAY & LESBIAN TRAVELERS

London has one of the most active gay and lesbian scenes in the world; we've recommended a number of the city's best gay clubs (at least as of press time) in chapter 8, "London After Dark." For up-to-the-minute information on activities, we recommend the monthly **Gay Times** (London) for 2.50¢ ($4.15).

There are also two good, biannual English-language gay guidebooks, both focused on gay men but including information for lesbians as well. You can get the **Spartacus International Gay Guide** or **Odysseus** from most gay and lesbian bookstores, or order them from **Giovanni's Room** (☎ **215/923-2960**), or **A Different Light Bookstore** (☎ **800/343-4002** or 212/989-4850). Both lesbians and gays might want to pick up a copy of *Gay Travel A to Z* ($16). The **Ferrari Guides** (www.q-net.com) is yet another very good series of gay and lesbian guidebooks. A new guide is the recently published **Frommer's Gay & Lesbian Europe.**

Out and About, 8 W. 19th St. #401, New York, NY 10011 (☎ **800/929-2268** or 212/645-6922), offers guidebooks and a monthly newsletter. A year's subscription to the newsletter costs $49. **Our World,** 1104 North Nova Rd., Suite 251, Daytona Beach, FL 32117 (☎ **904/441-5367**), is a slicker monthly magazine promoting and highlighting travel bargains and opportunities. Annual subscription rates are $35 in the U.S., $45 outside the U.S.

Lesbian and Gay Switchboard (☎ **020/7837-7324**) is open 24 hours a day, providing information about gay-related activities in London. London's best gay-oriented bookstore is **Gay's the Word,** 66 Marchmont St., WC1 (☎ **0171/278-7654;** Tube: Russell Square), the largest such store in Britain. The staff here is really friendly and helpful and will offer advice about the ever-changing gay scene in London.

FOR SENIORS

Many discounts are available to seniors. Be advised, however, that in England you often have to be a member of an association to obtain discounts. Public-transportation reductions, for example, are available only to holders of British Pension books. However, many attractions do offer discounts for senior citizens (women 60 or over and men 65 or over). Even if discounts aren't posted, you might ask if they're available.

If you're over 60, you're eligible for special 10% discounts on **British Airways** through its Privileged Traveler program. You also qualify for reduced restrictions on APEX cancellations. Discounts are also granted for BA tours and for intra-Britain air tickets that are booked in North America.

British Rail offers seniors discounted rates on first-class rail passes for travel around Britain. See the discussion under "Getting There by Train" below.

Members of the **American Association of Retired Persons (AARP),** 601 E St. NW, Washington, D.C. 20049 (☎ **800/ 424-3410** or 202/434-2277), get discounts not only on hotels but on airfares and car rentals, too. AARP offers members a wide range of special benefits, including *Modern Maturity* magazine and a monthly newsletter.

The National Council of Senior Citizens, 8403 Colesville Rd., Suite 1200, Silver Springs, MD 20910 (☎ **301/578-8800**), a non-profit organization, offers a newsletter six times a year (partly devoted to travel tips) and discounts on hotel and auto rentals; annual dues are $13 per person or couple.

FOR FAMILIES

On airlines, you must request a special menu for children at least 24 hours in advance. Bring your own baby food, though; you can ask a flight attendant to warm it to the right temperature.

Arrange ahead of time for such necessities as a crib, bottle warmer, and car seat (in England, small children aren't allowed to ride in the front seat). If you're staying with friends, you can rent baby equipment from **Chelsea Baby Hire,** 83 Burntwood Lane, SW17 OAJ (☎ 020/8540-8830). The **London black cab** is a lifesaver for families; the roomy interior allows a stroller to be lifted right into the cab without unstrapping baby.

If you want a night out without the kids, you're in luck: London has its own children's hotel, **Pippa Popins,** 430 Fulham Rd., SW6 1DU (☎ 020/7385-2458), which accommodates children overnight in a wonderful nursery filled with lots of toys and caring minders. Other recommendable babysitting services are **Babysitters Unlimited** (☎ 020/8892-8888) and **Childminders** (☎ 020/7935-2049 or 0171/935-3000). Babysitters can also be found for you at most hotels.

To find out what's on for kids while you're in London, pick up the leaflet **Where to Take Children,** published by the London Tourist Board. If you have specific questions, ring **Kidsline** (☎ 020/7222-8070) Monday to Friday 4 to 6pm and summer holidays 9am to 4pm or the **London Tourist Board's** special children's information lines (☎ 0839/123-425) for listings of special events and places to visit for children. The number is accessible in London at 50p (85¢) per minute.

6   Getting There

BY PLANE

If given a choice, opt to land at Heathrow Airport, London's main airport. Gatwick Airport, where most charters land, requires a train trip into London.

FROM THE UNITED STATES   American Airlines (☎ 800/433-7300; www.americanair.com) offers daily routes to London Heathrow Airport from five U.S. gateways: New York's JFK (six times daily), Chicago's O'Hare and Boston's Logan (twice daily), Miami International and Los Angeles International (each once daily).

British Airways (☎ 800/247-9297; www.british-airways.com) offers mostly nonstop flights from 18 U.S. cities to Heathrow and Gatwick Airports. With more add-on options than any other airline, British Airways can make a visit to Britain cheaper than you might have expected. The 1993 union of some of BA's functions and routings with US Airways has opened additional North American gateways to BA, improved services, and reduced some of its fares. Of particular interest are the "Value Plus," "London on the Town," and "Europe Escorted" packages that include both airfare and discounted accommodations throughout Britain.

Continental Airlines (☎ 800/525-0280; www.flycontinental.com) flies daily to Gatwick Airport from Newark, Houston, and Cleveland.

Depending on day and season, **Delta Air Lines** (☎ 800/241-4141; www.delta-air.com) runs either one or two daily nonstop flights between Atlanta and Gatwick. Delta also offers nonstop daily service from Cincinnati.

Northwest Airlines (☎ 800/447-4747; www.nwa.com) flies nonstop from both Minneapolis and Detroit to Gatwick, with connections possible from other cities, such as Boston and New York.

TWA (☎ 800/221-2000; www.twa.com) flies nonstop to Gatwick every day from its hub in St. Louis. Connections are possible through St. Louis from most of North America.

United Airlines (☎ 800/538-2929; www.ual.com) flies nonstop from New York's JFK and Chicago's O'Hare to Heathrow two or three times a day, depending on the season. United also offers nonstop service twice a day from Dulles Airport, near Washington, D.C., plus once-a-day service from Newark, Los Angeles, and San Francisco to Heathrow.

Virgin Atlantic Airways (☎ 800/862-8621; www.fly.virgin.com) flies daily to either Gatwick or Heathrow from Boston, Newark, New York's JFK, Los Angeles, San Francisco, Washington's Dulles, Miami, and Orlando.

FROM CANADA   **Air Canada** (☎ 800/776-3000; www.aircanada.ca) flies daily to London Heathrow nonstop from Vancouver, Montreal, and Toronto. There are also frequent direct flights from Calgary, and Ottawa.

FROM AUSTRALIA   **Qantas** (☎ 131211; www.qantas.com) flies from both Sydney and Melbourne daily. **British Airways** (☎ 02/92583300 or 03/96031133; www.british-airways.com) has five to seven flights weekly from Sydney and Melbourne.

TIPS FOR GETTING THE BEST AIRFARES

Periodically airlines lower prices on their most popular routes. Check your newspaper for advertised discounts or call the airlines directly and ask if any **promotional rates** or special fares are available.

Consolidators, also known as bucket shops, are a good place to find low fares. Consolidators buy seats in bulk from the airlines,

Cyberdeals for Net Surfers

It's possible to get some great deals on airfare, hotels, and car rentals via the Internet. The Web sites highlighted below are worth checking out, since all services are free. Always check the lowest published fare, however, before you shop for flights online.

Arthur Frommer's Budget Travel (www.frommers.com), home of the Encyclopedia of Travel and *Arthur Frommer's Budget Travel* magazine, offers detailed information on 200 cities and islands around the world.

Microsoft Expedia (www.expedia.com) is a multipurpose travel site featuring the "Fare Tracker": once a week, they'll e-mail you the best airfare deals on up to three destinations.

Travelocity (www.travelocity.com) is one of the best sites for finding cheap airfare.

Several major airlines offer a free e-mail service called E-Savers that sends you their best bargain airfares on a regular basis.

and then sell them back to the public at prices below even the airlines' discounted rates. Before you pay a consolidator, however, ask for a record locator number and confirm your seat with the airline itself.

Council Travel (☎ **800/226-8624;** www.counciltravel.com) and **STA Travel** (☎ **800/781-4040;** www.sta.travel.com) cater especially to young travelers, but their bargain-basement prices are available to people of all ages. **Travel Bargains** (☎ **800/ AIR-FARE;** www.1800airfare.com) was formerly owned by TWA, but now offers the deepest discounts on many other airlines, with a 4-day advance purchase. Other reliable consolidators include **1-800-FLY-CHEAP** (www.1800flycheap.com); **TFI Tours International** (☎ **800-745-8000** or 212/736-1140), which serves as a clearinghouse for unused seats; or "rebators" such as **Travel Avenue** (☎ **800/333-3335** or 312/876-1116) and the **Smart Traveller** (☎ **800/448-3338** or 305/448-3338; www.smarttraveller@ juno.com), which rebate part of their commissions to you.

Charter flight operators advertise and sell their seats through travel agents. Before deciding to take a charter flight, however, check the restrictions on the ticket. If the charter doesn't fill up, it may be canceled up to 10 days before departure. Summer charters fill up more quickly than others and are almost sure to fly.

BY TRAIN

VIA THE CHUNNEL FROM THE CONTINENT   Rail Europe
(☎ **800/94-CHUNNEL** for information) sells tickets on the *Eurostar*
direct train service between Paris or Brussels and London. A round-
trip, first-class fare between Paris and London, for example, costs
$438 ($298 in second class); but you can cut costs to $218 with a
second-class, 14-day advance purchase (nonrefundable) round-trip fare.
In London, make reservations for *Eurostar* at ☎ **0990/300003;** in
Paris, at ☎ **01-44-51-06-02;** and in the United States, at ☎ **800/
EUROSTAR.** *Eurostar* trains arrive and depart from London's Waterloo
Station, Paris's Gare du Nord, and Brussels' Central Station.

VIA BRITRAIL FROM OTHER PARTS OF ENGLAND   A
BritRail Classic Pass allows unlimited rail travel during a set time
period (8 days, 15 days, or 1 month). (Eurailpasses aren't accepted
in Britain.) For 8 days, a pass costs $400 in first class, and $265 in
standard class; for 15 days, it's $600 and $400, respectively; for 22
days, it's $760 and $505; and for 1 month, it's $900 and $600. If
a child age 5 to 15 is traveling with a full-fare adult, the fare is half
the adult fare. Children under 5 travel free if not occupying a seat.
Senior citizens (60 and over) qualify for discounts only on first-class
travel. Travelers between 16 and 25 can purchase a BritRail Classic
Youth Pass, which allows unlimited second-class travel: $215 for 8
days, $280 for 15 days, $355 for 22 days, or $420 for 1 month.

You must purchase your BritRail pass before you leave home.
Contact **BritRail Travel International,** 500 Mamaroneck Ave.,
Suite 314, Harrison, NY 10528 (☎ **800/677-8585** in the U.S.,
800/555-2748 in Canada), or you can get booking information on
the Internet at www.raileurope.com.

BY CAR & FERRY

If you plan to take a rented car across or under the Channel, check
carefully with the rental company about license and insurance re-
quirements before you leave.

FERRIES FROM THE CONTINENT   There are many "drive-
on, drive-off" car-ferry services across the Channel.

P&O Stena Lines (☎ **0990/980980**) operates car and passenger ferries between Calais (France) and Dover (England) only. Trip
time is 75 minutes. **P&O European Ferry** (☎ **0870/242-4999**)
operates ferry service from Cherbourg (France) to Portsmouth
(England). Depending on the vessel, this trip can take from 2 hours
and 45 minutes to up to 5 hours.

HoverSpeed operates at least 6 daily 35-minute hovercraft crossings, as well as slightly longer crossings via Seacat (a catamaran propelled by jet engines; these go four times daily and take about 50 minutes), between Boulogne and Folkestone. For reservations and information, call **HoverSpeed** at ☎ **0870/5240241.** Typical one-way fares are £15 to £20 ($24.75 to $33) per person.

LE SHUTTLE   Le Shuttle (☎ **0990/353535**) not only accommodates trains but passenger cars, charter buses, taxis, and motorcycles, under the English Channel from Calais, France, to Folkestone, England. It operates 24 hours a day, 365 days a year, running every 15 minutes during peak travel times and at least once an hour at night. Before boarding Le Shuttle, you pay at a toll booth and then pass through Immigration for both countries. You'll travel in bright, air-conditioned carriages. The total travel time between the French and English highway system is about 1 hour.

The cost of moving a car on Le Shuttle varies, according to the season and the day of the week. Count on at least £84.50 ($139.40) each way. Discounts are granted to passengers who return to France with their cars within 5 days of their departure; otherwise, the round-trip fare is twice the price of the one-way fare.

BY BUS

Bus connections to Britain from the Continent are generally not very comfortable. One line with a relatively good reputation is **Euroways Eurolines, Ltd.,** 52 Grosvenor Gardens, London SW1W OAU (☎ **020/7730-8235**). They book passage on buses traveling two times a day between London and Paris (9 hours); three times a day from Amsterdam (12 hours); three times a week from Munich (24 hours); and three times a week from Stockholm (44 hours).

3

Getting to Know London

*E*urope's largest city is like a great wheel, with Piccadilly Circus at the hub and dozens of communities branching out from it. Since London is such a conglomeration of sections, each with its own life and personality, first-time visitors may be intimidated until they get the hang of it. Most of the attractions are in the West End, with the exception of that historic part of London known as the City, where the Tower of London stands.

This chapter will help you get your bearings. It provides a brief orientation and a preview of the city's most important neighborhoods and tells you what you need to know about getting around London by public transportation or on foot. In addition, the "Fast Facts" section covers everything from babysitters to shoe repairs.

1 Orientation

ARRIVING
BY PLANE
LONDON HEATHROW AIRPORT Located west of London in Hounslow (☎ **0181/759-4321** for flight information), Heathrow is one of the world's busiest airports, with flights arriving from around the world. It's divided into four terminals, each relatively self-contained. Terminal 4, the most modern, handles the long-haul and transatlantic operations of British Airways. Most transatlantic flights of U.S.-based airlines arrive at Terminal 3. Terminals 1 and 2 receive the intra-European flights of several European airlines.

It takes 50 minutes by **Underground** and costs £3.40 ($5.60) to make the 15-mile trip from Heathrow to center city. You can also take the **Airbus,** which gets you into central London in about an hour and costs £6 ($9.90) for adults and £3 ($4.95) for children. A **taxi** is likely to cost at least £45 ($74.25). For more information about train or bus connections, call ☎ **020/7222-1234.**

The British Airport Authority now operates a **London-Heathrow Express** (☎ **0845/600-1515**), a 100-mile-an-hour train service running every 15 minutes daily from 5:10am until 11:40pm between Heathrow and Paddington Station in the center of London. Trips cost £10 ($16.50) each way in economy class, rising to £20 ($33) in first class. Children ages 5 to 15 go for half the fare (free for those 4 and under). The trip takes only 15 minutes each way between Paddington and Terminals 1, 2, and 3, or 20 minutes from Terminal 4. The trains have special areas for wheelchairs. From Paddington, passengers can connect to other trains or hail a taxi. You can buy tickets on the train or at self-service machines at Heathrow Airport (also available from travel agents). At Paddington, a bus link, Hotel Express, takes passengers from Paddington to a number of hotels in central London, costing £2.05 ($3.40) for adults, £1.05 ($1.75) children 5 to 15, and free for children under 4.

GATWICK AIRPORT   Many scheduled flights land at Gatwick (☎ 01293/535353 for flight information), located some 25 miles south of London in West Sussex. From Gatwick, **express trains** leave for Victoria Station in London every 15 minutes during the day and every hour at night. The charge is £9.50 ($15.65) for adults, half price for children 5 to 15, free for children under 5. There's also an express bus from Gatwick to Victoria, **Flightline Bus 777,** every hour from 5am to 8pm and every hour from 8 to 11pm; the fare is £7.50 ($12.40) per person. A **taxi** from Gatwick to central London usually costs £60 ($99)—you must negotiate a fare with the driver before you enter the cab since Gatwick is outside the Metropolitan Police District. For further transportation information, call ☎ **0345/484950** in London only.

BY TRAIN

All of London's train stations is connected to the city's vast bus and Underground network, and each has phones, restaurants, pubs, luggage-storage areas, and London Regional Transport Information Centres.

From Paris, you can take the Chunnel train directly to Waterloo Station in London.

BY CAR

Once you arrive on the English side of the channel, the M20 takes you directly into London. London is circled by two roadways: the A406 and A205 combination close in, and the M25 farther out. Determine which part of the city you wish to enter and follow signposts.

We suggest you confine driving in London to the bare minimum. Because of parking problems, narrow streets, and heavy traffic, getting around London by car is not a viable option. Also, driving on the *left* can be an additional cause for confusion.

VISITOR INFORMATION

The **British Travel Centre,** Rex House, 4–12 Lower Regent St., London SW1 4PQ (Tube: Piccadilly Circus), caters to walk-in visitors who need information about all parts of Britain. Telephone service has been suspended; you must show up in person and often wait in a lengthy line. On the premises you'll find a British Rail ticket office, travel and theater-ticket agencies, a hotel-booking service, a bookshop, and a souvenir shop. It's open Monday to Friday 9am to 6:30pm, Saturday and Sunday 10am to 4pm, with extended hours on Saturday from June to September.

London Tourist Board's **Tourist Information Centre,** Victoria Station Forecourt, SW1 (Tube: Victoria Station), can help you with almost anything. The center deals chiefly with accommodations in all price categories and can handle the whole spectrum of travelers' questions. It also arranges tour-ticket sales, theater reservations, and offers a wide selection of books and souvenirs. From Easter to October, the center is open daily 8am to 7pm; November to Easter, it's open Monday to Saturday 8am to 6pm and Sunday 9am to 4pm.

The tourist board also has offices at **Heathrow** Terminals 1, 2, and 3, and on the Underground concourse at **Liverpool Street Railway Station.**

CITY LAYOUT

While **Central London** doesn't formally define itself, most Londoners today would probably accept the Underground's Circle Line as a fair boundary. The city center is customarily divided into two areas, the **City** and the **West End.**

The City is where London began; it's the original square mile the Romans called Londinium, and still exists as its own self-governing entity. Rich in historical, architectural, and social interest, the City is now one of the world's great financial theaters.

The City and the West End are surrounded first by **Inner London** (which includes the East End), and then by the sprawling hinterland of **Outer London.** You'll find the greatest number of hotels in the west, in inner districts such as **Kensington, Chelsea,** and **Victoria,** and in the West End. Even though the City is jeweled with historic sights, it empties out in the evenings and on weekends.

FINDING YOUR WAY AROUND   It's not easy to find an address in London, as the city's streets—both names and house

London's Neighborhoods

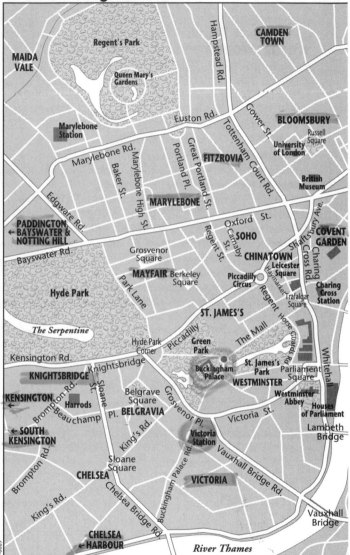

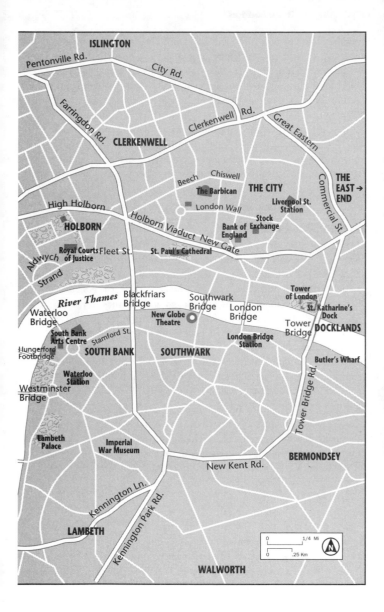

ISLINGTON

Pentonville Rd.

City Rd.

Farringdon Rd.

Clerkenwell Rd.

Great Eastern

CLERKENWELL

THE
EAST →
END

Commercial St.

Beech   Chiswell

The Barbican

THE CITY

Liverpool St.
Station

London Wall

High Holborn

Holborn Viaduct   New Gate

Stock
Exchange

Bank of
England

HOLBORN

Royal Courts
of Justice

Aldwych

Fleet St.

St. Paul's Cathedral

Strand

River Thames   Blackfriars
Bridge

Southwark
Bridge

London
Bridge

Tower
of London

St. Katharine's
Dock

Waterloo
Bridge

New Globe
Theatre

Tower
Bridge

DOCKLANDS

South Bank
Arts Centre

Stamford St.

London Bridge
Station

Hungerford
Footbridge

SOUTH BANK

SOUTHWARK

Butler's Wharf

Waterloo
Station

Westminster
Bridge

Tower Bridge Rd.

Lambeth
Palace

Imperial
War Museum

New Kent Rd.

BERMONDSEY

Kennington Ln.

Kennington Park Rd.

LAMBETH

0   1/4 Mi
0   .25 Km

WALWORTH

numbers—follow no pattern and London is checkered with squares, mews, closes, and terraces, which jut into, cross, overlap, or interrupt whatever street you're trying to follow. run in odds and evens, clockwise and counterclockwise—when they exist at all. Many establishments, such as the Four Seasons Hotel and Langan's Brasserie, don't have lnumbers, even though the building right next door is numbered.

If you plan on exploring London in any depth, you'll need a detailed street map with an index. And no Londoner is without a **London A to Z,** the ultimate street-by-street reference guide, available at bookstores and newsstands everywhere.

LONDON'S NEIGHBORHOODS IN BRIEF

WEST END NEIGHBORHOODS

MAYFAIR   Bounded by Piccadilly, Hyde Park, and Oxford and Regent Streets, this is the most elegant, fashionable section of London, filled with luxury hotels, Georgian town houses, and swank shops. Grosvenor Square (*Grov*-nor) is nicknamed "Little America" because it's home to the American Embassy and a statue of Franklin D. Roosevelt; Berkeley Square (*Bark*-ley) was made famous by the song. One of the curiosities of Mayfair is **Shepherd Market,** a tiny village of pubs, two-story inns, restaurants, and book and food stalls, all sandwiched within Mayfair's grandness. If Bond Street shopping, tony boutiques, and art galleries, along with tree-filled squares, warm the cockles of your heart, by all means check in.

MARYLEBONE   Most first-time visitors head to Marylebone to explore Madame Tussaud's waxworks or walk along Baker Street in the make-believe footsteps of Sherlock Holmes. The streets here form a near-perfect grid, with the major ones running north–south from Regent's Park toward Oxford Street. Architect Robert Adam laid out Portland Place, one of the most characteristic squares, from 1776 to 1780, and it was at Cavendish Square that Mrs. Horatio Nelson waited—often in vain—for the return of the admiral. Marylebone Lane and High Street still retain some of their former village atmosphere, but this is otherwise a rather anonymous area. Dickens (who seems to have lived everywhere) wrote nearly a dozen books when he resided here. At Regent's Park, you can visit Queen Mary's Gardens or, in summer, see Shakespeare performed in an open-air theater.

ST. JAMES'S   Often called "Royal London," St. James's has associations from the "merrie monarch" Charles II to Elizabeth II, who lives at its most famous address, Buckingham Palace. The neighborhood begins at Piccadilly Circus and moves southwest, incorporating Pall Mall, The Mall, St. James's Park, and Green Park, including such addresses as American Express on Haymarket and many of London's leading department stores. Be sure to stop in at **Fortnum & Mason,** 181 Piccadilly, the world's most luxurious grocery store. Launched in 1788, the store sent hams to the duke of Wellington's army, baskets of tinned goodies to Florence Nightingale in the Crimea, and packed a picnic basket for Stanley when he went looking for Livingstone. If you want to live in the same section as the Queen, you can find a scattering of hotels here.

PICCADILLY CIRCUS & LEICESTER SQUARE   Piccadilly Circus is the heart and soul of London. The circus isn't Times Square yet, but its traffic, neon, and jostling crowds might indeed make "circus" an apt word here. Piccadilly, traditionally the western road out of town, was named for the "picadil," a ruffled collar created by Robert Baker, a 17th-century tailor. If you want a little more grandeur, retreat to the Regency promenade of exclusive shops, the **Burlington Arcade,** designed in 1819. Some 35 shops, housing a treasure trove of expensive goodies, await you. A bit more tawdry is **Leicester Square,** a center of theaters, restaurants, movie palaces, and nightlife. The square is no longer the chic address it was when William Hogarth or Joshua Reynolds lived here. The square changed forever in the Victorian era, when four towering entertainment halls were opened (even Queen Victoria came to see a circus here on occasion). In time the old palaces changed from stage to screen; three of them are still showing films.

SOHO   A nightclubber's paradise, especially if you're gay, Soho is a confusing grid of densely packed streets, famous for their gloriously cosmopolitan mix of people and trades. A decade ago, much was heard about the decline of Soho when the thriving sex industry threatened to engulf it. Respectable businesses have returned, and fashionable restaurants and shops prosper; it's now the heart of London's expanding gay life. Soho starts at Piccadilly Circus and spreads out, more-or-less bordered by Regent Street, Oxford Street, Charing Cross Road, and Shaftesbury Avenue. Carnaby Street, a block from Regent Street, was the center of the universe in the Swinging Sixties. Across Shaftesbury Avenue, a busy street lined with theaters, is London's **Chinatown,** centered on Gerrard Street. It's small, authentic, and packed with excellent restaurants. But Soho's heart—with marvelous French and Italian delicatessens, fine butchers, fish stores, and wine merchants—is farther north, on Brewer, Old Compton, and Berwick Streets; Berwick is also a wonderful open-air fresh food market. To the north of Old Compton Street, Dean, Frith, and Greek Streets have fine little restaurants, pubs, and clubs.

BLOOMSBURY   This district, a world within itself, lies northeast of Piccadilly Circus, beyond Soho. It is, among other things, the academic heart of London; here you'll find the University of London and many bookstores. Despite its student population, this neighborhood is fairly staid. The novelist Virginia Woolf and her husband, Leonard, were once unofficial leaders of a group of artists and writers here, known as "the Bloomsbury Group." The heart of Bloomsbury is Russell Square, whose outlying streets are lined with moderately priced to inexpensive hotels and B&Bs. It's a rather noisy but very central place to stay. Most visitors come to the neighborhood to visit the British Museum, one of the world's greatest repositories of treasures.

Nearby is **Fitzrovia,** bounded by Great Portland, Oxford, and Gower Streets, and reached by the Goodge Street Tube. Goodge Street, with its many shops and pubs, forms the heart of the "village," once the stamping ground of writers Ezra Pound, Wyndham Lewis, and George Orwell. The bottom end of Fitzrovia is a virtual extension of Soho, with a cluster of Greek restaurants.

CLERKENWELL   This was the site of London's first hospital. It evolved into a muck-filled 18th-century cattle yard that was home to cheap gin distilleries, but by the 1870s, London's new socialist movement centered itself here. It was home to John Stuart Mill's London Patriotic Club in 1872 and William Morris's socialist press of the 1890s; Lenin lived and worked here editing *Iskra.* In later years, the neighborhood dwindled, but it's recently been reinvented by the moneyed and groovy—a handful of hot new restaurants and clubs have sprouted up, and art galleries now line St. John's Square and the border of Clerkenwell Green. But lorries still rumble into Smithfield Market throughout the night, unloading thousands of beef carcasses, and the church of St. Bartholomew-the-Great, built in 1123, still stands as London's oldest church.

HOLBORN   The old borough of Holborn (*ho*-burn), which abuts the City to the west, is the heart of legal London. Still Dickensian in spirit, the area preserves the Victorian author's footsteps in the two Inns of Court and the Bleeding Heart Yard of *Little Dorrit* fame. A 14-year-old Dickens was once employed as a solicitor's clerk at

Lincoln's Inn Fields. The Old Bailey has stood for English justice down through the years; Fagin went to the gallows from this site in *Oliver Twist.* Everything in Holborn seems steeped in history. Even as you're quenching your thirst with a half-pint of bitter at the **Viaduct Tavern,** 126 Newgate St. (Tube: St. Paul's), you learn the pub was built over the notorious Newgate Prison (which specialized in death by pressing) and was named after the Holborn Viaduct, the world's first overpass.

COVENT GARDEN & THE STRAND   The flower, fruit, and "veg" market is long gone (since 1970), but memories of Professor Higgins and his "squashed cabbage leaf," Eliza Doolittle, linger on. **Covent Garden** now contains the city's liveliest group of restaurants, pubs, and cafés outside Soho, as well as some of the city's hippest shops—including the world's only Dr. Marten's Super Store. The restored marketplace with its glass and iron roofs has been called a magnificent example of urban recycling. Covent Garden is tradition-ally London's theater area. The Royal Opera House is here, and Inigo Jones's St. Paul's Covent Garden is known as the actors' church; over the years it has attracted everybody from Ellen Terry to Vivien Leigh and is still attended by actors and artists. The Theatre Royal Drury Lane was where Charles II's mistress Nell Gwynne made her debut in 1665. The place is not packed with hotel beds, but there are a few choice ones, if you want a fashionable address that's less obvious than Mayfair.

Beginning at Trafalgar Square, the **Strand** runs east into Fleet Street and borders Covent Garden to the south. It's flanked with theaters, shops, first-class hotels, and restaurants. The Strand runs parallel to the River Thames, and to walk it is to follow in the foot-steps of Dr. Johnson, Charles Lamb, Mark Twain, Henry Fielding, James Boswell, and William Thackeray. The Savoy Theatre helped make Gilbert and Sullivan household names.

WESTMINSTER   Westminster has been the seat of the British government since the days of Edward the Confessor. Dominated by the Houses of Parliament and Westminster Abbey, the area runs along the Thames to the east of St. James's Park. **Trafalgar Square,** at the area's northern end and one of the city's major landmarks, remains a testament to England's victory over Napoléon in 1805, and the paintings in its landmark National Gallery will restore your soul. Whitehall is the main thoroughfare, linking Trafalgar Square with Parliament Square. You can visit Churchill's Cabinet War Rooms and walk down Downing Street to see no. 10, the world's most famous street address, home to Britain's prime minister. No visit is complete without a call at **Westminster Abbey,** one of the greatest Gothic churches in the world. It has witnessed a parade of English history, beginning when William the Conqueror was crowned here on Christmas Day, 1066.

Westminster also encompasses **Victoria,** an area that takes its unofficial name from bustling Victoria Station, known as "the gateway to the Continent." Because of its location near the rail station, many B&Bs and hotels have sprouted up here. It's not a tony address, but it's cheap to moderate in price for living, if you don't mind the noise and crowds.

THE CITY & ENVIRONS

THE CITY   When the Londoners speak of "the City" (EC2, EC3), they don't mean all of London; they mean the original square mile, site of Londinium, as it was called by its Roman conquerors. Now, of course, it's the British version of Wall Street. The institutions here are known all over the world: the Bank of England, the London Stock Exchange, and the financially troubled Lloyd's of London. The City doesn't easily reveal its past; much of it was swept away by the Great Fire of 1666, the Blitz of 1940, and the zeal of modern developers. Still, it retains some older landmarks, including St. Paul's Cathedral—the masterpiece of Sir Christopher Wren. Some 2,000 years of history unfold at the Museum of London. The Barbican Centre, opened by Queen Elizabeth in 1982, is a major performing arts venue. At the Guildhall, the first lord mayor of London was installed in 1192.

Fleet Street has been London's journalistic hub since William Caxton printed the first book in English here. *The Daily Consort,* the first daily newspaper printed in England, was launched at Ludgate Circus in 1702. However, most of the London tabloids have abandoned Fleet Street for the Docklands development across the river.

The City of London still prefers to function on its own, separate from the rest of the city; in keeping with its independence, it maintains its own **Information Centre** at St. Paul's Churchyard, EC4 (☎ **020/7332-1456**).

DOCKLANDS   In 1981, the London Docklands Development Corporation (LDDC) was formed to redevelop Wapping, the Isle of Dogs, the Royal Docks, and Surrey Docks in the largest, the most ambitious scheme of its kind in Europe. The area is bordered roughly by Tower Bridge to the west and London City Airport and the Royal Docks to the east. Many businesses have moved here;

Thames-side warehouses have been converted to Manhattan-style lofts; and museums, entertainment complexes, shops, and an ever-growing list of restaurants have popped up at this 21st-century river city in the making. **Canary Wharf,** on the Isle of Dogs, is the heart of Docklands; this huge 71-acre site is dominated by an 800-foot-high tower, the tallest building in the United Kingdom, designed by Cesar Pelli. The Piazza is lined with shops and restaurants. On the south side of the river at Surrey Docks, the Victorian warehouses of **Butler's Wharf** have been converted by Sir Terence Conran into offices, workshops, houses, shops, and restaurants. Butler's Wharf is also home to the Design Museum.

To get to Docklands, take the Underground to Tower Hill and pick up the **Docklands Light Railway** (☎ **020/7363-9696**), which operates Monday to Friday from 5:30am to 12:30am, with selected main routes now offering weekend service from 6am to 12:30pm Saturday and 7:30am to 11:30pm Sunday.

THE EAST END   Traditionally, this was one of London's poorest districts, and was nearly bombed out of existence in World War II. It extends from the City Walls east encompassing Stepney, Bow, Poplar, West Ham, Canning Town, and other districts. The East End is the home of the Cockney, London's most colorful character. To be a true Cockney, it's said that you must have been born "within the sound of Bow Bells," a reference to a church, St. Mary-le-Bow, rebuilt by Sir Christopher Wren in 1670. Many immigrants to London have found a home here.

SOUTH BANK   Although not officially a district like Mayfair, South Bank is the setting today for the **South Bank Arts Centre,** now the largest arts center in Western Europe and still growing. Reached by Waterloo Bridge or on foot by Hungerford Bridge, it lies across the Thames from the Victoria Embankment. Culture buffs flock to its many galleries and halls, including the National Theatre, Queen Elizabeth Hall, Royal Festival Hall, and the Hayward Gallery. It's also the setting of the National Film Theatre and the Museum of the Moving Image (MOMI). Nearby are such neighborhoods as Elephant and Castle and Southwark, home to grand Southwark Cathedral. To get here, take the Tube to Waterloo Station.

CENTRAL LONDON BEYOND THE WEST END

KNIGHTSBRIDGE   Knightsbridge is a top residential and shopping district, just south of Hyde Park. **Harrods** on Brompton Road is its chief attraction. Nearby, Beauchamp Place (*Bee*-cham) is one of London's most fashionable shopping streets, a Regency-era boutique-lined little street with a scattering of restaurants. Shops include Bruce Oldfield at 27 Beauchamp Place, where the likes of Joan Collins come for evening wear. And, at the end of a shopping day, if Harrods' five restaurants and five bars haven't tempted you, retreat to Bill Bentley's at 31 Beauchamp Place for a dozen oysters, washed down with a few glasses of muscadet. If you're checking in, Knightsbridge, in spite of its commercial overtones, is still a swank address. Most hotels are deluxe or first class, although a few moderately priced ones do exist.

BELGRAVIA   South of Knightsbridge, this area has long been the aristocratic quarter of London, rivaling Mayfair in grandness. Although it reached its pinnacle of prestige during the reign of Queen Victoria, it's still a chic address if you're looking for a hotel; the duke and duchess of Westminster, one of England's richest families, still live at Eaton Square. The area's centerpiece is Belgrave Square (1825–35).

CHELSEA   This stylish Thames-side district lies south of Belgravia. It begins at Sloane Square, with Gilbert Ledward's Venus fountain playing watery music and flower sellers hustling their wares. The area has always been a favorite of writers and artists, including Oscar Wilde (who was arrested here), George Eliot, James Whistler, J.M.W. Turner, Henry James, Augustus John, and Thomas Carlyle (whose former home can be visited). Mick Jagger and Margaret Thatcher (not together) have been more recent residents, and the late Princess Diana and her "Sloane Rangers" of the 1980s gave it even more fame. There are some swank hotels here and a scattering of modestly priced ones. The main drawback of Chelsea is inaccessibility— it has only one tube stop, Sloane Square. Its major boulevard is **King's Road,** where Mary Quant launched the miniskirt in the 1960s and where the English punk look began. King's Road runs the entire length of Chelsea; it's at its liveliest on Saturday. The hip-hop of King's Road isn't typical of otherwise upmarket Chelsea, an elegant village filled with town houses and little mews dwellings.

On the Chelsea/Fulham border is **Chelsea Harbour,** a luxury development of apartments and restaurants with a private marina. You can spot its tall tower from far away; the golden ball on top moves up and down to indicate the tide level. Driving by the Chelsea Harbour Club in the mid-1990s you could often see paparazzi perched on ladders, trying to get a shot of the late Princess Di entering or exiting the exclusive gym.

KENSINGTON   This Royal Borough (W8) lies west of Kensington Gardens and Hyde Park and is traversed by two of London's major shopping streets, Kensington High Street and Kensington Church Street. Since 1689, when asthmatic William III fled Whitehall Palace for Nottingham House (where the air was fresher), the district has enjoyed royal associations. In time, Nottingham House became Kensington Palace, and the royals grabbed a chunk of Hyde Park to plant their roses. Queen Victoria was born here. "KP," as the royals say, is still home to Princess Margaret (20 rooms with a view), Prince and Princess Michael of Kent, and the duke and duchess of Gloucester. It was also the residence of the late Princess of Wales. Kensington Gardens is now open to the public. Kensington Square has attracted artists and writers. Thackeray wrote *Vanity Fair* while living here. With all those royal associations, Kensington is a fashionable hotel address.

If you're a frugal traveler and would like to live in the area, head for **South Kensington,** southeast of Kensington Gardens and Earl's Court. Primarily residential South Kensington is often called "museumland" because it's dominated by a complex of museums that include the Natural History Museum, the Victoria and Albert Museum, and the Science Museum; nearby is Royal Albert Hall. South Kensington is also home to some fashionable restaurants and town house hotels, many converted to B&Bs. One of the district's chief curiosities is the Albert Memorial, completed in 1872 by Sir George Gilbert Scott; for sheer excess, the Victorian monument is unequaled in the world.

EARL'S COURT   Below Kensington, bordering the western half of Chelsea, and for decades a staid residential district, Earl's Court now attracts a new and younger crowd (often gay), particularly at night, to its pubs, wine bars, and coffeehouses. It's long been a popular base for budget travelers (particularly Australians, for reasons known only to them), thanks to its wealth of B&Bs and budget hotels, and its convenient access to central London: A 15-minute Tube ride will take you into the heart of Piccadilly.

Once regarded as "the boondocks," nearby **West Brompton** is seen today as an extension of central London. It lies directly south of Earl's Court (take the Tube to West Brompton) and directly southeast of West Kensington. Its focal point is the sprawling Brompton Cemetery, a flower-filled "green lung." It also has many good restaurants, pubs, and taverns, as well as some budget hotels.

NOTTING HILL   Increasingly fashionable Notting Hill is bounded on the east by Bayswater and on the south by Kensington, hemmed in on the north by West Way and on the west by the Shepherd's Bush ramp leading to the M40. It has many turn-of-the-century mansions and small houses sitting on quiet, leafy streets, plus a growing number of hot restaurants and clubs. Gentrified in recent years, it's becoming an extension of central London. Living in one of the few hotels in Notting Hill would brand you a hip hotel shopper.

On the north end, across Notting Hill Gate and west of Bayswater, is the hip neighborhood known as **Notting Hill Gate.** Portobello Road is home to one of London's most famous street markets. The area Tube stops are Notting Hill Gate, Holland Park, or Ladbroke Grove. Nearby **Holland Park** is a chi-chi residential neighborhood visited chiefly by the chic guests of Halcyon Hotel, one of the grandest of London's small hotels.

PADDINGTON & BAYSWATER   The **Paddington** section centers around Paddington Station, north of Kensington Gardens and Hyde Park. It's one of the major centers in London, attracting budget travelers who fill up the B&Bs in Sussex Gardens and Norfolk Square. After the first railway was introduced in London in 1836, it was followed by a circle of sprawling railway termini, including Paddington Station in 1838, which spurred the growth of this middle-class area, which is now blighted in parts.

Just south of Paddington, north of Hyde Park, and abutting more fashionable Notting Hill to the west is **Bayswater,** a sort of unofficial area, with a large number of B&Bs attracting budget travelers.

Nearby is **Maida Vale,** a village that, like St. John's Wood and Camden, has been absorbed by central London. Maida Vale lies directly west of Regent's Park, north of Paddington, and next to the more prestigious address of **St. John's Wood** (home to the Beatles' Abbey Road Studios). The whole area is very sports oriented; if you take the Tube to Maida Vale, you'll find Paddington Recreation Ground, plus a smaller "green lung," Paddington Bowling and Sports Club. It's also home to some of the BBC studios.

FARTHER AFIELD

GREENWICH   To the southeast of London, this suburb— ground zero for use in the reckoning of terrestrial longitudes— enjoyed its heyday under the Tudors. Henry VIII and both of his daughters, Mary I and Elizabeth I, were born here. Greenwich Palace, Henry's favorite, is long gone, though; today's visitors come to this lovely port village for nautical sights along the Thames, including the 1869 tea clipper, *Cutty Sark,* and the tiny *Gipsy Moth IV,* a 54-foot ketch in which Sir Francis Chichester sailed solo around the world in 1966–67. Other attractions in the district include the National Maritime Museum. Because Greenwich was selected as the site of the Millennium Dome, it will be overwhelmed with visitors in the year 2000, many of whom will be flocking here even if they have to skip the British Museum and the Tower of London.

HAMPSTEAD   This residential suburb of north London, beloved by Keats and Hogarth, is a favorite excursion spot for Londoners on the weekend. Everybody from Sigmund Freud to D.H. Lawrence to Anna Pavlova to John Le Carré has lived here, and it's still one of the most desirable districts in the Greater London area to call home. It has very few hotels, however, and is quite far from central London. Its centerpiece is Hampstead Heath, nearly 800 acres of rolling meadows and woodland with panoramic views; it still maintains its rural atmosphere even though engulfed by cityscapes on all sides. The hilltop village is filled with cafés, tearooms, and restaurants, and there are pubs galore, some with historic pedigrees. Take the Northern Line to Hampstead Heath station.

2 Getting Around

Travel Information Centres are located in the Underground stations at Hammersmith, King's Cross, Oxford Circus, St. James's Park, Liverpool Street Station, and Piccadilly Circus, as well as in the British Rail stations at Euston and Victoria and in each of the terminals at Heathrow Airport. They take reservations for London Transport's guided tours and offer free Underground and bus maps and other information leaflets. A **24-hour information service** is available (☎ **020/7222-1234**). You can get information before you go by writing **London Transport,** Travel Information Service, 55 Broadway, London SW1H 0BD.

London Transport offers a number of discount travel passes. **Travelcards** for use on bus, Underground, and British Rail services in Greater London are sold in combinations of adjacent zones, and are available for a minimum of 7 days or for any period from a month to a year. A Travelcard allowing travel in two zones for 1 week costs adults £17.60 ($29.05), children £6.50 ($10.75). Travelcards must be used in conjunction with a Photocard, issued free along with your Travelcard—bring a photo from one of the instant photo booths in London's train stations. Buy your

Travelcard at main post offices in the London area, the ticket window of any Tube station, or at the Travel Information Centres of London Transport (see above).

For shorter stays in London, the **One-Day Off-Peak Travelcard** can be used on most bus, Underground, and British Rail services throughout Greater London Monday to Friday after 9:30am and at any time on weekends and bank holidays. It's available from Underground ticket offices, Travel Information Centres, and some newsstands. For two zones, the cost is £3.80 ($6.25) for adults and £1.90 ($3.15) for children 5 to 15. Children 4 and under travel free.

Visitor Travelcard is worthwhile if you plan to travel a lot within Greater London. This card allows unlimited transport within all six zones of Greater London's Underground and bus network (including Heathrow). You must buy this pass in North America; it's not available in England. A pass good for 3 consecutive days of travel is $32 for adults, $14 for children 5 to 15; for 4 consecutive days of travel, it's $41 for adults, $16 for children; and for 7 consecutive days of travel, it's $63 for adults, $24 for children. Contact **BritRail Travel International,** 500 Mamaroneck Ave., Suite 314, Harrison, NY 10528 (☎ **800/677-8585;** 800/555-2748 in Canada).

The 1-day **Family Travelcard** is a go-as-you-please ticket, allowing as many journeys as you wish on the Tube, buses (excluding night buses) displaying the London Transport bus sign, the Docklands Light Railway, or any rail service within the travel zones designated on your ticket. The family card is valid Monday to Friday after 9:30am and all day on weekends and public holidays. It's available for families at a cost of £3 to £3.20 ($4.95 to $5.30) per adult, 60p ($1) per child. A final discount pass is the **Weekend Travelcard,** which allows you 2 days of weekend transportation on the Underground or buses. The cost ranges from £5.70 to £6 ($9.40 to $9.90) for adults or £2.80 ($4.60) for children. These passes are available at all Underground stations.

You can also buy **Carnet** tickets, a booklet of 10 single Underground tickets valid for 12 months from the issue date, but only in Zone 1 (Central London). They cost £10 ($16.50) for adults and £5 ($8.25) for children (up to 15). A book of Carnet tickets gives you a savings of £2 ($3.30) over the cost of 10 separate single tickets.

THE UNDERGROUND

The Underground, or Tube, is the fastest and easiest way to get from place to place. All Tube stations are clearly marked with a red circle and blue crossbar.

You pick the station for which you're heading on the large diagram displayed on the wall, which includes an alphabetic index. Note the color of the line (Bakerloo is brown, Central is red, and so on). Then, by merely following the colored band, you can see at a glance how many stops are between you and your destination or where you'll have to change. Some stations also have push-button information machines.

You can get your ticket from a vending machine or at the ticket office. You can transfer as many times as you like as long as you stay in the Underground. The flat fare for one trip within the Central zone is £1.40 ($2.30). Trips from the Central zone to destinations in the suburbs range from £1.40 to £4.70 ($2.30 to $7.75) in most cases.

Slide your ticket into the slot at the gate, and pick it up as it comes through on the other side and hold on to it—it must be presented when you exit the station at your destination. If you're caught without a valid ticket, you'll be fined £10 ($16.50) on the spot. If you owe extra money, you'll be asked to pay the difference by the attendant at the exit. The Tube runs roughly 5am to 11:30pm. After that you must take a taxi or night bus to your destination. For information on the London Tube system, call the **London Underground** at ☎ **020/7222-1234,** but expect to stay on hold for a good while before a live person comes on the line.

Scheduled for completion in early 2000, the **Jubilee Underground** line extension will open south of the river, providing much-needed fast access from central London to Greenwich, site of the Millennium Dome, and the Docklands.

BUSES

The first thing you learn about London buses is that you must "queue up"—that is, form a single-file line—for boarding at the bus stop.

The comparably priced bus system is almost as good as the Underground and gives you better views of the city. To find out about current routes, pick up a free bus map at one of London Transport's Travel Information Centres, listed above. The map is available in person only, not by mail.

London still has some old-style Routemaster buses, with both driver and conductor: If you board one of these buses, a conductor will come to your seat; you pay a fare based on your destination and receive a ticket in return. This type of bus is being phased out and replaced with buses that have only a driver; pay the driver as you enter and you exit via a rear door. As with the Underground, the fares vary according to distance traveled. Generally, bus fares are 50p to £1.20 (85¢ to $2)—less than Tube fares. If you travel for two or three stops, the cost is 60p ($1); longer runs within Zone 1 cost £1 ($1.65). If you want your stop called out, simply ask the conductor or driver.

Buses generally run between about 5am and 11:30pm. There are a few night buses on special routes, running once an hour or so; most pass through Trafalgar Square. Keep in mind that night buses are often crowded (especially on weekends) and unable to pick up passengers. You may find yourself waiting a long time. Consider taking a taxi. Call the 24-hour **hot line** (☎ **020/7222-1234**) for schedule and fare information.

TAXIS

London cabs are among the most comfortable and best-designed in the world. You can pick one up either by heading for a cab rank or by hailing one in the street (the taxi is available if the yellow taxi sign on the roof is lighted); once they have stopped for you, taxis are obliged to take you anywhere you want to go within 6 miles of the pick-up point, provided it's within the metropolitan area. For a **radio cab**, call ☎ **020/7272-0272** or 020/7253-5000.

The minimum taxi fare is £5 ($8.25), with the meter starting at £3.80 ($6.25), with increments of 20p (35¢) thereafter, based on distance or time. Each additional passenger is charged 40p (65¢). Passengers pay 10p (15¢) for each piece of luggage in the driver's compartment and any other item more than 2 feet long. Surcharges are imposed after 8pm and on weekends and public holidays. All these tariffs include VAT. Fares usually increase annually. It's recommended that you tip 10% to 15% of the fare. If you call for a cab, the meter starts running when the taxi receives instructions from the dispatcher, so you could find £1.40 ($2.25) or more already on the meter when you step inside.

Minicabs are also available, and they're often useful when the regular taxis become scarce or when the Tube stops running. These cabs are meterless, so the fare must be negotiated in advance. Unlike regular cabs, minicabs are forbidden by law to cruise for fares. They operate from sidewalk kiosks, such as those around Leicester Square. If you need to call one, try **Brunswick Chauffeurs/ Abbey Cars** (☎ **0181/969-2555**) in west London; **Greater London Hire** (☎ **0181/340-2450**) in north London; **London Cabs, Ltd.** (☎ **0181/778-3000**) in east London; or **Newname Minicars** (☎ **0181/472-1400**) in south London. Minicab kiosks can be found near many Tube or BritRail stops, especially in outlying areas.

Country & City Codes

The country code for the United Kingdom is 44. The two London city codes—171 for central London (within a 4-mile radius of Charing Cross), and 181 for outer London—have been replaced by 20, followed by an eight-digit number beginning with 7 (for the old 171 numbers) or 8 (for the old 181 numbers). The original seven digits of the numbers remain unchanged. The old area codes will continue to work alongside the new code until midsummer of 2000.

When calling London from inside the United Kingdom, use 020 followed by the eight-digit number. If you're calling from within London, leave off the area code and simply dial the 8-digit number.

If you have a complaint about taxi service, or if you leave something in a cab, contact the **Public Carriage Office,** 15 Penton St., N1 9PU (Tube: Angel Station). If it's a complaint, you must have the cab number, which is displayed in the passenger compartment. Call ☎ **020/7230-1631** with complaints.

Cab sharing is permitted in London, as British law allows cabbies to carry two to five persons. Taxis accepting such riders display a notice on yellow plastic, with the words "Shared Taxi." Each of two riders sharing is charged 65% of the fare a lone passenger would be charged. Three persons pay 55%, four pay 45%, and five (the seating capacity of all new London cabs) pay 40% of the single-passenger fare.

FAST FACTS: London

American Express   The main AmEx office is at 6 Haymarket, SW1 (☎ **020/7930-4411;** Tube: Piccadilly Circus). Full services are available Monday to Friday 9am to 5:30pm and Saturday 9am to 4pm. At other times—Saturday 4pm to 6pm and Sunday 10am to 4pm—only the foreign-exchange bureau is open.

Business Hours   Banks are usually open Monday to Friday 9:30am to 3:30pm. Pubs and bars are allowed to stay open from 11am to 11pm on Monday to Saturday and from noon to 10:30pm on Sunday. London stores generally open at 9am and close at 5:30pm, staying open until 7pm on Wednesday or Thursday. Most central shops close on Saturday around 1pm. Some stores now have Sunday hours.

Currency Exchange   See "Money" in chapter 2.

Dentists   For dental emergencies, call **Eastman Dental Hospital** (☎ 020/7915-1000; Tube: King's Cross).

Doctors   In an emergency, contact **Doctor's Call** (☎ 07000/372255). Some hotels also have physicians on call. **Medical Express,** 117A Harley St., W1 (☎ 020/7499-1991; Tube: Regent's Park), is a private clinic (not part of the free British medical establishment). For filling the British equivalent of a U.S. prescription, there's sometimes a surcharge of £20 ($33) on top of the cost of the medications. The clinic is open Monday to Friday 9am to 6pm and Saturday 9:30am to 2:30pm.

Drugstores   In Britain they're called **chemist shops.** Every police station in the country has a list of emergency chemists (dial "0" and ask the operator for the local police). A centrally located chemist with long hours is **Bliss the Chemist,** 5 Marble Arch, W1 (☎ 020/7723-6116; Tube: Marble Arch), open daily 9am to midnight.

Electricity   British current is 240 volts, AC cycle, roughly twice the voltage of the North American current, which is 115 to 120 volts, AC cycle. You'll need a transformer for your American appliances, available at electrical supply shops. Some (but not all) hotels will supply them for guests.

Embassies & High Commissions   In case you lose your passport or have some other emergency, here's a list of addresses and phone numbers:

- **Australia**   The high commission is at Australia House, Strand, WC2 (☎ 020/7379-4334; Tube: Charing Cross or Aldwych); it's open Monday to Friday from 10am to 4pm.
- **Canada**   The high commission is located at MacDonald House, 38 Grosvenor Sq., W1 (☎ 020/7258-6600; Tube: Bond Street); it's open Monday to Friday from 8 to 4pm.
- **Ireland**   The embassy is at 17 Grosvenor Place, SW1 (☎ 020/7235-2171; Tube: Hyde Park Corner); it's open Monday to Friday from 9:30am to 1pm and 2:15 to 5pm.
- **New Zealand**   The high commission is at New Zealand House, 80 Haymarket at Pall Mall, SW1 (☎ 020/7930-8422; Tube: Charing Cross or Piccadilly Circus); it's open Monday to Friday from 9am to 5pm.
- **The United States**   The embassy is located at 24 Grosvenor Sq., W1 (☎ 020/7499-9000; Tube: Bond Street). For passport and visa information go to the U.S. Passport & Citizenship Unit, 55–56 Upper Brook St., W1 (☎ 020/7499-9000, ext. 2563

or 2564; Tube: Marble Arch or Bond Street). Hours are Monday to Friday from 8:30am to 5:30pm.

Emergencies   For police, fire, or an ambulance, dial ☎ **999** (no coins required).

Hospitals   The following offer emergency care in London 24 hours a day, with the first treatment free under the National Health Service: **Royal Free Hospital,** Pond Street, NW3 (☎ **020/ 7794-0500;** Tube: Belsize Park), and University College Hospital, Grafton Way, WC1 (☎ **020/7387-9300;** Tube: Warren Street or Euston Square). Many other London hospitals also have accident and emergency departments.

Hot Lines   For police or medical emergencies, dial ☎ **999**. For legal emergencies, call **Release** at ☎ **020/7729-9904,** 24 hours a day. The Rape Crisis Line is ☎ **020/7837-1600,** accepting calls after 6pm. **Samaritans**, 46 Marshall St., W1 (☎ **020/7734-2800;** Tube: Oxford Circus or Piccadilly Circus), maintains a crisis hot line that helps with all kinds of trouble; doors open from 9am to 9pm daily, but phones are 24 hours. **Alcoholics Anonymous** (☎ **020/7833-0022**) answers its hot line daily from 10am to 10pm. The **AIDS** 24-hour hot line is ☎ **0800/567-123.**

Liquor Laws   No alcohol is served to anyone under 18. Children under 16 aren't allowed in pubs. Penalties for drunk driving are stiff, even if you're an overseas visitor. Restaurants are allowed to serve liquor during the same hours as pubs (Monday to Saturday from 11am to 11pm and Sunday noon to 10:30pm), but only to those eating a sit-down meal on the premises. In hotels, liquor may be served from 11am to 11pm to both residents and nonresidents; after 11pm, only residents may be served.

Mail   An airmail letter to North America costs 43p (70¢) for 10 grams and postcards require a 39p (65¢) stamp; letters generally take 7 to 10 days to arrive from the United States. See "Post Offices" below for locations.

Money   See "Money," in chapter 2.

Newspapers/Magazines   *The Times, Daily Telegraph, Daily Mail,* and *Guardian* are all dailies carrying the latest news. The *International Herald Tribune,* published in Paris, and an international edition of *USA Today,* beamed via satellite, are available daily. Copies of *Time* and *Newsweek* are also sold at most newsstands. Magazines such as *Time Out, City Limits,* and *Where* contain lots of useful information about the latest happenings in London.

Police   In an emergency, dial ☎ **999** (no coins required). You can also go to one of the local police branches in central London, including New Scotland Yard, Broadway, SW1 (☎ **020/ 7230-1212;** Tube: St. James's Park).

Post Offices   The main post office is at 24 William IV St. (☎ **020/7484-9307;** Tube: Charing Cross), open Monday to Friday 8am to 8pm and Saturday 9am to 8pm. Other post offices are open Monday to Friday 9am to 5:30pm and on Saturday 9am to 12:30pm. Some post offices close for an hour at lunchtime.

Rest Rooms   They're marked by "Public Toilets" signs in streets, parks, and Tube stations and are safe to use; many are automatic, which are sterilized after each use. You'll also find well-maintained lavatories in all larger public buildings, such as museums and art galleries, large department stores, and railway stations. Public lavatories are usually free, but you may need a small coin to get in or to use a proper washroom.

Smoking   London, like the rest of Europe, isn't a particularly friendly place for the non-smoker. Most restaurants have no-smoking tables, but they're usually separated from the smoking section by only a little space. No-smoking rooms are available in the bigger hotels.

Taxes   A 17.5% national value-added tax (VAT) is added to all hotel and restaurant bills, and will be included in the price of many items you purchase. This can be refunded if you shop at stores that participate in the Retail Export Scheme (signs are posted in the window). See the "How to Get Your VAT Refund" box in chapter 7.

A departure tax of £10 ($16.50) is charged for flights within Britain and the European Union. For passengers flying elsewhere, including to the United States, the tax is £20 ($33). Your airline ticket may or may not include this tax. Ask in advance. The government also levies a 25% tax on gasoline ("petrol").

Telephone   For directory assistance in London, dial ☎ **142;** for the rest of Britain, **192.** To call London from the United States, dial 011 (international code), 44 (Britain's country code), 171 or 181 (London's area codes), and the seven-digit local phone number. Note that these area codes will change in 2000; see the box above.

There are three types of public pay phones: those taking only coins, those accepting only phonecards (called Cardphones), and those taking both phonecards and credit cards. At coin-operated phones, insert your coins before dialing. The minimum charge is 10p (15¢).

Phonecards are available in four values—£2 ($3.30), £4 ($6.60), £10 ($16.50), and £20 ($33)—and are reusable until the total value has expired. Cards can be purchased from newsstands and post offices. Finally, the credit-call pay phone operates on credit cards—Access (MasterCard), Visa, American Express, and Diners Club—and is most common at airports and large railway stations.

Phone numbers in Britain outside of the major cities consist of an exchange name plus telephone number. To dial the number, you'll need the code of the exchange being called. Information sheets on call-box walls give the codes in most instances. If your code isn't there, call the operator by dialing 100.

In London, phone numbers consist of the exchange code and number (seven digits or more). These digits are all you need to dial if you are calling from within the same city. If you're calling from elsewhere, you will need to prefix them with the dialing code for the city. Again, you'll find these codes on the call-box information sheets or by dialing the operator (100).

To make an international call from London, dial the international access code (00), then the country code, then the area code, and finally the local number. Or call through one of the following long-distance access codes: AT&T USA Direct (☎ **0800/890011**), Canada Direct (☎ **0800/890016**), Australia (☎ **0800/890061**), and New Zealand (☎ **0800/890064**). Common country codes are: USA and Canada, 1; Australia, 61; New Zealand, 64; South Africa, 27.

Time England follows Greenwich Mean Time (5 hours ahead of Eastern Standard Time). Since the dates of Daylight Savings Time differ slightly in the U.S. and Britain, there's a brief period (about a week) in autumn when Britain is only 4 hours ahead of New York, and in spring when it's 6 hours ahead of New York.

Tipping In restaurants, service charges in the 15% to 20% range are usually added to the bill. Sometimes this is clearly marked; at other times, it isn't. When in doubt, ask. If service isn't included, it's customary to add 15% to the bill. Sommeliers get about £1 ($1.65) per bottle of wine served. There's no tipping in pubs. In cocktail bars, the server usually gets about 75p ($1.25) per round of drinks.

Hotels, like restaurants, often add a service charge of 10% to 15% to most bills. In smaller B&Bs, the tip isn't likely to be included. Therefore, tip for special service, such as for the person who served you breakfast. If several persons have served you in a B&B, many guests ask that 10% or 15% be added to the bill and divided among the staff.

It's standard to tip taxi drivers 10% to 15% of the fare, although a tip for a taxi driver should never be less than 30p (50¢), even for a short run. Barbers and hairdressers expect 10% to 15%. Tour guides expect £2 ($3.30), although it's not mandatory. Today petrol (gas) station attendants are rarely tipped and theater ushers don't expect tips.

Weather   Call ☎ 020/7922-8844 for current weather information, but chances are the line will be busy.

4

Accommodations

With the millennium upon London, the year 2000 brings hoteliers a daunting challenge. Will London have enough beds for the anticipated invasion of 30 million visitors?

With all the vast improvements and upgrades done in the 1990s, chances are you'll like your room. What you won't like is the price, and that's almost guaranteed. Even if a hotel remains scruffy and shabby, London hoteliers, operating in a seller's market, have little embarrassment about jacking up prices. Hotels in all categories remain vastly overpriced as European capitals go.

Face it—you're just going to pay more than you'd like for a hotel room in London. London boasts some of the most famous hotels in the world—such hallowed temples of luxury as Claridge's, the Dorchester, the Park Lane, and the Savoy—and they're all superlative. The problem (and it's a serious one) is that there are too many of them and not enough of the moderately priced options so typical of other European capitals.

Even at the luxury level, you might be surprised at what you don't get at a London hotel. Many are stately Victorian and Edwardian gems so steeped in tradition that they still lack most or all of the modern conveniences that come standard in the luxury hotels of, say, New York. Some have gone to no end to modernize, but others have remained at Boer War vintage. London does have some cutting-edge, chintz-free hotels that seem shifted bodily from Los Angeles—complete with high-end sound systems and gadget-filled marble baths—but they're not necessarily superior; what the others lack in streamlining and convenience they frequently make up in personal service and spaciousness. It all depends on what you like.

If you're looking for reasonably priced options, don't despair. London does have some good value options in the lower price ranges. An affordable way to go is to book a **bed-and-breakfast.** At their best, they're clean, comfortable, and friendly. Currently, however, good B&Bs are in short supply in London; don't reserve a room at one without a recommendation you can trust. The following services will arrange a B&B room for you: **Bed & Breakfast**

A Note About Prices

Unless otherwise noted, prices are published rack prices for rooms with private bathrooms. Many include breakfast (often continental instead of English) and a 10% to 15% service charge. The British Government also imposes a VAT (value added tax) that adds 17.5% to your bill. This must be added to the prices quoted in the guide. Always ask for a better rate, particularly at the first-class and deluxe hotels (B&Bs generally charge a fixed rate). Be aware that you may not get it, particularly in the busy summer season or during certain trade fairs, when practically every room in the city is booked. But it never hurts to ask. You can sometimes negotiate a 20% to 30% discount in winter. Parking rates are per night.

It is generally cheaper to book a hotel through a travel agent than on your own. In most cases travel agents have access to wholesale rates which can be significantly less expensive than hotel rack rates. Sometimes, however, hotels may offer "spot specials," which may be even cheaper than the discounted rates offered by a travel agent. Getting the cheapest deal on a hotel is always tricky business. Regardless of how you try, you'll probably run into a client paying a cheaper rate than you agreed to. With time consideration a factor, it is always advised to shop around for the best rate.

(☎ **800/367-4668** or 423/690-8484), **Worldwide Bed & Breakfast Association** (☎ **800/852-2632** in the U.S., or 020/8742-9123; fax 020/8749-7084), and **The London Bed and Breakfast Agency Limited** (☎ **0207/586-2768;** fax 0207/586-6567) another reputable agency that can provide inexpensive accommodations in selected private homes.

1 West End Hotels

MAYFAIR
VERY EXPENSIVE

✪ **Brown's Hotel.** 29–34 Albemarle St., London W1X 4BP. ☎ **020/ 7493-6020.** Fax 020/7493-9381. www.brownshotel.com. E-mail: brownshotel@ukbusiness.com. 118 units. A/C MINIBAR TV TEL. £265–£285 ($437.25–$470.25) double; from £415 ($684.75) suite. AE, DC, MC, V. Off-site parking £32 ($52.80). Tube: Green Park.

Almost every year a hotel sprouts up trying to evoke an English country house ambience with Chippendale and chintz; this quintessential town house hotel watches these competitors come and go, and always comes out on top. Brown's was founded by James Brown, a former manservant of Lord Byron's, who knew the tastes of well-bred gentlemen and wanted to create a dignified, club-like place for them. He opened its doors in 1837, the same year Queen Victoria took the throne.

Brown's, which occupies 14 historic houses just off Berkeley Square, is still a thorough realization of its founder's vision. The guest rooms vary considerably and are a tangible record of England's history, showing restrained taste in decoration and appointments; even the washbasins are antiques. Accommodations, which range in size from small to extra spacious, have such extras as voice mail, dual-phone lines, and data ports; each is equipped with a luxurious mattress, even if the bed is antique. Bathrooms come in a variety of sizes, but are beautifully equipped with robes, luxurious cosmetics, hair dryers, and a rack of fluffy towels. In keeping with the atmosphere of the rest of the hotel, the inviting lounges pay homage to the past: They include the Roosevelt Room (Theodore Roosevelt spent his honeymoon at Brown's in 1886), the Rudyard Kipling Room (the famous author was a frequent visitor), and the paneled St. George's Bar for the drinking of spirits.

Dining: The dining room has a quiet dignity and unmatched service. Afternoon tea is served in the **Albemarle Room.** See "Teatime," in chapter 5.

Amenities: 24-hour room service, dry cleaning and laundry service, babysitting, secretarial services, valet, men's hairdresser, tour desk, business center; health club nearby.

Claridge's. Brook St., London W1A 2JQ. ☎ **800/223-6800** or 020/ 7629-8860. Fax 020/7409-6335. E-mail: info@claridges.co.uk. 190 units. A/C MINIBAR TV TEL. £320–£335 ($528–$552.75) double; from £450 ($742.50) suite. AE, DC, MC, V. Tube: Bond St.

This is *the* hotel for *Pax Britannia* nostalgists. Although other upper-crust addresses conjure up images of Empire, nobody does it better than Claridge's, which has cocooned royal visitors in an ambience of discreet elegance since the time of the Battle of Waterloo. This is stuffy British formality at its appealing best: As a reviewer once wrote, the "staff here will never try to be your friends"—as they might at, say, the Dorchester.

The hotel took on its present modest exterior in 1898. Inside, an art deco look was added in the 1930s; much of it still exists agreeably alongside antiques and TVs. The guest rooms are spacious, many with generous-size bathrooms complete with dressing rooms and other extras. About half the units are in a chic art deco style, the

West End Hotels

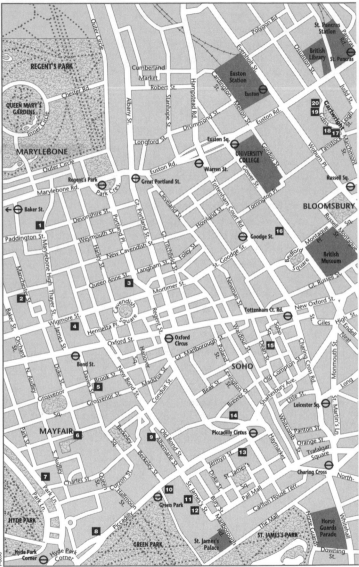

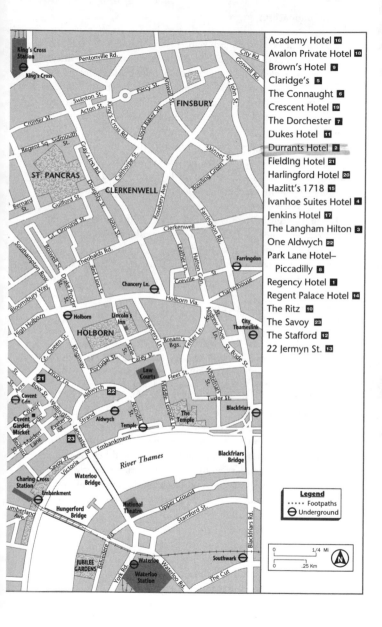

Academy Hotel **16**
Avalon Private Hotel **18**
Brown's Hotel **9**
Claridge's **5**
The Connaught **6**
Crescent Hotel **19**
The Dorchester **7**
Dukes Hotel **11**
Durrants Hotel **2**
Fielding Hotel **21**
Harlingford Hotel **20**
Hazlitt's 1718 **15**
Ivanhoe Suites Hotel **4**
Jenkins Hotel **17**
The Langham Hilton **3**
One Aldwych **22**
Park Lane Hotel–
   Piccadilly **8**
Regency Hotel **1**
Regent Palace Hotel **14**
The Ritz **10**
The Savoy **23**
The Stafford **12**
22 Jermyn St. **13**

Legend
···· Footpaths
⊖ Underground

0   1/4 Mi
0   .25 Km

others more in a classic English vein. Tasteful fabrics and extremely comfortable beds with state-of-the-art mattresses and quality linens are in each unit, along with double glazing, private safes, call buttons, and mirrored closets, plus dual-line phones with data ports. Most of the rooms are air-conditioned. The combination shower and tub baths have been called "sybaritic," with tubs big enough for the late Churchill to float in, and water pressure with the force of a fire hydrant. Everything lush and plush is here from the thick towels to the deluxe toiletries, from the hair dryers to the big robes. The emphasis is on old-fashioned room layouts instead of modern comforts, so you may feel embarrassed if you check in without your valet, à la Prince Charles.

Dining: Excellent food is stylishly served in the intimacy of the **Causerie,** renowned for its lunchtime smorgasbord and pre-theater suppers, and the more formal **Restaurant,** with English and French specialties. The strains of the Hungarian Quartet, a Claridge's institution since 1902, can be heard in the adjacent foyer during lunch and dinner.

Amenities: 24-hour room service, valet, laundry service, babysitting, on-call physician, concierge, currency exchange, basic secretarial services, salon, travel and theater desk, health club.

The Connaught. Carlos Place, W1Y 6AL. ☎ **020/7499-7070.** Fax 020/ 7495-3262. www.savoy_group.co.uk. E-mail: info@the_connaught.co.uk. 90 units. A/C TV TEL. £335–£395 ($552.75–$651.75) double; from £630 ($1,039.50) suite. AE, DC, MC, V. Parking: £32 ($52.80). Tube: Green Park.

This elegant hotel evoking an English country house and siting in the heart of Mayfair is one of Europe's most prestigious addresses. Not the most glamorous, nor even the most fashionable hotel in London, it nonetheless coddles you in comfort and luxury, with a hospitality that's legendary and guarantees privacy even if you're a film star sex symbol. Near Grosvenor Square, this brick-built house is somewhat like a club, many repeat guests demanding their favorite room. You enter a world of fresh flowers, crystal chandeliers, Wedgwood, and antiques. There is something of an aura of aristocratic decay here, just as the country gentry like it.

Rooms range from medium to large, and are a world of antiques, chintz, tasteful appointments such as gilt-trimmed white paneling, and sumptuous beds with grand mattresses and the finest of Irish linen bed clothing. Marble fireplaces, ornate plasterwork, and oak paneling add to its allure. The large, old-fashioned baths are still intact, and are outfitted with robes, a hair dryer, and thick fluffy towels.

Dining/Diversions: The on-site **Grill Connaught Restaurant,** with its mahogany paneling, and the smaller Georgian-style **Grill Room** are among the premier dining venues of London. Under the guidance of chef Michel Bourdin, they both offer the same menu but may have different daily specials. Classical French dishes and old-fashioned English cookery are combined to entice tout London. Yes, they still serve Irish stew on Tuesday, but they can also dazzle with the finest haute cuisine of the Escoffier tradition. One loyal patron who comes here twice a week to dine told us, "I picked up the habit from my great-grandfather." The bar and lounges appear as if waiting for the arrival of an ambassador.

Amenities: Concierge, 24-hour room service, dry cleaning and laundry service, babysitting, access to nearby health club.

✪ **The Dorchester.** 53 Park Lane, London W1A 2HJ. ☎ **800/727-9820** or 020/7629-8888. Fax 020/7409-0114. E-mail: info@dorchesterhotel.com. 248 units. A/C MINIBAR TV TEL. £295–£325 ($486.75–$536.25) double; from £415 ($684.75) suite. AE, DC, MC, V. Parking £27 ($44.55). Tube: Hyde Park Corner or Marble Arch.

This is among the best of today's London hotels. It has all the elegance of Claridge's, but without the upper-crust attitude that can verge on snobbery. Few hotels have the time-honored experience of "The Dorch," which has maintained a tradition of fine comfort and cuisine since it opened its doors in 1931.

Breaking from the neoclassical tradition, the most ambitious architects of the era designed a building of reinforced concrete clothed in terrazzo slabs. Within you'll find a 1930s take on Regency motifs: The monumental arrangements of flowers and the elegance of the gilded-cage promenade seem appropriate for a diplomatic reception, yet convey a kind of comfort in which guests from all over the world feel at ease.

The Dorchester boasts guest rooms outfitted with Irish linen sheets on deluxe mattresses, plus all the electronic gadgetry you'd expect, and double- and triple-glazed windows to keep out noise, along with plump armchairs, cherrywood furnishings, and, in many cases, four-poster beds piled high with pillows. The large bathrooms are equally stylish, with mottled carrara marble and Lalique-style sconces, plus hair dryers, thick towels, makeup mirrors, and posh toiletries. The best rooms open onto views of Hyde Park.

Dining: The hotel's restaurant, **The Grill Room,** is among the finest dining establishments in London, and the **Dorchester Bar** is a legendary meeting place. The promenade, with its glorious lush sofas, is the ideal setting to enjoy afternoon tea and watch the world go by. The hotel also offers Cantonese cuisine at **The Oriental,** London's most exclusive—and expensive—Chinese restaurant.

Amenities: 24-hour room service; dry cleaning and laundry service; one of the best-outfitted health clubs in London, the Dorchester Spa; barbershop; hairdresser; tour desk; secretarial services; and babysitting.

✪ **Park Lane Hotel.** Piccadilly, London W1Y 8BX. ☎ **800/325-3535** or 020/7499-6321. Fax 020/7499-1965. www.sheraton.com. 305 units. A/C MINIBAR TV TEL. £260 ($429) double; from £360 ($594) suite. AE, DC, MC, V. Parking £28 ($46.20). Tube: Hyde Park Corner or Green Park.

The most traditional of the Park Lane mansions, and once the lone holdout against chain management, the Park Lane Hotel was sold in 1996 to the Sheraton Corporation, which upgraded it but maintained its quintessential Britishness. Launched in 1913 but kept empty for years, the Park Lane finally opened in 1924 under the leadership of Bracewell Smith, one of London's leading hoteliers. Today, its Silver Entrance remains an art deco marvel that has been used as a backdrop in many films, including the classic BBC miniseries *Brideshead Revisited.*

Designed in a U shape, with a view overlooking Green Park, the hotel offers luxurious accommodations that are a surprisingly good deal—they're among the least expensive on Park Lane. Many of the suites have marble fireplaces and original marble bathrooms. The rooms have benefited from an impressive refurbishment—they're larger, and the decor is lighter in tone. All have double-glazed windows to block out noise.

Dining/Diversions: On site is a **Brasserie,** serving French cuisine. A harpist plays in the **Palm Court Lounge** every Sunday and tea is served daily. For more information, see "Teatime" in chapter 5.

Amenities: 24-hour room service, concierge, dry cleaning and laundry service, babysitting, secretarial services, fitness center, beauty salon, business center, safety-deposit boxes, gift and newspaper shop, barbershop, women's salon, and Daniele Ryman Aromatherapy Shop. Some bedrooms are larger and better appointed than others, with higher ceilings and taller windows. In the more deluxe rooms, you get trouser presses and better views. The most tranquil rooms open onto the rear, but those opening onto the court are dark. Mattresses have been renewed and are deluxe. Bathrooms are generally spacious and well equipped with fluffy towels and hair dryers; many units also have robes.

INEXPENSIVE

Ivanhoe Suite Hotel. 1 St. Christopher's Place, Barrett St. Piazza, London W1M 5HB. ☎ **020/7935-1047.** Fax 020/7224-0563. www.scoot.co.uk/ivanhoe_suite_hotel. 8 units. MINIBAR TV TEL. £79 ($130.35) double, £89 ($146.85) triple. Rates include continental breakfast. AE, DC, MC, V. Tube: Bond St.

Born-to-shop buffs flock to this little hidden discovery located in a part of town off Oxford Street not known for its hotels. "It's like having my own little flatlet every time I come to London," one satisfied guest told us. "If you dare tell anybody about it, I might have to get out the old horse whip or at least scold you." Situated above a restaurant on a pedestrian street of boutiques and restaurants and close to the shop-flanked New and Old Bond streets, this townhouse hotel has attractively furnished small and medium-size singles and doubles, each with a sitting area. Each stylish room has its own entry, security video, trouser press, and beverage-making facilities along with a fridge/bar, plus a wide selection of videotapes. Its bedrooms were redecorated in 1998, the mattresses renewed. The newly tiled baths are small—half with a shower, half with a tub-shower combination, plus hair dryers, trouser presses, and a rack of medium-size towels. Breakfast is served in a very small area at the top of the first flight of stairs, and you can stop off for a nightcap at the corner pub, a real neighborhood locale. The Ivanhoe offers a number of services including room service, babysitting, secretarial service, laundry, and sightseeing tour and theater reservations. *Note:* The four-floor hotel doesn't have an elevator.

MARYLEBONE

To locate these hotels, see the map, "Marylebone, Paddington, Bayswater & Notting Hill Gate Hotels" on p. 94.

VERY EXPENSIVE

✪ **The Langham Hilton.** 1 Portland Place, London W1N 4JA. ☎ **020/7636-1000.** Fax 020/7323-2340. www.hilton.com. 379 units. A/C MINIBAR TV TEL. £280 ($462) double; £365 ($602.25) executive room; from £670 ($1,105.50) suite. Rates include breakfast for executive room and suite. AE, DC, MC, V. Tube: Oxford Circus.

When this extremely well-located hotel was inaugurated in 1865 by the Prince of Wales, it was a suitably fashionable address for aristocrats seeking respite from their country estates. After it was bombed in World War II, it languished as dusty office space for the BBC until the early 1990s, when Hilton International took it over. Its restoration was painstaking; today, it's Hilton's European flagship. The Langham's public rooms reflect the power and majesty of the British Empire at its apex. Guest rooms are somewhat less opulent, but they're still attractively furnished and comfortable, featuring French provincial furniture and red oak trim. Major refurbishment to the bedrooms was carried out in 1999 to be ready for the millennium. Mattresses are of extremely high quality, and the small bathrooms contain hair dryers, robes, trouser presses, and an array of fluffy towels. And the location is still terrific: within easy reach of Mayfair and Soho restaurants and theaters and Oxford and Regent Street shopping; Regent's Park is just blocks away.

Dining/Diversions: Vodka, caviar, and champagne flow liberally at the **Tsar's Russian Bar and Restaurant.** Drinks are served in the **Chukka Bar,** a re-creation of a private polo club. The most upscale restaurant is a high-ceilinged Victorian fantasy called **Memories,** featuring patriotic nostalgia and cuisine from the far corners of the British Commonwealth. Afternoon tea is served amid the potted palms of the Edwardian-style **Palm Court.**

Amenities: 24-hour room service, concierge, health club, business center, beauty salon.

EXPENSIVE

✪ **Dorset Square Hotel.** 39–40 Dorset Sq., London NW1 6QN. ☎ **020/ 7723-7874.** Fax 020/7724-3328. www.firmdale.com. E-mail: Dorset@ afirmdale.com. 38 units. MINIBAR TV TEL. £130–£195 ($214.50–$321.75) double; from £215 ($354.75) suite. AE, MC, V. Parking £25 ($41.25). Tube: Baker St. or Marylebone.

Situated in a lovely Regency Square steps away from Regent's Park, this is one of London's best and most stylish "house hotels," overlooking Thomas Lord's first cricket pitch. Hot hoteliers Tim and Kit Kemp have furnished the interior of these two Georgian town houses in a comfy mix of antiques, reproductions, and chintz that will make you feel like you're in an elegant private home. All the impressive guest rooms come with marble baths; about half are air-conditioned. All units are decorated in a personal yet extravagantly beautiful style—the owners are interior decorators known for their taste, which is often bold and daring. Eight offer crown-canopied beds, but all have firm and very high-quality mattresses. The baths are exquisite in taste with robes, hair dryers, and fluffy towels.

Dining: The menu at the **Potting Shed** changes seasonally and features the best of English cuisine as well as a wide selection of champagnes and wines. The restaurant occupies an old servants' hall, with a trompe l'oeil mural of a cricket pitch and a sisal-decked floor.

Amenities: 24-hour room service, babysitting, dry cleaning and laundry service, massage, and secretarial services. You can ride in the owner's chauffeured vintage Bentley for a fee; it'll make you feel like Norma Desmond in *Sunset Boulevard.*

MODERATE

Bryanston Court Hotel. 56–60 Great Cumberland Place, London W1H 7FD. ☎ **020/7262-3141.** Fax 020/7262-7248. www.bryanstonhotel.com. E-mail: hotel@bryanstonhotel.com. 54 units. TV TEL. £110 ($181.50) double; £125 ($206.25) triple. Rates include continental breakfast. AE, DC, MC, V. Tube: Marble Arch.

This hotel is ideally located in a neighborhood with many lovely squares. Three individual houses were cleverly joined to form the hotel about two centuries ago. Today, it's one of the finest moderately priced hotels in the area, thanks to the refurbishing and maintenance efforts of the Theodore family. Family owned and operated, it offers bedrooms that, although small, are comfortably furnished and well maintained, with good mattresses. Bathrooms are small, but adequate for the job, with medium-sized towels. *Warning:* Don't let them send you down to the basement room, or you'll feel like Cinderella before she met Prince Charming.

On chilly nights, we like to retreat to the bar, in the rear of a comfortable lounge, and relax with a pint in front of the roaring fireplace. Your hosts are happy to arrange theater and tour bookings for you.

Durrants Hotel. George St., London W1H 6BJ. ☎ **020/7935-8131.** Fax 020/7487-3510. 92 units. TV TEL. £135–£180 ($222.75–$297) double; £175 ($288.75) family room for 3; from £275 ($453.75) suite. AE, MC, V. Tube: Bond St.

This historic hotel off Manchester Square (established in 1789) with its Georgian-detailed facade is snug, cozy, and traditional—almost like a poor man's Brown's. We find it to be one of the most quintessentially English of all London hotels and a soothing retreat on a cold, rainy day. In the 100 years that the Miller family has owned the hotel, several neighboring houses have been incorporated into the original structure. A walk through the pine-and-mahogany–paneled public rooms is like stepping back into another time: You'll even find an 18th-century letter-writing room. The rooms are rather bland except for elaborate cove moldings and very comfortable furnishings, including good beds. They exude an aura of solidity; some are air-conditioned. Alas, all of them are small. Bathrooms are also tiny, but nearly all of them have both tubs and showers, but not much room to maneuver around. Each has a set of medium-size towels, but few other amenities except a bidet.

The in-house restaurant serves full afternoon tea and satisfying French or traditional English cuisine in one of the most beautiful Georgian rooms in the neighborhood. The less formal breakfast room is ringed with 19th-century political cartoons by a noted Victorian artist. The pub, a neighborhood favorite, has Windsor chairs, an open fireplace, and decor that hasn't changed much in two centuries. Services include 24-hour room service, laundry service, and babysitting.

INEXPENSIVE

Edward Lear Hotel. 28–30 Seymour St., London W1H 5WD. ☎ **020/ 7402-5401.** Fax 020/7706-3766. www.edlear.com. E-mail: edwardlear@ aol.com. 31 units (12 with bathroom). TV TEL. £60 ($99) double without bathroom, £79.50–£89.50 ($131.15–$147.65) double with bathroom; from £105 ($173.25) suite. Rates include English breakfast. MC, V. Tube: Marble Arch.

This popular hotel one block from Marble Arch is made all the more desirable by the bouquets of fresh flowers in the public rooms. It occupies a pair of brick town houses, both of which date from 1780. The western house was the London home of the 19th-century artist and poet Edward Lear, famous for his nonsense verse; his illustrated limericks adorn the walls of one of the sitting rooms. Steep stairs lead up to the cozy rooms, which are fairly small but comfortable, with firm mattresses. One major drawback: This is an extremely noisy part of London. Rooms in the rear are quieter. Bathrooms are tidily arranged and well maintained, complete with hair dryers and medium-size towels.

Hart House Hotel. 51 Gloucester Place, Portman Sq., London W1H 3PE. ☎ **020/7935-2288.** Fax 020/7935-8516. 16 units. TV TEL. £95 ($156.75) double; £115 ($189.75) triple; £130 ($214.50) quad. Rates include English breakfast. AE, MC, V. Tube: Marble Arch or Baker Street.

Hart House has been a longtime favorite with Frommer's readers. In the heart of the West End, this well-preserved historic building (one of a group of Georgian mansions occupied by exiled French nobles during the French Revolution) lies within easy walking distance of many theaters, as well as some of the most sought-after shopping areas and parks in London. Cozy and convenient, it's run by Andrew Bowden, one of Marylebone's best B&B hosts. The rooms—done in a combination of furnishings, ranging from Portobello antique to modern—are spic-and-span, each one with a different character. Favorites include no. 7, a triple with a big bath and shower. Ask for no. 11, on the top floor, if you'd like a brightly lit aerie. Housekeeping rates high marks here, and the bedrooms are comfortably appointed with chairs, an armoire, a desk, a chest of

♟ Frommer's Family Friendly Hotels

Although the bulk of their clients are business travelers, each of the major international hotel chains does its best to create the impression that its fully geared for family fun. Look for special summer packages at most hotel chains between June and August. Some of the most consistently generous offers come from **Travelodge** (☎ 800/435-4542) and **Hilton International** (☎ 800/445-8667) chains, but it all depends on the specific branch. For best results, call the 800 number and ask about special family packages.

- **Hart House Hotel** (Marylebone; see p. 64) This small, family-run B&B is right in the center of the West End, near Hyde Park. Many of its rooms are triples; if you need even more room, special family suites with connecting rooms can be arranged.

- **Sandringham Hotel** (3 Holford Rd., London NW3 1AD. ☎ 020/7435-1569. Fax 020/7431-5932. E-mail: sandringham.hotel@virgin.net). Out in Hampstead, where children have plenty of room to play on the heath, this hotel offers both triple and family rooms that comfortably accommodate four to five people.

drawers, and a good bed with a firm mattress. Bathrooms, though small, are efficiently organized with a hair dryer and a set of medium-size towels. Guest services include babysitting, dry cleaning and laundry service, and massage service. Literary buffs, take note: Poet Elizabeth Barrett resided at no. 99 with her family for many years.

Regency Hotel. 19 Nottingham Place, London W1M 3FF. ☎ **020/ 7486-5347.** Fax 020/7224-6057. 20 units. MINIBAR TV TEL. £85 ($140.25) double; £125 ($206.25) family room. Rates include English breakfast. AE, DC, MC, V. Parking £18 ($28.80) nearby. Tube: Baker St. or Regent's Park.

This centrally located hotel was built, along with most of its neighbors, in the late 1800s. Although it has functioned as some kind of hotel since the 1940s, in 1991 it was gutted and tastefully renovated into its upgraded present format. One of the better hotels on the street, it offers simple, conservatively decorated modern bedrooms scattered over four floors, and a breakfast room set in what used to be the cellar. Each room has a radio, hair dryer, coffeemaker, trouser press, and ironing board. Baths, although small, are well kept and come with a set of adequate-size towels and a hair dryer. Room service is available. The neighborhood is protected as a historic district, and Marble Arch, Regent's Park, and Baker Street all lie within a 12-minute walk. Hotel services include daily maid service and room service.

ST. JAMES'S
VERY EXPENSIVE

The Ritz. 150 Piccadilly, London W1V 9DG. ☎ **800/525-4800** or 020/ 7493-8181. Fax 020/7493-2687. www.ritzhotel.co.uk. E-mail: enquire@ ritzhotel.co.uk. 130 units. A/C MINIBAR TV TEL. £245–£355 ($404.25–$585.75) double; from £385 ($635.25) suite. Children under 12 stay free in parents' room. AE, DC, MC, V. Parking £45 ($74.25). Tube: Green Park.

Built in the French-Renaissance style and opened by César Ritz in 1906, this hotel overlooking Green Park is synonymous with luxury: Gold-leafed molding, marble columns, and potted palms abound, and a gold-leafed statue, *La Source,* adorns the fountain of the oval-shaped Palm Court. After a major restoration, the hotel is better than ever: New carpeting and air-conditioning have been installed in the guest rooms, and an overall polishing has recaptured much of the Ritz's original splendor. Still, this Ritz lags far behind the much grander one in Paris (to which it is not affiliated). The belle époque guest rooms, each with its own character, are spacious and comfortable. Many have marble fireplaces, elaborate gilded plasterwork, and a decor of soft pastel hues. A few rooms have their original brass beds and marble fireplaces. Beds are deluxe with luxury mattresses, and the bathrooms are elegantly appointed in either tile or marble and filled with fluffy towels, robes, phones, deluxe toiletries, and a hair dryer.

Dining: The Ritz is still the most fashionable place in London to meet for afternoon tea at the **Ritz Palm Court** (see "Teatime," in chapter 5). The **Ritz Restaurant,** one of the loveliest dining rooms in the world, has already been faithfully restored to its original splendor. Service is efficient yet unobtrusive, and the tables are spaced to allow the most private of conversations (perhaps the reason Edward and Mrs. Simpson dined here so frequently before they married). The Palm Court also serves coffee and breakfast. Remember, both venues are very formal and require jacket and tie for gentlemen.

Amenities: 24-hour room service, valet, laundry service, babysitting, concierge, turndown, in-room massage, twice-daily maid service, express checkout, salon fitness center, business center.

The Stafford. 16–18 St. James's Place, London SW1A 1NJ. ☎ **800/525-4800** or 020/7493-0111. Fax 020/7493-7121. E-mail: info@thestaffordhotel.co.uk. 81 units. A/C TV TEL. £230–£260 ($379.50–$429) double; from £330 ($544.50) suite. AE, DC, MC, V. Tube: Green Park.

Famous for its American Bar, its clubby St. James's address, its discretion, and the warmth of its Edwardian décor, the Stafford is in a cul-de-sac off one of London's most centrally located and busiest neighborhoods. It's reached via St. James's Place or by a cobble-covered courtyard designed as a mews and known today as the Blue Ball Yard. The recently refurbished late-19th-century hotel has retained a country-house atmosphere, with touches of antique charm and modern amenities. It's not the Ritz, but the Stafford competes well with Dukes and 22 Jermyn Street (both highly recommendable as well) for a tasteful, discerning clientele. All the guest rooms are individually decorated, reflecting the hotel's origins as a private home. Many singles contain queen-size beds. Most of the units have king-size or twin beds, however, and all contain quality mattresses for a good night's sleep. Some of the deluxe units also offer four-posters, making you feel like Henry VIII. Nearly all the baths are clad in marble with tubs and stall showers, a hair dryer, a private bath, fluffy towels, toiletries, and quality chrome fixtures. A few of the hotel's newest and plushest accommodations in the historically restored stable mews require a walk across the yard. These rooms in some ways are even superior to those in the main building, and much has been saved to preserve their original style, including A-beams on the upper floors. But no horse in the 18th century ever slept like this. Units come with electronic safes, disc and stereo systems, and quality furnishings, mostly antique reproductions.

Dining: Classic international dishes are prepared from select fresh ingredients at the elegant **Stafford Restaurant,** lit with handsome chandeliers and accented with flowers, candles, and white linen. The famous **American Bar,** which brings to mind the memento-packed library of an English country house, is an especially cozy place serving light meals and cocktails.

Amenities: 24-hour room service, babysitting, concierge, secretarial services, laundry service, maid service, privileges at a nearby health club.

EXPENSIVE

✪ **Dukes Hotel.** 35 St. James's Place, London SW1A 1NY. ☎ **800/381-4702** or 020/7491-4840. Fax 020/7493-1264. www.dukeshotel.co.uk. E-mail: dukeshotel@csi.com. 81 units. A/C TV TEL. £245 ($392) double; from £265 ($437.25) suite. AE, DC, MC, V. Parking £32 ($52.80). Tube: Green Park.

Dukes provides elegance without ostentation in what was presumably someone's *Upstairs–Downstairs* town house. Along with its nearest competitors, the Stafford and 22 Jermyn Street, it caters to those looking for charm, style, and tradition in a hotel. A hotel since

1908 (last renovated in 1994), it stands in a quiet courtyard off St. James's Street with turn-of-the-century gas lamps that create the appropriate mood for what's coming once you walk through the front door. Each well-furnished guest room is decorated in the style of a particular English period, ranging from Regency to Edwardian. All rooms are equipped with marble baths, satellite TV, air-conditioning, and private bars, plus luxurious mattresses. Bathrooms are small but clad in marble, with robes, soft fluffy towels, and hair dryers. A short walk away are Buckingham Palace, St. James's Palace, and the Houses of Parliament, shoppers will be near Bond Street and Piccadilly, and literature buffs will be interested to note that Oscar Wilde lived and wrote in St. James's Place for a time.

Dining: Dukes' Restaurant is small, tasteful, and elegant, combining classic British and continental cuisine. The hotel also has a club-like bar, which is known for its rare collection of vintage ports, Armagnacs, and cognacs.

Amenities: Even though it's claustrophobically small—it was once described as England's smallest castle—Dukes offers full hotel services, including 24-hour room service, car-rental and ticket services, photocopying and typing services, babysitting, dry cleaning and laundry service, a small health spa, conference rooms.

✪ **22 Jermyn Street.** 22 Jermyn St., London SW1Y 6HL. ☎ **800/682-7808** or 020/7734-2353. Fax 020/7734-0750. www.22jermyn.com. E-mail: togna@ 22jermyn.com. 18 units. MINIBAR TV TEL. £205 ($338.25) double; from £280 ($462) suite. AE, DC, MC, V. Valet parking £30 ($48). Tube: Piccadilly Circus.

This is London's premier town house hotel, a gem of elegance and discretion. Set behind a facade of gray stone with neoclassical details, this structure, only 50 yards from Piccadilly, was built in 1870 as an apartment house for English gentlemen doing business in London. Since 1915, it has been administrated by three generations of the Togna family, whose most recent scion closed it for a radical restoration in 1990. Now reveling in its new role as a chic and upscale boutique hotel, 22 Jermyn offers an interior filled with greenery, the kind of art you might find in an elegant private home, and the best "information superhighway services" of any hotel in London. This hotel doesn't have the bar or restaurant facilities of The Stafford or Dukes, but its rooms are even more richly appointed, done in traditional English style with masses of fresh flowers and chintz. Beds are exceedingly luxurious with deluxe mattresses, and the bathrooms are clad in granite and equipped with fluffy robes and towels, luxurious toiletries, phones, and hair dryers.

Amenities: 24-hour room service; concierge; babysitting; dry cleaning and laundry service; secretarial services; fax; videophones; video library; CD-ROM library; Internet access; and a weekly newsletter that keeps guests up to date with restaurants, theater, and exhibitions. Access to a nearby health club.

PICCADILLY CIRCUS
INEXPENSIVE

Regent Palace Hotel. 12 Sherwood St., London W1A 4BZ. ☎ **020/ 7734-7000.** Fax 020/7734-6435. www.forte-hotels.com. 842 units (none with bathroom). TV TEL. Sun–Thurs £54 ($89.10) double, Fri–Sat £94 ($155.10) double. Rates include English breakfast. AE, DC, MC, V. Parking £35 ($56). Tube: Piccadilly Circus.

The Regent Palace, a major focal point since it was built in 1915 at the edge of Piccadilly Circus, is one of the largest hotels in Europe, a beacon for those who want to be near the bright lights of London's theaterland. It's certainly a comedown from the deluxe Mayfair palaces recommended above, but you can't expect the same kinds of service, ambience, and amenities at these prices. This hotel is known for staunch loyalty to its original design: None of the simply furnished rooms have private bathrooms. The shared facilities in the hallways are adequate, though, and each room has a sink with hot and cold running water and coffee- and tea-making facilities. Here's your chance to live as your great, great-grandfather did when he visited London and headed down the corridor to the shared bath, towel in hand.

Calahan's, the Irish pub on site, is the most central in London, in the very heart of the city actually, drawing a mixed crowd of friendly locals and visitors from all parts of the globe. Marco Pierre White, the leading chef of London, has also chosen this site to launch his first venture in the medium-priced dining field: **Titanic,** and it's not sinking.

SOHO
MODERATE

✪ **Hazlitt's 1718.** 6 Frith St., London W1V 5TZ. ☎ **020/7434-1771.** Fax 020/7439-1524. E-mail: reservation@hazlitts.co.uk. 23 units. TV TEL. £180 ($297) double; £260 ($429) suite. AE, DC, MC, V. Tube: Leicester Sq. or Tottenham Court Rd.

This gem, housed in three historic homes on Soho Square—the most fashionable address in London two centuries ago—is one of London's best small hotels. Built in 1718, the hotel is named for William Hazlitt, who founded the Unitarian church in Boston and wrote four volumes on the life of his hero, Napoléon; the essayist died here in 1830.

Hazlitt's is a favorite with artists, actors, media people, and models. It's eclectic, filled with odds and ends picked up around the country at estate auctions. Some find the Georgian decor a bit spartan, but the 2,000 original prints hanging on the walls brighten it considerably. Many bedrooms have four-poster beds, and some bathrooms have their original claw-footed tubs (only one unit has a shower). If you can afford it, opt for the elegant Baron Willoughby suite, with its giant four-poster bed and wood-burning fireplace. Some of the floors dip and sway and there's no elevator, but it's all part of the charm. Some rooms are a bit small, but most of them are spacious, and all contain state-of-the-art mattresses. Most of the bathrooms have 19th-century styling but up-to-date plumbing with oversize tubs and old brass fittings; the showers, however, are mostly hand-held. A rack of medium-size towels greets you. Amenities include a concierge, room service, babysitting, dry cleaning and laundry service, and a discounted rate on a car or limousine. Swinging Soho is at your doorstep; the young, hip staff will be happy to direct you to the local hot spots.

BLOOMSBURY
MODERATE

Academy Hotel. 17–21 Gower St., London WC1E 6HG. ☎ **800/678-3096** or 020/7631-4115. Fax 020/7636-3442. E-mail: academy@aol.com. 48 units. A/C TV TEL. £125–£145 ($206.25–$239.25) double; £185 ($305.25) suite. AE, DC, MC, V. Tube: Tottenham Court Rd., Goodge St., or Russell Sq.

Right in the heart of London's publishing district, the Academy attracts budding British John Grishams who haven't hit the big time yet. If you look out your window, you'll see where Virginia Woolf and other literary members of the Bloomsbury Group used to pass by every day. Many were headed for the British Museum, and you can follow in their footsteps. Many of the original architectural details were preserved when these three 1776 Georgian row houses were joined. The hotel was substantially upgraded in the 1990s, with a bathroom added to every bedroom (whether there was space or not). Fourteen have a tub-shower combination; the rest have showers only, but all contain a rack of medium-size towels. The beds, so they say, were built to "American specifications." True or not, they assure you of a restful night's sleep. Grace notes include the glass panels, colonnades, and intricate plasterwork on the facade. Rooms with their overstuffed armchairs and half-canopied beds sometimes evoke English country-house living, but that of the poorer relations. The theater district and Covent Garden are within walking distance. The in-house, award-winning restaurant, **Alchemy,** has been recently refurbished to a much more modern design and offers a reasonably priced menu of modern European food. Other facilities include an elegant bar, a library room, a secluded patio garden, concierge, room service, and dry cleaning and laundry service.

INEXPENSIVE

Avalon Private Hotel. 46–47 Cartwright Gardens, London WC1H 9EL. ☎ **020/7387-2366.** Fax 020/7387-5810. www.scoot.co.uk/avalon-hotel. E-mail: avalonhotellondon@compuserve.com. 28 units (5 with shower). TV. £62 ($102.30) double without shower, £78 ($128.70) double with shower; £84 ($138.60) triple without shower, £96 ($158.40) triple with shower; £96 ($158.40) quad without shower, £108 ($178.20) quad with shower. Rates include English breakfast. AE, DC, MC, V. Tube: Russell Sq., King's Cross, or Euston.

One guidebook from Victoria's day claimed Bloomsbury attracted "Medical and other students of both sexes and several nationalities, American folk passing through London, literary persons 'up' for a week or two's reading in the British Museum, and Bohemians pure and simple." The same might be said for today's patrons of this hotel, built in 1807 as two Georgian houses in residential Cartwright Gardens. Guests feel privileged because they have use of a semi-private garden across the street with tennis courts. Top-floor rooms, often filled with students, are reached via impossibly steep stairs, but bedrooms on the lower levels have easier access. The place obviously didn't hire a decorator; everything is wildly mismatched in the bedrooms and the droopy lounge—but the price is right. The bedrooms were recently renewed with new mattresses and fresh curtains were added. Private baths with shower are extremely small. Most guests in bathless rooms have to use the corridor baths, which are generally adequate and maintained well. Towels are a bit thin. Services include concierge, dry cleaning and laundry service, and a tour desk.

Crescent Hotel. 49–50 Cartwright Gardens, London WC1H 9EL. ☎ **020/7387-1515.** Fax 020/7383-2054. 24 units, 18 with bathroom (some with shower only, some with tub only). TV TEL. £80 ($132) double with bathroom. Rates include English breakfast. MC, V. Tube: Russell Sq., King's Cross, or Euston.

Although John Ruskin, Percy Bysshe Shelley, Leonard Woolf, and Dorothy Sayers no longer pass by the door, the Crescent still stands in the heart of academic London. The private square is owned by the City Guild of Skinners and guarded by the University of London, whose student residential halls are just across the street. You have access to the gardens with their private tennis courts. Mrs. Bessolo and Mrs. Cockle, the managers, are the kindest hosts along the street; they view Crescent as an extension of their private home and welcome you to its comfortably elegant Georgian surroundings, which date from 1810. Some guests have been returning for four decades. Bedrooms range from small singles with shared bathrooms to more spacious twin and double rooms with private plumbing. All rooms have good mattresses, plus TV and beverage makers; other thoughtful extras include alarm clocks and hair dryers. Twins and doubles have very tiny baths. Many rooms are singles, however, ranging in price from £40 to £60 ($66 to $99), depending on the plumbing. You're given a set of medium-size towels. The good ladies will even let you do your ironing so that you'll look sharp when you go out on the town.

Harlingford Hotel. 61–63 Cartwright Gardens, London WC1H 9EL. ☎ **020/ 7387-1551.** Fax 020/7387-4616. 44 units. TV TEL. £80 ($132) double; £90 ($148.50) triple; £100 ($165) quad. Rates include English breakfast. AE, DC, MC, V. Tube: Russell Sq., King's Cross, or Euston.

This hotel is composed of three town houses built in the 1820s that were joined together around 1900 via a bewildering array of staircases and meandering hallways. Set in the heart of Bloomsbury, it's run by a management that seems genuinely concerned about the welfare of their guests, unlike many of their neighboring rivals. (In a scene straight from Dickens, they distribute little mincemeat pies to their guests during the Christmas holidays.) Double-glazed windows cut down on the street noise, and all the bedrooms are generally comfortable and inviting, especially the firm mattresses. Bathrooms are small, however, since the house wasn't originally designed for them. The most comfortable rooms are on the second and third levels; otherwise, expect to climb some steep English stairs (there's no elevator). Still, say no to the rooms on ground level, as they are darker and have less security. The tiny bathrooms have medium-size towels and hair dryers. You'll have use of the tennis courts in Cartwright Gardens.

Jenkins Hotel. 45 Cartwright Gardens, London WC1H 9EH. ☎ **020/7387-2067.** Fax 020/7383-3139. E-mail: reservations@jenkinshotel.demon.co.uk. 15 units (6 with bathroom). MINIBAR TV TEL. £62 ($102.30) double without bathroom, £72 ($118.80) double with bathroom; £83 ($136.95) triple with bathroom. MC, V. Rates include English breakfast. Tube: Russell Sq., King's Cross, or Euston.

Followers of the Agatha Christie TV series *Poirot* might recognize this Cartwright Gardens residence—it was featured in the series. The antiques are gone and the rooms are small, but some of the original charm of the Georgian house remain—enough so that the London *Mail on Sunday* recently proclaimed it one of the "ten best hotel values" in the city. All the rooms have been redecorated and many completely refurbished, with firm mattresses added to all the beds. Only a few rooms have private baths, and they're quite small, but the corridor baths are adequate and well maintained. Towels are medium size, and each guest room has a hair dryer. The location is great, near the British Museum, London University, theaters, and antiquarian bookshops. There are some drawbacks—no lift and no reception or sitting room, but it's a place where you can settle in and feel at home.

COVENT GARDEN
VERY EXPENSIVE

One Aldwych. 1 Aldwych, London WC2B 4BZ. ☎ **800/447-7462** in the U.S., or 020/7300-1000. www.onealdwych.co.uk. E-mail: sales@ onealdwych.co.uk. 105 units. A/C MINIBAR TV TEL. £265–£320 ($437.25–$528) double; from £395 ($651.75) suite. AE, DC, MC, V. Parking £25 ($41.25). Tube: Temple.

Of the many hotels that compete for five-star ratings within London, this is the newest, and the one infused with a décor affected by the calm and simplicity of the Zen aesthetic. Just east of Covent Garden, it occupies the classic-looking Edwardian building that was erected in 1907 as the headquarters for the (now-defunct) *Morning Post,* and was designed, ironically enough, by the same architect who created the Ritz Hotels in London, Paris, and Madrid. Prior to its re-inauguration as a hotel in 1998, all but a fraction of its interior was stripped and gutted, and replaced with an artful simplicity. Bedrooms are outfitted with simple lines and rich color schemes of sage, purple, burnt orange, and deep reds, and accessorized with raw silk curtains, computer modems, and electrical outlets that can handle both North American and European electrical currents. The bedrooms are sumptuous with quality mattresses; bathrooms are deluxe, with hair dryers, robes, phones, fluffy towels, and luxurious toiletries.

Dining/Diversions: There's an all-day café and bistro, **Indigo,** that serves California-inspired platters daily, plus the more formal **Axis,** featuring a modern British and Pacific Rim cuisine.

Amenities: On site is a state-of-the-art health club and a pool almost 60 feet long, 24-hour room service, laundry and dry cleaning, concierge, babysitting.

MODERATE

✪ **Fielding Hotel.** 4 Broad Court, Bow St., London WC2B 5QZ. ☎ **020/ 7836-8305.** Fax 020/7497-0064. 24 units. TV TEL. £95–£120 ($156.75–$198) double. AE, DC, MC, V. Tube: Covent Garden.

One of London's more eccentric hotels, the Fielding is cramped, quirky, and quaint, but an enduring favorite nonetheless. The hotel is named after novelist Henry Fielding of *Tom Jones* fame, who lived in Broad Court. It lies on a pedestrian street still lined with 19th-century gas lamps; the Royal Opera House is across the street; and the pubs, shops, and restaurants of lively Covent Garden are just beyond the front door. Rooms are a little less than small, but they're charmingly old-fashioned and traditional. Some of the units are redecorated or at least "touched up" every year, and the mattresses are renewed as frequently as needed. Bathrooms are minuscule, and very few rooms have anything approaching a view; floors dip and sway, and the furnishings and fabrics have known better times—so be duly warned. The bathrooms have a set of good-size towels, but if you want a hair dryer you'll have to request one from the front desk. But with a location like this, in the very heart of London, the Fielding keeps guests coming back; many love the hotel's rickety charm. There's no room service or restaurant, but breakfast is served. Be sure to introduce yourself to Smokey the African Grey parrot in the bar; he's the hotel's oldest resident.

ALONG THE STRAND
VERY EXPENSIVE

✪ **The Savoy.** The Strand, London WC2R 0EU. ☎ **800/63-SAVOY** or 020/7836-4343. Fax 020/7240-6040. www.savoy-group.co.uk. E-mail: info@ the-savoy.co.uk. 207 units. A/C MINIBAR TV TEL. £310–£325 ($511.50–$536.25) double; from £395 ($651.75) suite. AE, DC, MC, V. Parking £24 ($39.60). Tube: Charing Cross or Covent Garden.

Although not as swank as the Dorchester, this London landmark is the premier address if you want to be in the Strand and Covent Garden area. Impresario Richard D'Oyly Carte built the hotel in 1889 as an annex to his nearby Savoy Theatre, where many Gilbert and Sullivan operettas were originally staged. Eight stories of glazed tiles rising in ponderous dignity between the Strand and the Thames, it dwarfs all of its nearby competition, including the Waldorf at Aldwych and the Howard on Temple Place. Each guest room is individually decorated with color-coordinated accessories, solid and comfortable furniture, large closets, and an eclectic blend of antiques, such as gilt mirrors, Queen Anne chairs, and Victorian sofas; 48 have their own sitting rooms. The handmade beds, real luxury models, have top-of-the-line crisp linen clothing and luxury mattresses. Some baths have shower stalls, but most have a combination shower and tub. Bathrooms are spacious with hair dryers, deluxe toiletries, and a set of gargantuan towels. The expensive river-view suites are the most sought after, and for good reason—the views are the best in London.

Dining: The world-famous **Savoy Grill** has long been popular with the theater crowd; Sarah Bernhardt was a regular. The even more elegant **River Restaurant** has tables overlooking the Thames; there's dancing to live band music in the evening. The room known as **Upstairs** specializes in champagne, Chablis, and seafood.

Amenities: 24-hour room service, nightly turndown, same-day dry cleaning and laundry service, secretarial service, hairdresser, news kiosk, the city's best health club—the pool has fabulous views.

WESTMINSTER/VICTORIA
EXPENSIVE

Goring Hotel. 15 Beeston Place, Grosvenor Gardens, London SW1W 0JW. ☎ **020/7396-9000.** Fax 020/7834-4393. www.goringhotel.co.uk. E-mail: reception@goringhotel.co.uk. 75 units. A/C TV TEL. £195–£235 ($321.75–$387.75) double; from £230–£290 ($379.50–$478.50) suite. AE, DC, MC, V. Parking £25 ($41.25). Tube: Victoria.

For tradition and location, the Goring is our premier choice in the Westminster area—even better than the nearby Stakis London St. Ermins, its closest competitor. Located just behind Buckingham Palace, it lies within easy reach of the royal parks, Victoria Station, Westminster Abbey, and the Houses of Parliament. It also happens to offer the finest personal service of all its nearby competitors.

Built in 1910 by O. R. Goring, this was the first hotel in the world to have central heating and a private bathroom in every room. Today's well-furnished guest rooms still offer all the comforts, including refurbished bathrooms—which are most luxurious, with extra-long tubs, red marble walls, dual pedestal basins, bidets, deluxe toiletries, fluffy towels, hair dryers, and power showerheads. There is an ongoing refurbishment of all the bedrooms, including replacement of mattresses whenever needed. The beds, in fact, are among the most comfortable in London. Preferred is one of the rooms overlooking the garden. Queen Anne and Chippendale are usually the decor style. Maintenance is so high here that some discerning English clients call it "bang up to date." The charm of a traditional English country hotel is evoked in the paneled drawing room, where fires crackle in the ornate fireplaces on nippy evenings. The adjoining bar overlooks the rear gardens.

Dining: At the restaurant, the chef uses only the freshest ingredients in his classic English recipes; specialties include venison with a brussels sprout compote, roast breast of pheasant, rump of English lamb with bubble and squeak (cabbage and potatoes) and rosemary jus, and grilled Dover sole. The restaurant also offers one of the most extensive wine lists in London. Afternoon tea is served in the lounge.

Amenities: 24-hour room service, valet service, concierge, dry cleaning and laundry service, babysitting, secretarial services, free use of local health club.

MODERATE

The Sanctuary House Hotel. 33 Tothill St., London, SW1H 9LA. ☎ **020/ 7799-4044.** Fax 020/7799-3657. 33 units. A/C TV TEL. £72.50–£99. 50 ($119.65–$164.15) double. AE, DC, MC, V. Parking: £20 ($33). Tube: St. James's Park.

The hotel is in an historic building close to Westminster Abbey. Only in the new London where hotels are bursting into bloom like spring daffodils would you expect to find a hotel so close to Westminster Abbey—a pub hotel, no less! It has been converted into traditional English-inn–style, with a pub downstairs and the rooms above. Rooms reflect this style and have a rustic feel, but they have first-rate beds and mattresses along with newly restored bathrooms with state-of-the-art plumbing, plus fluffy towels. The building was converted by Fuller Smith and Turner, a traditional brewery group in Britain. Downstairs a pub/restaurant, part of The Sanctuary, offers hearty old-style British meals that have ignored changing culinary fashions of the past quarter of a century. "We like tradition," one of the perky staff members told us. "Why must everything be trendy? Some people come to England nostalgic for the old. Let others be trendy." Actually the food is excellent if you like the roast beef, Welsh lamb, and Dover sole known to Churchill's palate. Naturally, there's always plenty of brew on tap. The reception is open 24 hours a day.

Tophams Belgravia. 28 Ebury St., London SW1W 0LU. ☎ **020/7730-8147.** Fax 020/7823-5966. www.tophams.com. E-mail: tophams_belgravia@ compuserve.com. 40 units (34 with bathroom). TV TEL. £120 ($198) double without bathroom; £130–£140 ($214.50–$231) double with bathroom; £170 ($280.50) triple. AE, DC, MC, V. Tube: Victoria.

Tophams came into being in 1937, when five small row houses were interconnected; with its flower-filled window boxes, the place still has a country-house flavor. It was completely renovated in 1997. The petite informal reception rooms are done in flowery chintzes and antiques. All rooms have coffeemakers, firm mattresses, hair

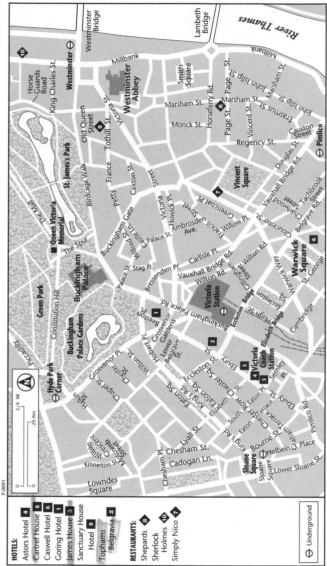

HOTELS:
Astors Hotel **4**
Cartref House **5**
Caswell Hotel **6**
Goring Hotel **1**
James House **3**
Sanctuary House Hotel **9**
Tophams Belgravia **2**

RESTAURANTS:
Shepards **8**
Sherlock Holmes **10**
Simply Nico **7**

◆ Underground

dryers, and satellite TV; the best of the bunch are comfortably appointed with private bathrooms containing medium-size towels and four-poster beds. Not all the rooms have private bathrooms—ask for one when making reservations. The restaurant offers both traditional and modern English cooking for lunch and dinner. And the location is great, especially if you're planning to cover a lot of ground by Tube or train: It's only a 3-minute walk to Victoria Station. Services include concierge, room service, dry cleaning and laundry service, and babysitting.

INEXPENSIVE

Astors Hotel. 110–112 Ebury St., London SW1W 9QD. ☎ **020/7730-3811.** Fax 020/7823-6728. 22 units (12 with bathroom). TV. £58 ($95.70) double without bathroom, £70 ($115.50) double with bathroom; from £140 ($231) family unit with bathroom. Rates include English breakfast. MC, V. Parking £15 ($24.75) nearby. Tube: Victoria.

This well-located choice is a stone's throw from Buckingham Palace and just a 5-minute walk from Victoria's main line and Tube stations. The brick-fronted Victorian was once home to Margaret Oliphant (1828–97), a popular Victorian novelist; Noël Coward was a neighbor for 20 years, and H. G. Wells, Yeats, Bennett, and Shaw called down the street at no. 153 when poet, novelist, and racy autobiographer George Moore (1852–1933) was in residence. The guests today don't have such pedigrees, but are frugal travelers looking for a decent, affordable address in pricey London. Although more functional than glamorous, the rooms are satisfactory in every way. By the end of 1998, much of the hotel had been completely renovated. Each unit is fitted with a comfortable mattress, and the bathrooms have been renewed, each well maintained and containing a rack of medium-size towels. Since space and furnishings vary greatly, ask to take a little peek before committing yourself to a room. (As the hotel is often full, that won't always be possible.)

Caswell Hotel. 25 Gloucester St., London SW1V 2DB. ☎ **020/7834-6345.** 18 units (7 with bathroom). MINIBAR TV. £56 ($92.40) double without bathroom, £76 ($125.40) double with bathroom. Rates include English breakfast. MC, V. Tube: Victoria.

Run with consideration and thoughtfulness by Mr. and Mrs. Hare, Caswell lies on a cul-de-sac, a calm oasis in an otherwise busy area. Mozart lived nearby while he completed his first symphony, and that "notorious couple," Harold Nicholson and Victoria Sackville-West, are long departed, but this is still a choice address. Beyond the chintz-filled lobby, the decor is understated: There are four floors of well-furnished but not spectacular bedrooms, each with such amenities as hair dryers and beverage makers. Mattresses are worn but still have much comfort left in them. Private baths are very small units with a shower stall and few amenities except a hair dryer; however, corridor baths are adequate and well maintained. Guests receive a set of medium-size towels. How do they explain the success of the place? One staff member said, "This year's guest is next year's business."

✪ **James House/Cartref House.** 108 and 129 Ebury St., London SW1W 9QD. James House ☎ **020/7730-7338;** Cartref House ☎ **020/7730-6176.** Fax 020/7730-7338. E-mail: jamescartref@compuserve.com. 21 units (11 with bath). TV. £62 ($102.30) double without bathroom, £73 ($120.45) double with bathroom; £104 ($171.60) quad with bathroom. Rates include English breakfast. AE, MC, V. Tube: Victoria.

Hailed by many publications, including the *Los Angeles Times,* as one of the top 10 B&B choices in London, James House and Cartref House (across the street) deserve their accolades. Derek and Sharon James have real dedication in their work, and have the ability to make everyone feel right at home, even the first-time visitor to London. They're the finest hosts in the area, and they're constantly refurbishing, so everything looks up to date. Each room is individually designed; some of the large ones have bunk beds that make them suitable for families, although these mattresses are a bit thin; mattresses on the other beds are firm. Maintenance is exceedingly high. Clients in rooms with a private bath will find somewhat cramped quarters, but each room is tidily arranged. Corridor baths are adequate and frequently refurbished, and each guest is given a set of medium-size towels. The English breakfast is so generous that you might end up skipping lunch. There's no elevator, but the happy guests don't seem to mind. Don't worry about which house you're assigned; each one's a winner. Smokers be warned, both houses are no-smoking environments. You're just a stone's throw from Buckingham Palace should the Queen invite you over for tea.

2 In & Around Knightsbridge

VERY EXPENSIVE

The Capital. 22–24 Basil St., London SW3 1AT. ☎ **800/926-3199** in the U.S., or 020/7589-5171. Fax 020/7225-0011. www.capitalhotel.co.uk. E-mail: capitalhotel.co.uk. 48 units. A/C MINIBAR TV TEL. £235–£305 ($387.75–$503.25) double; from £350 ($577.50) suite. AE, DC, MC, V. Parking £20 ($33). Tube: Knightsbridge.

One of the most personalized hotels in the West End, this small, modern place is a stone's throw from Harrods. It doesn't have the

Hotels from Knightsbridge to Earl's Court

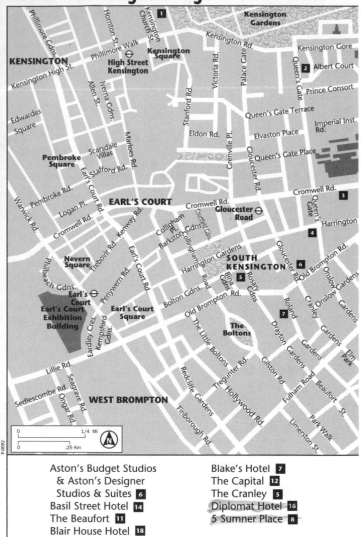

Aston's Budget Studios
& Aston's Designer
Studios & Suites **6**
Basil Street Hotel **14**
The Beaufort **11**
Blair House Hotel **18**

Blake's Hotel **7**
The Capital **12**
The Cranley **5**
Diplomat Hotel **16**
5 Sumner Place **8**

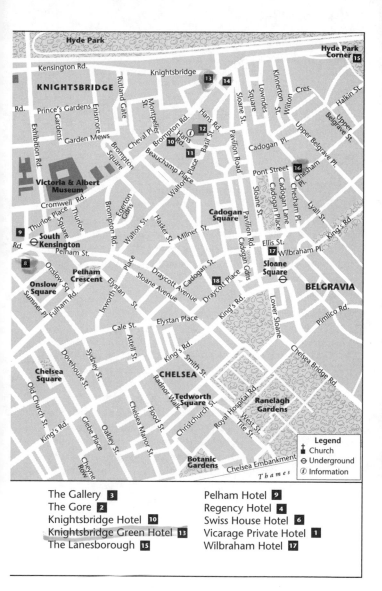

The Gallery **3**
The Gore **2**
Knightsbridge Hotel **10**
Knightsbridge Green Hotel **13**
The Lanesborough **15**

Pelham Hotel **9**
Regency Hotel **4**
Swiss House Hotel **6**
Vicarage Private Hotel **1**
Wilbraham Hotel **17**

five-star quality of the nearby Hyatt, but the cuisine is far better than at many of London's more highly rated hotels. With extensive refurbishment, the owner, David Levin, has created a warm townhouse ambience with an elegant fin-de-siècle décor, matched by the courtesy and professionalism of the staff. Lined with original oils, the corridors and staircase literally function as an art gallery. The guest rooms are tastefully decorated, often with Ralph Lauren furnishings. The objets d'art and original paintings adorning the rooms were selected by the owners. Beds are comfortable with luxurious mattresses, and the bathrooms are equipped with powerful showers, a hair dryer, bathrobes, and a range of deluxe toiletries.

Dining: The Capital Restaurant was refurbished in the early 1990s in a vaguely French style, with David Linley panels for the windows (Linley is Princess Margaret's son). Under the direction of chef Phillip Britton, it's among the finest restaurants in London, specializing in seafood and offering exquisitely prepared French cuisine.

Amenities: 24-hour room service, concierge, dry cleaning and laundry service, babysitting, secretarial service, valet.

EXPENSIVE

Basil Street Hotel. 8 Basil St., London SW3 1AH. ☎ **020/7581-3311.** Fax 020/7581-3693. E-mail: thebasil@aol.com. 92 units. TV TEL. £210 ($346.50) double; £280 ($462) family room. AE, DC, MC, V. Parking £28–£30 ($46.20–$49.50) at 24-hour lot nearby. Tube: Knightsbridge.

The Basil, an Edwardian charmer, has long been a favorite for those who make an annual pilgrimage to Harrods—"just 191 steps away"— and the Chelsea Flower Show. (Harvey Nichols is also nearby.) Several spacious, comfortable lounges are furnished in a fitting style and accented with 18th- and 19th-century accessories; off the many rambling corridors are smaller sitting rooms. No room is standardized: they come in varying shapes and dimensions, evocative of the Edwardian era when hotels housed everyone from grand dukes to their valets in the upper floors. Nearly all units are traditional (they even have TVs that broadcast the original *I Love Lucy* series). Persons with disabilities should check in elsewhere because the steps and stairs in all directions make this hotel an Olympic feat to traverse. Even so, older clients particularly like this hotel, which calls itself a "Hotel for Those Who Hate Hotels." We love its old-fashioned and fading Edwardian gentility, even the antiquated bathrooms that still function perfectly, and hold a rack of thick towels.

Dining: In the restaurant, candlelight and piano music re-create the atmosphere of a bygone era. **The Parrot Club,** a rendezvous reserved only for women, is ideal for afternoon tea.

Amenities: 24-hour room service, evening maid service, conference facilities, babysitting, dry cleaning and laundry service, shoe cleaning.

The Beaufort. 33 Beaufort Gardens, London SW3 1PP. ☎ **800/888-1199** or 020/7584-5252. Fax 020/7589-2834. www.thebeaufort.co.uk/index.htm. E-mail: thebeaufort@nol.co.uk. 28 units. TV TEL. £200–£290 ($330–$478.50) double; £325 ($536.25) junior suite. Rates include breakfast and afternoon tea. AE, DC, MC, V. Tube: Knightsbridge.

If you'd like to stay at one of London's finest boutique hotels, offering personal service in an elegant, tranquil town house atmosphere, head to the Beaufort—they're a market leader. The Beaufort, only 200 yards from Harrods, sits on a cul-de-sac behind two Victorian porticoes and an iron fence. Owner Diana Wallis, a television producer, combined a pair of adjacent houses from the 1870s, ripped out the old decor, and created a stylish hotel of merit and grace that has the feeling of a private house in the heart of London. You register at a small desk extending off a bay-windowed parlor, and then climb the stairway used by the queen of Sweden during her stay. Each guest room is bright and individually decorated in a modern color scheme and adorned with several well-chosen paintings by London artists; they come with earphone radios, flowers, and a selection of books. Bedrooms are exceedingly small, but tasteful and efficiently organized with luxurious mattresses. The most deluxe and spacious rooms are in the front. Units contain such thoughtful extras as fax machines and trouser presses. Baths are adequate, not special in any way, but contain a set of medium-size towels and have tidy maintenance, plus a hair dryer. The all-female staff is exceedingly helpful—a definite plus.

Dining: Light meals are available from room service. There's a 24-hour honor bar.

Amenities: Concierge, theater-ticket service, car rental, secretarial services, fax machines, sightseeing, babysitting, massage, room service. Access to nearby health club for a small fee; laundromat nearby.

MODERATE

Knightsbridge Green Hotel. 159 Knightsbridge, London SW1X 7PD. ☎ **020/7584-6274.** Fax 020/7225-1635. E-mail: theKGHotel@aol.com. 28 units. A/C MINIBAR TV TEL. £135 ($222.75) double; £160 ($264) suite. AE, DC, MC, V. Tube: Knightsbridge.

Many return guests from around the world view this dignified 1890s structure as their home away from home. In 1966, when it was converted into a hotel, the developers were careful to retain its wide baseboards, cove moldings, high ceilings, and spacious proportions.

Even without kitchens, the well-furnished suites come close to apartment-style living; all have trouser presses and hair dryers in the well-appointed marble bathrooms with fluffy towels, a hair dryer, and power showers. Most of the rooms are quite spacious, with decorator colors and adequate storage space. Bedrooms are often individualized—one has a romantic sleigh bed, for example—and each comes with a deluxe mattress. This is still a solid choice, and it's just around the corner from Harrods. Coffee, tea, and pastries are available throughout the day; babysitting, dry cleaning, and laundry service are other perks.

Knightsbridge Hotel. 12 Beaufort Gardens, London SW3 1PT. ☎ **020/ 7589-9271.** Fax 020/7823-9692. www.knightsbridge.co.uk. E-mail: reception@knightsbridgehotel.co.uk. 40 units. MINIBAR TV TEL. £135 ($222.75) double. Rates include English or continental breakfast. AE, DC MC, V. Parking free on street from 6pm to 8am. Tube: Knightsbridge.

The Knightsbridge Hotel attracts visitors from all over the world seeking a small hotel in a high-rent district. It's fabulously located, sandwiched between fashionable Beauchamp Place and Harrods, and with many of the city's top theaters and museums close at hand, including the Royal Albert Hall and Madame Tussaud's. Built in the early 1800s as a private town house, this family-run place sits on a tranquil, tree-lined square, free from traffic. Small and unpretentious, with a subdued Victorian ambience, it's been recently renovated to a high standard: All the well-furnished rooms have private bathrooms, coffeemakers, trouser presses, and safety-deposit boxes. Most bedrooms are spacious and furnished with traditional English fabrics. The best are numbers 311 and 312 at the rear, each with a pitched ceiling and a small sitting area. Bathrooms are clad in marble or tile and contain medium-size towels and hair dryers. Amenities include room service, laundry service, and a concierge. There's also a small health club with a steam room and a spa for guests' use.

IN NEARBY BELGRAVIA
VERY EXPENSIVE

✪ **The Lanesborough.** Hyde Park Corner, London SW1X 7TA. ☎ **800/ 999-1828** or 020/7259-5599. Fax 020/7259-5606. www.lanesborough.co.uk. 95 units. A/C MINIBAR TV TEL. £310–£410 ($511.50–$676.50) double; from £470 ($775.50) suite. AE, CB, DC, MC, V. Parking £2.50 ($4.15) hour. Tube: Hyde Park Corner.

One of London's grandest hotels was created from the dreary hospital wards that Florence Nightingale made famous. This Regency-style, four-story hotel vies with the Dorchester for sophistication (although it falls short of the Dorch's time-honored experience). When

Rosewood Hotels and Resorts (known for managing top hotels like the Bel-Air in Los Angeles and Dallas's Mansion on Turtle Creek) upgraded the building into a luxury hotel, most of the Georgian details were retained. The guest rooms are as opulent and antique-stuffed as the public spaces; each has electronic sensors to alert the staff as to when a resident is in or out, a CD player, VCR, personal safe, fax machine, 24-channel satellite TV, triple glazing on the windows, and the services of a personal butler. Most accommodations are spacious suites with high ceilings. The beds are luxurious, and the bathrooms are opulently clad in milk marble with deluxe toiletries, hair dryers, robes, fluffy towels, and generous shelf space. Security is tight—there are at least 35 surveillance cameras.

Dining: The Conservatory is an elegant restaurant with decor inspired by the Chinese, Indian, and Gothic motifs of the Brighton Pavilion. **The Library Bar**—which opens into a Regency-era hideaway, charmingly named "The Withdrawing Room"—re-creates the atmosphere of an elegant private club.

Amenities: Personal butlers, concierges, room service, dry cleaning and laundry service, massage, babysitting, secretarial services, car rental, business center, small fitness studio. Exercise equipment (Stairmasters, stationary bicycles) can be delivered directly to your room.

MODERATE

Diplomat Hotel. 2 Chesham St., London SW1X 3DT. ☎ **020/7235-1544.** Fax 020/7259-6153. www.btinternet.com/-diplomat.hotel. E-mail: diplomat.hotel@btinternet.com. 27 units. TV TEL. £125–£155 ($206.25–$255.75) double. Rates include English buffet breakfast. AE, CB, DC, MC, V. Tube: Sloane Sq. or Knightsbridge.

Part of the Diplomat's charm is that it is a small and reasonably priced in an otherwise prohibitively expensive neighborhood of privately owned Victorian homes and first-class, high-rise hotels. Only minutes from Harrods, it was built in 1882 as a private residence by the noted architect Thomas Cubbitt. It's very well appointed: The registration desk is framed by the sweep of a partially gilded circular staircase; above it, cherubs gaze down from a Regency-era chandelier. The staff is helpful, well mannered, and discreet. The high-ceilinged guest rooms are tastefully done in Victorian style; many were renovated in 1996. You get good—not grand—comfort here. Rooms are a bit small and usually furnished with twin beds with exceedingly good mattresses. Bathrooms are also small but well maintained with medium-size towels and hair dryers. Amenities include a concierge, massage service, business center, afternoon tea, and a snack menu available daily from 1 to 8:30pm. A health club is located nearby. As a special feature, the hotel offers a complimentary 15-minute back and neck Shiatsu massage to its arriving guests.

3 Chelsea

MODERATE

Blair House Hotel. 34 Draycott Place, London SW3 2SA. ☎ **020/7581-2323.** Fax 020/7823-7752. 11 units. TV TEL. £105–£115 ($173.25–$189.75) double. Extra bed £18 ($29.70). AE, DC, MC, V. Tube: Sloane Sq.

If you can't afford a luxury hotel, this comfortable B&B-style hotel in the heart of Chelsea near Sloane Square is a good alternative. It's hard finding reasonably priced lodgings in this fashionable neighborhood, stamping ground of everybody from Oscar Wilde to Baroness Margaret Thatcher. A boutique hostel nearby charges rates six times the tariff here, so you get good value. Its ideal for shoppers—trendy King's Road and Peter Jones Department Store are a short walk away. It's been completely refurbished inside. The small rooms are individually decorated, but may have too many flowery prints for most tastes. They all come with coffeemakers and trouser presses, plus a tiny bath with medium-size towels and a hair dryer. Although most singles are small, some rooms are spacious enough to accommodate four. Babysitting and laundry service can be arranged. Only breakfast is served. If you're bothered by noise, ask for a quieter room in the back.

INEXPENSIVE

Wilbraham Hotel. 1–5 Wilbraham Place (off Sloane St.), London SW1X 9AE. ☎ **020/7730-8296.** Fax 020/7730-6815. 46 units. TV TEL. £100–£112 ($165–$184.80) double. No credit cards. Parking £17.50 ($28.90). Tube: Sloane Sq.

This dyed-in-the-wool British hotel is set on a quiet residential street, just a few hundred yards from Sloane Square. Occupying three Victorian town houses, it's a bit faded; but the traditionally furnished, wood-paneled bedrooms are well maintained and have fireplaces and leaded-glass windows. There are even heated towel racks in the bathroom—a lovely comfort on a cold gray London morning. Expect sagging beds, somewhat on the order of a London town house at the turn of the century. Accommodations vary widely in size from small to spacious. The plumbing is antiquated in the charmingly old-fashioned baths, but still works smoothly. The best double—certainly the most spacious—is no. 1. There's an attractive old-fashioned lounge where you can order drinks, simple lunches, and traditional English dinners. Despite its small size, guest services include room service, babysitting, dry cleaning and laundry service.

4 Kensington & South Kensington

KENSINGTON
INEXPENSIVE

✪ **Vicarage Private Hotel.** 10 Vicarage Gate, London W8 4AG. ☎ **020/ 7229-4030.** Fax 020/7792-5989. www.londonvicaragehotel.com. E-mail: reception@londonvicaragehotel.com. 18 units (none with bathroom). £68 ($112.20) double; £89 ($146.85) triple; £100 ($165) family room for 4. Rates include English breakfast. No credit cards. Tube: High St. Kensington or Notting Hill Gate.

Eileen and Martin Diviney have a host of admirers on all continents. Their hotel is tops for old-fashioned English charm, affordable prices, and hospitality. Situated on a residential garden square close to Kensington High Street, not far from Portobello Road Market, this Victorian town house retains many original features. Individually furnished in a country-house style, the bedrooms can accommodate up to four. If you want a little nest to hide away in, opt for the top floor aerie (no. 19), a private retreat such as Noël Coward used to occupy before "I got rich enough to move downstairs." By the time you arrive, some small private baths may be added. For the moment, guests find the corridor baths adequate, and they are well maintained. Each year a few rooms are refurbished, and beds have decent mattresses. Guests meet in a cozy sitting room for conversation and to watch the telly. As a thoughtful extra, hot drinks are available 24 hours a day. In the morning, a hearty English breakfast awaits.

SOUTH KENSINGTON
VERY EXPENSIVE

✪ **Blake's Hotel.** 33 Roland Gardens, London SW7 3PF. ☎ **800/926-3173** or 020/7370-6701. Fax 020/7373-0442. E-mail: blakes@easynet.co.uk. 51 units. MINIBAR TV TEL. £210–£310 ($346.50–$511.50) double; from £485 ($800.25) suite. AE, DC, MC, V. Parking £15–£30 ($24.75–$49.50). Tube: South Kensington or Gloucester Rd.

This opulent and highly individual creation of actress Anouska Hempel-Weinberg is one of London's best small hotels. No expense was spared in converting this former row of Victorian town houses into one of the city's most original hotels. It's now Oriental nights down in old Kensington: The richly appointed lobby boasts British Raj–era furniture from India; individually decorated, elaborately appointed rooms contain such treasures and touches as Venetian glassware, cloth-covered walls, swagged draperies, even Empress Josephine's daybed. Live out your fantasy: Choose an ancient Egyptian funeral barge or a 16th-century Venetian boudoir. Rooms in the older section have the least space and aren't air-conditioned, but are chic nevertheless. Beds are deluxe, and the marble baths are richly appointed with fluffy towels, toiletries, robes, and hair dryers; rooms have data ports and private safes. Although a formidable rival, the Pelham (see below) doesn't match Blake's in sophistication and style. Go for a deluxe room if you can manage it; the standard singles and doubles are tiny.

Dining: The stylish restaurant is one of the best in town. Neville Campbell's cuisine blends the finest of East and West, ranging from baked sea bass with a crispy fennel skin to chicken and crab shaped like a large delectable Fabergé egg. With cuisine this fabulous, it's no wonder that reservations are strictly observed.

Amenities: 24-hour room service, laundry service, babysitting, secretarial services, and an arrange-anything concierge. Access to a nearby health club for a fee.

EXPENSIVE

The Cranley. 10–12 Bina Gardens, London SW5 0LA. ☎ **800/553-2582** or 020/7373-0123. Fax 020/7373-9497. www.thecranley.co.uk. E-mail: thecranley@compuserve.com. 37 units. A/C TV TEL. £140–£170 ($231–$280.50) double; £180–£220 ($297–$363) suite. AE, DC, MC, V. Tube: Gloucester Rd.

A trio of adjacent 1875 town houses became the Cranley Hotel when its Michigan-based owners upgraded the buildings in South Kensington. All the high-ceilinged guest rooms have enormous windows, much of their original plasterwork, scattered antiques, and plush upholstery, and the public rooms are like a stage set for an English country house. It all adds up to a vivid 19th-century ambience that makes this feel more like a private residence than a hotel. All but one of the guest rooms have tiny kitchenettes; most units are spacious, although a few are small. Beds are first rate, and extras include trouser presses. Baths are small, tiled, and feature power showers, medium-size towels, and a hair dryer; some bathrooms even contain big mirrors bordered with Dutch tile. Ground-floor suites open onto a private terrace and have Jacuzzis.

Dining: There's no restaurant, but light meals are served in a small café.

Amenities: Room service daily from 7am to 11pm, dry cleaning and laundry service, secretarial services available during office hours. Access to a nearby health club.

✪ **The Gore.** 189 Queen's Gate, London SW7 5EX. ☎ **800/637-7200** or 020/7584-6601. Fax 020/7589-8127. www.gorehotel.co.uk. E-mail: reservations@gorehotel.co.uk. 54 units. MINIBAR TV TEL. £171–£236 ($282.15–$389.40) double; £257 ($424.05) The Tudor Room. AE, DC, MC, V. Tube: Gloucester Rd.

Once owned by the Marquess of Queensberry's family, the Gore has been a hotel since 1892—and it's always been one of our favorites. Victorians would still feel at home here among all the walnut and mahogany, Oriental carpets, and walls covered in antique photos and the hotel's collection of some 4,000 English prints. The Gore has always been known for eccentricity. Each room is different, so try to find one that suits your personality. The Venus Room has a bed once owned by Judy Garland. The dark-paneled Tudor Room is the most fascinating, with its gallery and fireplace. Rooms no longer go for the 1892 price of 50p, but they're still a good value. Although most are a bit small, there is still room for a sitting area. Well-maintained baths have thick towels, hair dryers, and custom brass taps. Some units contain a shower stall but no full tub, although most have a tub and shower combination. Some of the plumbing wares would be familiar to Queen Victoria, but everything works smoothly. Many rooms have four-poster beds or half testers, each with a good, firm mattress. Amenities include private safes.

Dining: It's worth a trip across town to dine at renowned chef Antony Worrall Thompson's **Bistro 190,** especially for the crispy squid, the chargrilled corn-fed chicken, and the seared tuna sashimi with spicy lentil relish.

Amenities: Concierge, room service daily from 7am to 12:20am, dry cleaning and laundry service. Newspaper delivery, babysitting, secretarial services, and express checkout may be arranged. Access to health club next door.

Pelham Hotel. 15 Cromwell Place, London SW7 2LA. ☎ **020/7589-8288.** Fax 020/7584-8444. www.firmdale.com. E-mail: pelham@firmdale.com. 50 units. A/C MINIBAR TV TEL. £175–£225 ($288.75–$371.25) double; from £285 ($470.25) suite. AE, MC, V. Parking £23.10 ($38.10) nearby. Tube: South Kensington.

This small hotel is sure to please discerning travelers. Hoteliers extraordinaire Kit and Tim Kemp preside over one of the most stunningly decorated establishments in London, formed from a row of early 19th-century terrace houses with a white portico facade. In the drawing room, 18th-century paneling, high ceilings, and fine moldings create a suitable backdrop for a collection of antiques and Victorian art; needlepoint rugs and cushions evoke a home-like warmth, and an honor bar completes the club-like atmosphere. The sumptuously decorated rooms are outfitted with Oriental carpets and unique oils; even the smallest room will have a handsome desk. Most of the units have high ceilings, with tasteful fabrics such as silks. Many of the beds are either canopied or four-posters; each has a luxurious mattress and an eiderdown duvet. Bathrooms are trimmed in mahogany and clad with polished granite, along with robes, deluxe toiletries, hair dryers, and fluffy towels. Some of the better accommodations have sitting areas as well. The location is ideal, close to the Victoria and Albert Museum, Hyde Park, and Harrods, and returning guests are welcomed here like part of an extended family.

Dining: Kemps is one of the finest restaurants in South Kensington.

Amenities: 24-hour room service, concierge, babysitting, dry cleaning and laundry service, maid service, business services. A health club is nearby.

MODERATE

5 Sumner Place. 5 Sumner Place, London SW7 3EE. ☎ **020/7584-7586.** Fax 020/7 823-9962. www.dspace.dial.pipex.com/no.5. E-mail: no.5@dial.pipex.com. 14 units. TV TEL. £130–£140 ($214.50–$231) double. Rates include English breakfast. AE, MC, V. Parking £20 ($33). Tube: South Kensington.

This little charmer is frequently cited as one of the best B&Bs in the greater Kensington area, and we agree. Completely restored in an elegant, classically English style that captures the flavor of its bygone era, this Victorian terrace house (ca. 1848) now enjoys landmark status. You'll feel the ambience as soon as you enter the reception hall and are welcomed by the graceful staff. After you register, you're given your own front-door key—and London is yours. An elevator will take you up to the guest floors, where the well-maintained rooms are tastefully done in traditional period furnishings; a few have refrigerators. Bedrooms are medium in size with extremely comfortable, soft beds where you may want to linger. Bathrooms are small but tidily kept and supplied with plenty of fluffy towels and a hair dryer. Hotel services include room service, massage, dry cleaning and laundry service, and concierge. Breakfast is served in a Victorian-style conservatory.

The Gallery. 8–10 Queensberry Place, London SW7 2EA. ☎ **020/7915-0000.** Fax 020/7915-4400. www.eeh.co.uk. E-mail: reservations@eeh.co.uk. 36 units. TV TEL. £115 ($189.75) double; £200 ($330) junior suite. Extra bed £35 ($57.75). Rates include buffet English breakfast. AE, DC, MC, V. Tube: South Kensington.

This is the place for you if you want to stay in an exclusive little townhouse hotel, but don't want to pay £300 a night for the privilege. Two splendid Georgian residences have been completely restored and converted into this remarkable hotel (which remains relatively unknown). The location is ideal, near the Victoria and Albert Museum, Royal Albert Hall, Harrods, Knightsbridge, and King's Road. Bedrooms are individually designed and elegantly decorated in

Laura Ashley style, with half-canopied beds with firm mattresses, plus luxurious marble-tiled bathrooms with brass fittings, thick towels, and hair dryers. The junior suites have private roof terraces, minibars, Jacuzzis, and air-conditioning. A team of butlers takes care of everything. The lounge, with its rich mahogany paneling and moldings and deep colors, has the ambience of a private club. The drawing room beckons you to a quiet corner. The Gallery Room displays works for sale by known and unknown artists. There's 24-hour room service, plus concierge, dry cleaning and laundry service, and babysitting.

The Regency Hotel. 100 Queen's Gate, London SW7 5AG. ☎ **800/ 223-5652** or 020/7370-4595. Fax 020/7370-5555. E-mail: regency.london@ dial.pipex.com. 209 units. A/C MINIBAR TV TEL. £147 ($242.55) double; from £215–£255 ($354.75–$420.75) suite. AE, DC, MC, V. Tube: South Kensington.

On a street lined with Doric porticoes, close to museums, Kensington, and Knightsbridge, six Victorian terrace houses were converted into one stylish, seamless whole. A Chippendale fireplace, flanked by wing chairs, greets you in the polished reception area. One of the building's main stairwells has what could be London's most unusual lighting fixture: five Empire chandeliers suspended vertically, one on top of the other. Most bedrooms are small and furnished in a standard modern idiom with trouser presses, bedside controls, and firm mattresses; maintenance is topnotch. Bathrooms are excellent with hair dryers, robes, and phones, and they're clad either in marble or tile. Suites also have a Jacuzzi bath, plus an iron and ironing board.

The **Pavilion** is a glamorous but reasonably priced restaurant specializing in international cuisine. Amenities include 24-hour room service; laundry service; babysitting; a health club with steam rooms, saunas, and sensory-deprivation tank; a mini gym; and a business center.

INEXPENSIVE

✪ **Aston's Budget Studios & Aston's Designer Studios and Suites.** 31 Rosary Gardens, London SW7 4NQ. ☎ **800/525-2810** in the U.S., or 020/ 7590-6000. Fax 020/7590-6060. www.astons_apartments.com. E-mail: sales@ astons_apartments.com. 76 units. A/C TV TEL. Budget Studios £65 ($107.25) double; £97 ($160.05) triple; £114 ($188.10) quad. Designer Studios £110 ($181.50) double. MC, V. Tube: Gloucester Rd.

This carefully restored row of Victorian town houses offers comfortably furnished studios and suites that are among London's best values. Heavy oak doors and 18th-century hunting pictures give the foyer a rich traditional atmosphere. Accommodations range in size and style from budget to designer; every one has a compact but complete kitchenette concealed behind doors. The air-conditioned designer studios and two-room designer suites are decorated with rich fabrics and furnishings and each has its own marble bathroom with a hair dryer and medium-size towels. Mattresses are good. Amenities include laundry service, secretarial services, guests' message line, fax machines, private catering on request, car and limousine service, and daily maid service in the designer studios and suites.

Swiss House Hotel. 171 Old Brompton Rd., London SW5 OAN. ☎ **020/ 7373-2769.** Fax 020/7373-4983. www.webscape.co.uk/swiss_house/ index.htmlssi. E-mail: recep@swiss-hh.demon.co.uk. 16 units (15 with bathroom). TV TEL. £77 ($127.05) double with bathroom; £98 ($161.70) triple with bathroom; £110 ($181.50) quad with bathroom. Rates include continental breakfast. AE, CB, DC, MC, V. Tube: Gloucester Rd.

This appealing B&B, in a Victorian row house with a portico festooned with flowers and vines in the heart of South Kensington, is close to the South Kensington museums, Kensington Gardens, and the main exhibition centers of Earl's Court and Olympia. Some of its individually designed country-style guest rooms have fireplaces, and there's enough chintz to please the most avid Anglophile. Try to avoid the rooms along the street—traffic is heavy, and even with double-glazing, they get noisy. Instead, book one of the rear bedrooms, which overlook a communal garden and have a view of the London skyline. Most of the rooms are small, but beds are fitted with good mattresses. Sometimes there's a private safe in the room. Baths are also small but contain medium-size towels and a hair dryer. And there's a luxury that you won't get in most B&Bs: Room service—nothing elaborate, just soups and sandwiches—is available from noon to 9pm. Additional services include babysitting, massage, tour desk, and laundry service.

5 Notting Hill

MODERATE

The Abbey Court. 20 Pembridge Gardens, London W2 4DU. ☎ **020/ 7221-7518.** Fax 020/7792-0858. www.telinco.co.uk/abbeycourt/. E-mail: abbey@ telinco.co.uk. 22 units. TV TEL. £130–145 ($214.50–$239.25) double; £175 ($288.75) suite with four-poster bed. AE, CB, DC, MC, V. Tube: Notting Hill Gate.

This first-rate hotel is a small white-fronted mid-Victorian town house with a flower-filled patio in front and a conservatory in back. Its recently renovated lobby has a sunny bay window, floral draperies, and a comfortable sofa and chairs. You'll always find fresh flowers in the reception area and the hallways. Each room, although small, has carefully coordinated fabrics and fine furnishings, mostly

18th- and 19th-century country antiques, plus excellent mattresses. Done in Italian marble, bathrooms are equipped with a Jacuzzi bath, shower, and heated racks of medium-size towels. Light snacks and drinks are available from room service 24 hours a day and breakfast is served in the newly renovated conservatory. Kensington Gardens is a short walk away, as are the antiques stores along Portobello Road and Kensington Church Street. Other amenities include a tour desk, dry cleaning, laundry service, and concierge.

Pembridge Court Hotel. 34 Pembridge Gardens, London W2 4DX. ☎ **020/ 7229-9977.** Fax 020/7727-4982. www.pemct.co.uk. E-mail: reservations@ pemct.co.uk. 20 units. A/C TV TEL. £145–£180 ($239.25–$297) double. Rates include English breakfast. AE, DC, MC, V. Tube: Notting Hill Gate.

This hotel presents an elegant cream-colored neoclassical facade in an increasingly fashionable Notting Hill Gate residential neighborhood. Avid antiques hunters like its proximity to Portobello Road. Most guest rooms contain at least one antique, as well as 19th-century engravings and plenty of warm-toned floral fabrics, plus first-rate mattresses. Some of the largest and most stylish rooms are on the top floor. Bathrooms are tiled in Italian marble, with hair dryers and medium-size towels. Three air-conditioned deluxe rooms, all with VCRs, overlook Portobello Road: The Spencer and Churchill Rooms are decorated in blues and yellows, and the Windsor Room has a contrasting array of tartans. Also called Spencer and Churchill are a pair of ginger cats, two of the most adorable in London. Churchill likes the pop stars who stay at the hotel; Spencer tries to avoid them.

Good international food is served at **Caps,** the hotel restaurant, which also boasts a well-chosen wine list; it's open to guests only from 4 to 11pm. Services include 24-hour room service, same-day dry cleaning and laundry service. A car-rental agency is on the premises, and day membership in a nearby health club is available.

The Portobello Hotel. 22 Stanley Gardens, London W11 2NG. ☎ **020/ 7727-2777.** Fax 020/7792-9641. 24 units. TV TEL. £150–£155 ($240–$248) double; £185–£240 ($296–$384). Rates include continental breakfast. Tube: Notting Hill Gate.

Mixing an eclectic medley of styles, two six-floor town houses dating from 1850 on an elegant Victorian terrace near the Portobello antiques market were combined to form a quirky property that doesn't please everybody, but has its devotees. We remember these rooms when they looked better; but although they're tattered here and there, they still have plenty of character—whimsy and a fair measure of flamboyance went into their design. Who knows what will show up in what nook? Perhaps a Chippendale, a multi-nozzle

Marylebone, Paddington, Bayswater & Notting Hill Gate Hotels

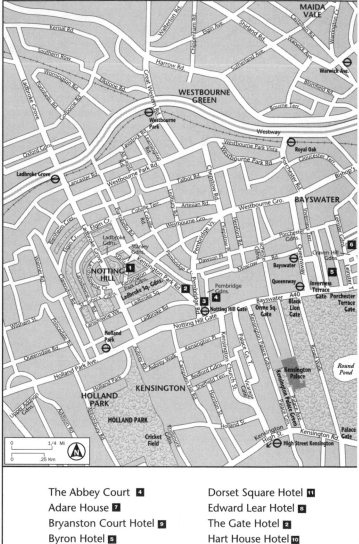

The Abbey Court **4**

Adare House **7**

Bryanston Court Hotel **9**

Byron Hotel **5**

Dorset Square Hotel **11**

Edward Lear Hotel **8**

The Gate Hotel **2**

Hart House Hotel **10**

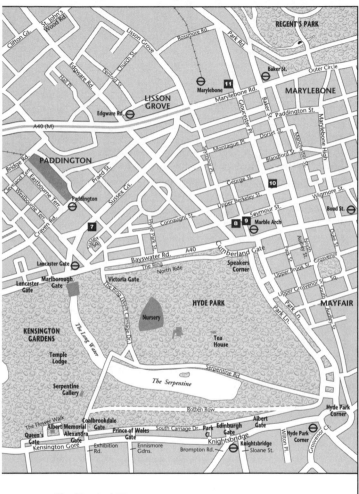

The Hempel 6
Pembridge Court Hotel 3
Portobello Hotel 1

clawfoot tub, or a round bed tucked under a gauze canopy. Try for no. 16, with a full-tester bed facing the garden. Some of the cheaper rooms are so tiny they're cabin-like garrets (some consider them romantic). But some of these have been combined into large doubles. The comfortable beds are standard throughout with decent mattresses, and most of the small bathrooms lack tubs (shower stalls instead) but have a rack of medium-size towels. An elevator will take you as far as the third floor; after that, it's the stairs. Some rooms are air-conditioned. Don't expect top-notch service; it's erratic at best. A 24-hour bar and restaurant in the basement is a local favorite, and provides hotel-room services.

INEXPENSIVE

The Gate Hotel. 6 Portobello Rd., London W11 3DG. ☎ **020/7221-2403.** Fax 020/7221-9128. www.go_london.co.uk/hp/gatehotel.html. E-mail: gatehotel@ aol.com. 6 units. TV TEL. £75–£78 ($123.75–$128.70) double. Rates include continental breakfast. MC, V. Tube: Notting Hill Gate.

This antiques-hunters' favorite is the only hotel along the entire length of Portobello Road—and because of rigid zoning restrictions, it will probably remain the only one for many years to come. It was built in the 1820s as housing for farmhands working the orchards and vegetable plots at the now-defunct Portobello Farms and has functioned as a hotel since 1932. It has two cramped but cozy bedrooms on each of its three floors, plus a renovated breakfast room in the cellar. Be prepared for some *very* steep English stairs. Rooms are color-coordinated, with a bit of style, and have such amenities as full-length mirrors, built-in wardrobes, and excellent mattresses. Bathrooms are small but adequate with a set of good-size towels; housekeeping is excellent. Especially intriguing are the wall paintings that show what the Portobello Market was in its early days: Every character looks straight from a Dickens novel. The on-site manager can direct you to the antiques markets and the attractions of Notting Hill Gate and nearby Kensington Gardens, both of which lie within a 5-minute walk.

6 Paddington & Bayswater

VERY EXPENSIVE

The Hempel. 31–35 Craven Hill Garden Square, London W2 3EA. ☎ **020/ 7298-9000.** Fax 020/7402-4666. www.hempelhotel.com. E-mail: the-hempel@easynet.co.uk. 47 units. A/C MINIBAR TV TEL. £220–£255 ($363–$420.75) double; from £370 ($610.50) suite. AE, CB, DC, DISC, MC, V. Tube: Lancaster Gate.

Set in a trio of nearly identical 19th-century row houses, this hotel is the newest statement of flamboyant interior designer Anouska Hempel-Weinberg. Don't expect the swags, tassels, and labyrinthine elegance of her better-established hotel, Blake's (see above)—the feeling here is radically different. The Hempel manages to combine a grand Italian sense of proportion with Asian simplicity, all meant for capitalists rich enough to afford it. Its artful simplicity is like that of a Zen temple. Soothing monochromatic tones prevail. The deliberately underfurnished lobby is flanked by symmetrical fireplaces; throughout the hotel are carefully positioned mementos from Asia, including Thai bullock carts that double as coffee tables. Bedrooms continue the minimalist theme, except for their carefully concealed battery of electronic accessories, which includes a VCR, satellite TV control, CD player, twin phone lines, and a modem hookup. Baths have cut-stone walls, with both the countertops and bathtubs crafted from the same material. Extras include a hair dryer, deluxe toiletries, robes, slippers, and a rack of fluffy towels. The hotel mostly caters to business travelers from around the world, most of whom appreciate its tactful service and undeniably snobbish overtones.

Dining: In the cellar is an innovative restaurant and bar, **I-Thai.**

Amenities: 24-hour room service, concierge, dry cleaning and laundry service, turndown and twice-daily maid service, massage, express checkout, limited business services; babysitting can be arranged. Conference rooms, access to nearby health club.

INEXPENSIVE

Adare House. 153 Sussex Gardens, London W2 2RY. ☎ **020/7262-0633.** Fax 020/7706-1859. www.freespace.virgin.net/adare.hotel. E-mail: adare.hotel@ virgin.net. 20 units. TV TEL. £69 ($113.85) double with shower (slightly less in winter). Rates include full English breakfast. MC, V. Tube: Paddington.

This longstanding bed-and-breakfast remains one of the best choices for the budget traveler along B&B-crazed Sussex Gardens; the place still has a little soul, even though so many of its neighbors have lost theirs. The property is well maintained and has been gradually improved over the years, with the addition of private bathrooms in admittedly cramped space. Each room has a hair dryer. The public areas are relatively modest, but smart Regency-era wallpaper and red carpeting give them a touch of class. Many of the homey rooms are quite small, but they're spic-and-span and comfortably furnished, each with a good mattress. All have beverage makers.

The Byron Hotel. 36–38 Queensborough Terrace, London W2 3SH. ☎ **020/ 7243-0987.** Fax 020/7792-1957. www.capricornhotels.co.uk. E-mail: byron@ capricornhotels.co.uk. 45 units. A/C TV TEL. £96–£105 ($158.40–$173.25) double; £120 ($198) triple; from £135 ($222.75) suite. Rates include English/ continental breakfast. AE, DC, MC, V. Tube: Bayswater or Queensway.

A mostly American clientele appreciates this family-run hotel just north of Kensington Gardens for its country-house atmosphere, its helpful staff (who spend extra time with guests hoping to make their stay in London special), and the good value it offers. This is one of the best examples of a Victorian house conversion that we've seen; it was modernized without ruining its traditional appeal. The interior was recently redesigned and refurbished, and the rooms are better than ever, with ample closets, fine mattresses, tile bathrooms with good-size towels and a hair dryer, good lighting, and extra amenities like trouser presses, coffeemakers, and safes. An elevator services all floors, and breakfast is served in a bright and cheery room. Services include concierge, room service (limited hours), and dry cleaning.

SMITHFIELD
EXPENSIVE

✪ **The Rookery.** 12 Peters Lane, Cowross Street, London EC1M 6DS. ☎ **020/7336-0931.** Fax 020/7336-0932. 33 units. A/C MINIBAR TV TEL. £170 ($280.50) double; £230 ($379.50) suite. AE, DC, MC, V. Tube: Farrington.

Newly fashionable Smithfield now has a quirky hotel worth considering as the center of your London sojourn. The only remaining Georgian houses in Peter's Lane have been united to form a delightful small hotel only a short walk from the Square Mile. The brainchild of Peter McKay and Douglas Blain, who gave the world the trendy Hazlitt's in Soho, the Rookery has been patiently restored with its period features relatively intact—even the coal-fired bread ovens still survive in the basement, which was a former bakery. They spent thousands of hours combing auction rooms, antiques shops, and flea markets for pictures, furniture, beds, and carpets to create maximum atmosphere. Regardless of where the bed came from, it is fitted with an absolutely superb mattress and fine bed linen. Each room is different and full of character. The Rook's Nest, for example, is on two levels with a 40-foot ceiling, boasting a panoramic view across London's rooftops from St. Paul's to the Old Bailey. The bathrooms are a special treat, all with Victorian cast-iron fittings, polished-copper pipe work, and an array of fluffy towels.

Dining: The owners say they're surrounded by wonderful places to eat (and they are)—"So why start another restaurant?" But there is an interesting menu served around the clock, and the fluffy breakfast croissants are baked on the premises.

Amenities: 24-hour room service, concierge, a tiny garden (unusual for a City location), dry cleaning, and laundry.

7 Near the Airports

NEAR HEATHROW

EXPENSIVE

London Heathrow Hilton. Terminal 4, Hounslow TW6 3AF. ☎ **020/ 8759-7755.** Fax 020/8759-7579. E-mail: gm_heathrow@comhilton.com. 395 units. A/C MINIBAR TV TEL. Sun–Thurs £160–£295 ($264–$486.75) double, Fri–Sat £110–£150 ($181.50–$247.50) double. Suite from £430 ($709.50) (all week). AE, DC, MC, V. Parking £6.50 ($10.75).

This eye-catching, first-class hotel with its five-story atrium evoking the feel of a hangar is linked to Heathrow's Terminal 4 by a covered walkway. A glass wall faces the runways, so you can see planes land and take off. You can take buses to Terminals 1, 2, or 3. Bedrooms are fairly standardized and medium in size, but comfortably decorated with built-in wood furniture, upholstered sofas, and first-class mattresses on the beds. Bathrooms are tiled and trimmed in marble, containing a phone, a hair dryer, and a set of fluffy towels. The best accommodations are on the fifth floor with private robes and better amenities such as a private lounge with airport vistas.

Dining/Diversions: An open brasserie lies in the main lobby, and is "shaded" by umbrellas and canopies. There's also a rather good Chinese and Thai restaurant on site, plus a standup bar with a grill section, decorated with a movie theme.

Amenities: Room service, concierge, TV with flight information, automated checkout.

Radisson Edwardian Heathrow. 140 Bath Rd., Hayes UB3 5AW. ☎ **020/ 8759-6311.** Fax 020/8759-4559. www.radisson.com. E-mail: resreh@ radisson.com. 459 units. A/C MINIBAR TV TEL. £180–£210 ($297–$346.50) double; from £383 ($631.95) suite. AE, DC, MC, V. Parking: £7 ($11.55). Heathrow Hopper bus service.

The poshest digs at Heathrow, this deluxe hotel lies just south of the M4 and about five minutes east of the long tunnel that leads to Terminals 1, 2, and 3. Since 1991 it has housed tired air travelers from all over the world. Its grand spa has a swimming pool and two bubbling whirlpools. You enter in a courtyard with potted trees and a koi pond. Persian rugs, brass-railed staircase, and chandeliers live up to the Edwardian in the hotel's name. Rooms are medium in size but richly adorned with hand-painted hardwood furnishings, including deluxe mattresses, and such extras as trouser presses and ironing boards, plus flight information broadcast on the TV. The baths are in tile and marble with robes, a hair dryer, and a set of fluffy towels.

Dining/Diversions: On site are both a formal restaurant and a cheaper garden-style brasserie, each serving from an international and British menu. The sportsy bar has a polo theme, with saddles instead of stools.

Amenities: Steam room, spa, sauna, plunge pool, room service, concierge.

MODERATE

Renaissance London Heathrow Hotel. Bath Rd., Houndslow, London TW6 2AQ. ☎ **020/8987-6363.** Fax 020/8897-1113. E-mail: 106047.3556@ compuserve.com. 650 units. A/C MINIBAR TV TEL. Sun–Thurs £139 ($229.35) double, Fri–Sat £82 ($135.30) double. All-week suite from £315 ($519.75). AE, DC, MC, V. Heathrow Hopper bus service to air terminals.

This is no airport sleeping dormitory. A bustling hotel factory, it lies just inside the perimeter of the airport and is spotted just before you reach the long airport entrance tunnel. Three cantilevered concrete floors attract a bevy of international travelers. Rooms have recently been renovated and are fairly standardized and a bit small, with coffeemakers, bedside controls, inlaid wood and laminate furnishings, and first-class mattresses, along with tiled combination baths (tub and shower), plus hair dryers, marble sinks, medium-size towels, and toilet articles. We prefer the units facing the airport itself (double glazing keeps down the noise). A brasserie serving international food overlooks the runaways, and there's also an international bar decorated with vintage aeronautical wall prints. Amenities include a solarium, sauna, gym, and restored health club.

Stanwell Hall. Town Lane, Stanwell, Staines, Middlesex TW19 7PW. ☎ **01784/252292.** Fax 01784/245250. 19 units (18 with bathroom). TV TEL. £100 ($165) double; £130 ($214.50) suite. Rates include breakfast. AE, DC, MC, V. Free parking.

This sunny Victorian house was purchased in 1951 by the Parke family, who converted it into a comfortable hotel. The cheery house with its side garden is located in a small village just minutes from Heathrow; it's perfect for business people who are tired of staying in standard airport hotels. About half the rooms have been fully renovated. The renovated rooms are comfortably furnished, papered in warm shades, and have chintz curtains covering the windows—a dramatic improvement over the washed-out, prerenovation rooms. All have coffeemakers and good mattresses. Bathrooms are efficiently organized and tidy, each with a hair dryer and a rack of medium-sized towels. **St. Anne's Restaurant,** located on the ground floor, is small but inviting and serves modern British cuisine. The bar, which is popular with locals, serves drinks and snacks at lunchtime. Basic services include dry cleaning and laundry.

NEAR GATWICK

EXPENSIVE

Gatwick Hilton International Hotel. South Terminal, Gatwick Airport, Gatwick, West Sussex RH6 0LL. ☎ **800/HILTONS** or 01293/518080. Fax 01293/528980. www.hilton.com. E-mail: gathitwrm@hilton.com. 550 units. A/C TV TEL. £187–£240 ($308.55–$396) double; from £260 ($429) suite. AE, DC, MC, V. Parking £10.40 ($17.15).

This deluxe five-floor hotel—Gatwick's most convenient resting place—is linked to the airport terminal with a covered walkway; an electric buggy service transports people between the hotel and airport. The most impressive part of the hotel is the first-floor lobby; its glass-covered portico rises four floors and contains a scale replica of the de Havilland Gypsy Moth airplane *Jason,* used by Amy Johnson on her solo flight from England to Australia in 1930. The reception area has a lobby bar and lots of greenery. The well-furnished, soundproofed rooms have triple-glazed windows, firm mattresses, and coffeemakers. Baths are tidily kept and equipped with a hair dryer and a rack of medium-size towels. Recently, 123 of the rooms were refurbished, in addition to the executive floor and all their junior suites. Now 300 of the rooms have minibars, stocked upon request.

Dining/Diversions: The American-themed restaurant **Amy's** serves buffet breakfasts, lunches, and dinners. **The Garden Restaurant,** outfitted in a formal English garden theme, serves drinks and full meals. There's also the 24-hour **Lobby Bar,** plus a polo-themed watering hole aptly named the **Jockey Bar.**

Amenities: Same-day dry cleaning and laundry service, up-to-date flight information channel, 24-hour room service, salon, bank, gift shop. Concierge, newspapers, babysitting, health club (sauna, steam room, massage room, swimming pool, gymnasium, Jacuzzi). Conference rooms, business center, shopping arcade.

5

Dining

*G*eorge Mikes, Britain's famous Hungarian-born humorist, once wrote about the culinary prowess of his adopted country: "The Continentals have good food. The English have good table manners."

Quite a lot has happened since.

London has emerged as one of the great food capitals of the world, more so at the millennium than ever before. In the last few years, both its veteran and upstart chefs are pioneering a new style of cooking called "Modern British" that is forever changing and yet comfortingly familiar. They're committed to centering their dishes around local ingredients, and have become daringly innovative with traditional recipes—too much so in the view of some critics, who don't like fresh mango over their blood pudding.

Traditional British cooking has made a comeback, too. The dishes that British mums nationwide have been forever feeding their reluctant families are fashionable again. Yes, we're talking British soul food: bangers and mash, Norfolk dumplings, nursery puddings, cottage pie—the works. This may be a rebellion against the excessive minimalism of the nouvelle cuisine that ran rampant over London in the 1980s, but who knows? Maybe it's just plain old nostalgia. Pig's nose with parsley-and-onion sauce may not be your idea of cutting-edge cuisine, but Simpson's-in-the-Strand is serving it for breakfast.

If you want a lavish meal, London is now the place: gourmet havens such as Le Gavroche or Chez Nico at Ninety Park Lane, and a half-dozen others you'll find reviewed in the following pages. For those of you who don't want to break the bank, we've included affordable restaurants where you can dine really well. You'll find that London's food revolution has infiltrated every level of the dining scene—even the lowly pub has entered the culinary sweepstakes. In some, standard pub grub has given way to Modern British and Mediterranean-style fare; in others, oyster bars have taken hold.

TAXES & TIPPING All restaurants and cafés are required to display prices of their food and drink in a place visible from outside the establishment. Charges for service as well as any minimum charge or cover charge must also be made clear. The prices shown must include 17¹/₂% VAT. Most of the restaurants add a 10% to 15% service charge to your bill, but you'll have to check to make sure of that. If nothing has been added to your bill, leave a 12% to 15% tip.

1 West End Restaurants

MAYFAIR
VERY EXPENSIVE

✪ **Chez Nico at Ninety Park Lane.** In Grosvenor House, 90 Park Lane, W1. ☎ **020/7409-1290.** Reservations required (at least 2 days in advance for lunch, 7 days for dinner). Fixed-price lunch £33 ($54.45) for 3 courses; à la carte dinner £54 ($89.10) for 2 courses, £66 ($108.90) for 3 courses. AE, DC, MC, V. Mon–Fri noon–2pm; Mon–Sat 7–11pm. Closed 10 days around Christmas/New Year's. Tube: Marble Arch. FRENCH.

Although the setting is as opulent as the cuisine, nothing takes precedence over food here. It's the work of one of London's supreme culinary artists, the temperamental but always amusing Nico Ladenis, assisted today by Paul Rhodes, who interprets the master's culinary ideas with flair and zest. Landenis, a former oil-company executive, self-taught cook, and economist, remains one of Britain's most talked-about chefs; his food is always impressive, always stylish, and he's constantly reinventing dishes we thought he had already perfected. As starters go, who can top his quail salad with sweetbreads, flavored with an almond vinaigrette? The main courses are a tour de force in the best post-nouvelle tradition, in which the tenets of classical cuisine are creatively and flexibly adapted to local fresh ingredients. With masterful technique, Nico's chefs dazzle with ever-changing fare, including a ravioli of langoustine that's a virtual signature dish. The chargrilled sea bass with basil purée or the Bresse pigeon are rivaled only by the work of Le Gavroche (see below). The only complaint we've ever heard about Chez Nico is that it attracts too many Michelin three-star groupies.

✪ **Le Gavroche.** 43 Upper Brook St., W1. ☎ **020/7408-0881.** Reservations required as far in advance as possible. Main courses £29.10–£36.80 ($48–$60.70); fixed-price lunch £37 ($61.05); menu exceptionnel, for entire table, £78 ($128.70) per person. AE, DC, MC, V. Mon–Fri noon–2pm and 7–11pm. Tube: Marble Arch. FRENCH.

Le Gavroche has long stood for quality French cuisine, perhaps England's finest, although Michelin gives it only two stars. Though it may have fallen off briefly in the early 1990s, it's fighting its way back to the stellar ranks. There's always something special coming out of the kitchen of Burgundy-born Michel Roux; the service is

West End Restaurants

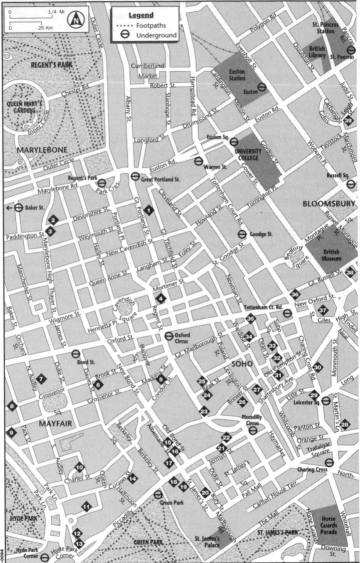

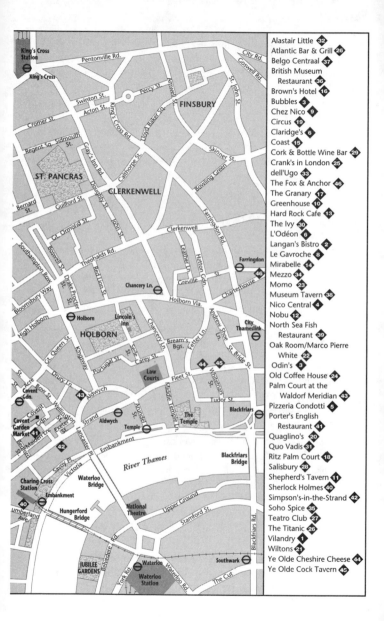

Alastair Little 32
Atlantic Bar & Grill 26
Belgo Centraal 37
British Museum
  Restaurant 36
Brown's Hotel 16
Bubbles 3
Chez Nico 9
Circus 19
Claridge's 6
Coast 15
Cork & Bottle Wine Bar 29
Crank's in London 25
dell'Ugo 33
The Fox & Anchor 46
The Granary 17
Greenhouse 10
Hard Rock Cafe 13
The Ivy 30
L'Odéon 6
Langan's Bistro 2
Le Gavroche 8
Mirabelle 14
Mezzo 34
Momo 23
Museum Tavern 38
Nico Central 4
Nobu 12
North Sea Fish
  Restaurant 39
Oak Room/Marco Pierre
  White 22
Odin's 3
Old Coffee House 24
Palm Court at the
  Waldorf Meridian 43
Pizzeria Condotti 5
Porter's English
  Restaurant 41
Quaglino's 20
Quo Vadis 31
Ritz Palm Court 18
Salisbury 28
Shepherd's Tavern 11
Sherlock Holmes 40
Simpson's-in-the-Strand 42
Soho Spice 35
Teatro Club 27
The Titanic 26
Vilandry 1
Wiltons 21
Ye Olde Cheshire Cheese 44
Ye Olde Cock Tavern 45

105

faultless and the ambience formally chic without being stuffy. The menu changes constantly, depending on the fresh produce that's available and the current inspiration of the chef. But it always remains classically French, although not of the "essentially old-fashioned bourgeois repertoire" that some critics suggest. There are signature dishes that have been honed over years of unswerving practice: Try the soufflé Suissesse, *papillote* of smoked salmon, or whole Bresse chicken with truffles and a Madeira cream sauce. Game is often served, depending on availability. New menu options include cassoulet of snails with frog thighs, seasoned with herbs; mousseline of lobster in champagne sauce; pavé of braised turbot with red Provençal wine and smoked bacon; and fillet of red snapper with caviar and oyster-stuffed tortellini. Desserts, including the sablé of pears and chocolate, are sublime. The wine cellar is among the most interesting in London, with many quality Burgundies and Bordeaux. The *menu exceptionnel* is, in essence, a tasting menu for the entire table. It usually consists of four to five smaller courses, followed by one or two desserts and coffee. At £78 ($128.70) per person, this may prove to be a smarter choice as opposed to the à la carte items.

✪ **Oak Room/Marco Pierre White.** in Le Méridien Piccadilly, 21 Piccadilly, W1. ☎ **020/7734-8000.** Reservations required as far in advance as possible. Fixed-price lunch £29.50 ($48.70); fixed-price dinners £80–£90 ($132–$148.50). AE, MC, V. Mon–Fri noon–2:15pm; Mon–Sat 7–11pm. Closed Christmas. Tube: Piccadilly Circus. MODERN BRITISH.

Put simply, "MPW" is the best chef in London. Picture Liam Neeson in a chef's jacket. The man's talent is prodigious and by 1995 he had become one of the few three-star Michelin chefs in Britain. Not bad for a lad born in working-class Leeds, and a high-school dropout at that. He serves London's finest cuisine in the city's most beautiful dining room, which has been restored to its original oak-and-gilt splendor and filled with art, including works by Cocteau and Chagall.

Creative, sophisticated, and bold, this daring chef claims he never apprenticed in France other than a couple of weeks of eating in Paris restaurants. Lavish in his choice of ingredients, White explores the depths of flavor in food. As you peruse the dozen or so appetizers, you'll note that most feature foie gras, caviar, and truffles. Afterward, you can proceed to such main courses as Bressole of Bresse pigeon (with foie gras again), or braised pig's trotter. Platters sometimes appear with brilliant colors, including a gratinée of brill with a soft herb crust, young spinach, and a sabayon of chives. Among all this fancy fare, Marco Pierre White makes the world's greatest mashed potatoes, which one diner claims were "sieved, puréed, and squeezed through silk stockings." White vies with Nico Ladenis as the most temperamental chef in London. In White's view, "I'd rather be arrogant than insecure." He's clearly a magician. If you can afford it, try to catch the "show" of London's chef du jour.

EXPENSIVE

✪ **Mirabelle.** 56 Cruzon St., W1. ☎ **020/7499-4636.** Reservations required. Main courses £14.50–£26 ($23.90–$42.90); set lunch £15.95–£18.95 ($26.30–$31.25). AE, MC, V. Daily noon–2:30pm and 6pm–midnight. Tube: Green Park. MODERN BRITISH.

Marlene Dietrich and Noël Coward have long faded, of course, but you are likely to encounter today's media tabloid fodder, including Johnny Depp, battling paparazzi outside. Inside Marco Pierre White, the high-school dropout from Leeds, now an acclaimed chef, has brought new life to this long-standing legend. The chef has become so famous in London he's often simply "MPW." He calls Mirabelle, former stamping ground of the likes of Princess Margaret or Aristole Onassis, "my little love affair." The fading vestige of the seventies is all gone now, with a smart new art deco glimmer, a sexy red leather floor, and a little English garden in the heart of Mayfair. He's known for throwing some of the biggest names in the world out of his restaurants, but claims they deserve it when he tosses them out. This master chef has long abandoned his well-publicized bouts with drugs and alcohol, and tired of old Mirabelle, has become a shining new star.

On his menu, he remains a French classicist who refuses to Anglicize or even diversify his complex cuisine. For starters, foie gras terrine appears with amber jelly, a delectable opening. For more daring selections, opt for the pork cheeks flavored with ginger and spices. His squid ink risotto with calamari is now a familiar feature at his restaurants, and his sea bass with fennel and Béarnaise is worth traveling through the Chunnel from France. His boneless oxtail, topped by a filigree potato galette, is the finest we've ever sampled. Save room for dessert, especially the bitter-chocolate tart with ice cream.

✪ **Nobu.** In the Metropolitan Hotel, 19 Old Park Lane, W1. ☎ **020/7447-4747.** Reservations required. Main courses £13–£27.50 ($21.45–$45.40); sushi and sashimi £2.50–£4.75 ($4.15–$7.85) per piece; fixed-price menu £60 ($99). AE, DC, MC, V. Mon–Fri noon–2:15pm; Mon–Fri 6–10:15pm, Sat 6–11:15pm, Sun 6–9:45pm. Tube: Hyde Park Corner. JAPANESE.

Robert de Niro and his restaurant gang of Nobu Matsuhisa and Como Holdings have taken their New York hot spot to London, where they offer an intensely innovative and experimental Japanese cuisine. With a beauty like Isabella Rossellini claiming that eating at Nobu keeps her lean and mean, how can you go wrong here?

The kitchen staff is brilliant and as finely tuned as their New York cousins. Sushi chefs don't just create sushi, but gastronomic pyrotechnics. Those on the see-and-be-seen circuit don't seem to mind the high prices that go with these incredibly fresh dishes. Elaborate preparations lead to perfectly balanced flavors. Where can you find a good sea urchin tempura these days but at Nobu? Salmon tartare with caviar is a brilliant appetizer, and Madonna agrees. Follow with a perfectly done fillet of sea bass in a sour bean paste or soft-shell crab rolls. The squid pasta is sublime, as is the black cod with miso, this latter dish incredibly popular and with good reason. Cold sake arrives in a green bamboo pitcher. If it's featured, finish with the savory ginger crème brûlée.

MODERATE

Greenhouse. 27A Hays Mews, W1. ☎ **0771/499-3331.** Reservations essential. Main courses £9.50–£18.50 ($15.65–$30.55). AE, DC, MC, V. Mon–Fri noon–2:45pm and 7–10:45pm; Sat 7–11pm; Sun 12:30–3pm and 7–10:30pm. Closed Christmas, bank holidays. Tube: Green Park. MODERN BRITISH.

Head chef Graham Grafton is quite inspired by modern British food. Grafton has a winning way with fish, if his poached skate is any example—and his deep-fried cod-and-chips is galaxies beyond what you'd get at the local chippie. But you may prefer the lip-smacking fare from the heart of England, which includes a roast breast of pheasant that Henry VIII would have loved, and grilled farmhouse pork—we're also fond of the wilted greens wrapped in bacon. The menu is backed up by a well-chosen wine list of some 20 selections. Some of the delightfully sticky desserts, including a moist bread-and-butter pudding and a ginger pudding with orange marmalade, would have pleased your Midlands grannie. It does look a bit like a greenhouse with plants scattered about. There are even prints of vegetables and flowers on the wall. Simply conceived dishes with a resolutely British slant draw a never-ending line of satisfied customers. The ingredients are first class and beautifully prepared, without ever destroying the natural flavor of a dish.

✪ Quaglino's. 16 Bury St., SW1. ☎ **020/7930-6767.** Reservations recommended. Main courses £11–£17 ($18.15–$28.05); fixed-price menu (available only for lunch and pre-dinner theater between 5:30 and 6:30pm) 2-courses £12.50 ($20.65), 3 courses £15 ($24.75). AE, DC, MC, V. Daily noon–3pm; Mon–Thurs 5:30–11:30pm, Fri–Sat 5:30pm–12:30am, Sun 5:30–10:30pm. Tube: Green Park. CONTINENTAL.

It's vast, it's convivial, it's fun. A restaurant on these premises was established in 1929 by Giovanni Quaglino, from Italy's Piedmont. Personalities who paraded through here in ermine and pearls could fill a between-the-wars roster of Who's Who for virtually every country of Europe. In 1993, noted restaurateur and designer Sir Terence Conran brought the place into the postmodern age with a vital new décor—eight artists were commissioned to decorate the octet of massive columns supporting the soaring ceiling. A mezzanine with a bar features live jazz every Friday and Saturday night and live piano music the rest of the week, and an "altar" in the back is devoted to the most impressive display of crustaceans and shellfish in Britain.

Everything seems to be served in bowls. Menu items have been criticized for their quick preparation and standardized format. But considering that on some nights up to 800 people might show up here for food, laughter, and gossip, the marvel is that the place functions as well as it does. That's not to say there isn't an occasional delay. Come for fun, not culinary subtlety and finesse. The menu changes often, but your choices might include goat cheese and caramelized onion tart; seared salmon with potato pancakes; crab tartlet with saffron; and roasted cod and ox cheek with chargrilled vegetables. The prawns and oysters—so delectable, so fresh—are the most ordered items.

INEXPENSIVE

✪ **Crank's In London.** 8 Marshall St., W1 ☎ **020/7437-9431.** Main courses £2.00–£3.65 ($3.30–$6). No credit cards. Mon–Tues 8am–8pm, Wed–Fri 8am–9pm. Tube: Oxford Circus. VEGETARIAN.

Located just off Carnaby Street, this is the headquarters of a chain of vegetarian restaurants with seven other branches in London. Outfitted in natural wood, wicker-basket lamps, pinewood tables, and handmade ceramic bowls and plates, Crank's is a completely self-service restaurant: You carry your own tray to one of the tables. Organic-white and stone-ground flour is used for breads and rolls. The uncooked vegetable salad is especially good, and there's always a hot stew of savory vegetables (with "secret" seasoning) served in a hand-thrown stoneware pot with a salad. Their couscous with asparagus is an original concoction, and their stir-fry vegetable dishes continue to draw a funky crowd of 25–to–35-year-olds. Homemade honey cake, cheesecake, tarts, and crumbles are featured. Bakery goods, nuts, and general health-food supplies are sold in an adjoining shop.

MARYLEBONE
MODERATE

Odin's. 27 Devonshire St., W1. ☎ **020/7935-7296.** Reservations required. Fixed-price 2-course lunch or dinner £24.95 ($41.15); fixed-price 3-course lunch or dinner £26.45 ($43.65). AE, DC, MC, V. Mon–Fri 12:30–2:30pm and 6:30–11pm. Tube: Regent's Park. INTERNATIONAL.

This elegant restaurant is one of at least four in London owned by chef Richard Shepherd and actor Michael Caine (whose stable includes Langan's Brasserie). Set adjacent to its slightly less expensive twin, Langan's Bistro (see below), it features ample space between tables and an eclectic decor that includes evocative paintings and deco accessories. As other restaurants nearby have come and gone, the cookery here remains solid and reliable, the standard of fresh ingredients and well-prepared dishes is always maintained. The menu changes with the seasons: Typical fare might include forest mushrooms in brioche, braised leeks glazed with mustard and tomato sauce, roast duck with apple sauce and sage and onion stuffing, or roast fillet of sea bass with a juniper cream sauce.

INEXPENSIVE

Langan's Bistro. 26 Devonshire St., W1. ☎ **020/7935-4531.** Reservations recommended. Fixed-price 2-course lunch or dinner £18.50 ($30.55); Fixed-price 3-course lunch or dinner £20.50 ($33.80). AE, DC, MC, V. Mon–Fri 12:30–2:30pm; Mon–Sat 6:30–11:30pm. Tube: Regent's Park. TRADITIONAL BRITISH/FRENCH.

This unpretentious restaurant has been a busy fixture on the London scene since the mid-1960s, when it was established by the late restaurateur Peter Langan with chef Richard Shepherd and actor Michael Caine. Of the several restaurants in this chain (see Odin's, above), it's the least expensive, but the most visually appealing. Set behind a brightly colored storefront on a residential street, the dining room is decorated with fanciful clusters of Japanese parasols, rococo mirrors, surrealistic paintings, and old photographs. The menu is "mostly English with a French influence"; it changes with the seasons, but might include as a starter red-pepper and Brie tarlets or grilled goat cheese with rocket salad. Long-time brasserie favorites here are reassuringly familiar, and just as good as they ever were. Always check out the dish of the day or opt for the chargrilled tuna Niçoise or the cod with an herb crust (served in a butter sauce). Chocaholics should finish off with the dessert extravaganza known as "Mrs. Langan's Chocolate Pudding."

PICCADILLY CIRCUS & LEICESTER SQUARE
EXPENSIVE

Coast. 26B Albemarle St., W1X 3FA. ☎ **020/7495-5999.** Reservations required. Main courses £13.50–£22.50 ($22.30–$37.15). AE, MC, V. Mon–Sat noon–3pm and 6pm–midnight, Sun noon–3:30pm and 6–11pm. Tube: Piccadilly Circus. MODERN INTERNATIONAL.

Coast is so cutting edge, so 21st century, that you might get the feeling that it strains a bit to maintain its hip image. Set in a former auto showroom with lots of parquet woodwork, it's painted in colors that resemble, according to your tastes, either spring green or the color of aged bilge water, and accented with lighting fixtures that protrude like alien bug eyes. There's only one piece of art (by the terribly fashionable artist Angela Bulloch), but it's a doozy: a drawing machine that uses a robotic arm to scribble a graph simulating the movement on an electronic screen—like a giant Etch-a-Sketch, it's wiped clean when it becomes unreadable.

With all this forced hipness, we didn't really want to like this place, but it won us over with its surprisingly good food. Innovative chef Bruno Loubet is an original (some say too innovative), but we liked his willingness to go where others fear to tread. He handles textures well and brings out the best of the flavors in the light cuisine, particularly the fish dishes. This is no beans-on-toast place. Loubet tempts with his seared salmon spring roll in fermented black bean aïoli, monkfish and pickled vegetable terrine, rabbit ravioli, or peppered Hereford duck with honey and Asian greens. Of course, none of these exact items will be on the menu presented to you, because Loubet will have long changed them, but expect a surprise and a delight to your palate regardless of what he's dishing out.

L'Odéon. 65 Regent St., W1. ☎ **020/7287-1400.** Reservations required. Main courses £14.50–£25 ($23.90–$41.25); fixed-price lunch £15.50 ($25.60) for 2 courses, £19.50 ($32.15) for 3 courses. AE, DC, MC, V. Mon–Sat and Sun noon–2:30pm; Mon–Sat 5:30–11:30pm. Tube: Piccadilly Circus. FRENCH.

When the Michelin-starred chef Bruno Loubet opened this chic 1930s-style brasserie, headlines read "Loubet Cooks for the Masses." His sous-chef, Erwan Louaisil, carries on since Loubet's departure. But the menu remains rooted in the Loubet repertoire. You can opt for a table looking out on Regent Street and its bright-red doubledeckers. In all, some 250 diners can pack this place (and often do).

The culinary style isn't as daring and provocative as before, and has switched to a more classic French cuisine. Opt for the panfried seam bream with a peppery butter sauce or else the roast farmhouse chicken with Parmesan, served with Basmatic rise. Louaisil learned a lot when he worked at Daniel's in New York and was a protégé of the great Pierre Garnier in Paris. Each dish reflects his own special taste, as evoked by his starters, a light mussel saffron mousse or a risotto of flap mushrooms with Parmesan shavings. For dessert, he dazzles, especially his poached apple in saffron with dried-fig ice cream or his roast papaya with whiskey-and-caramel ice cream.

✪ **Wiltons.** 55 Jermyn St., SW1. ☎ **020/7629-9955.** Reservations required. Jacket and tie required for men. Main courses £15–£25 ($24.75–$41.25). AE, DC, MC, V. Mon–Fri 12:30–2:30pm and 6–10:30pm, Sun 12:30–2:30pm and 6:30–10pm. Closed Sat. Tube: Green Park or Piccadilly Circus. TRADITIONAL BRITISH.

This is one of the top purveyors of traditional British cuisine and our favorite of the current bunch. Opened in 1742, this thoroughly British restaurant—it's been called "as British as a nanny"—is known for its fine fish and game. Gourmets flock here for the best oysters and lobsters in London, and they know it's the place to go to find unusual seafood. You might begin with an oyster cocktail and follow with Dover sole, plaice, salmon, or lobster, prepared in any number of ways. In season (from mid-August), there are such delights as roast partridge, pheasant, or grouse; you might even be able to order widgeon, a wild, fish-eating river duck (the chef might ask you if you want it "blue" or "black," a reference to roasting times). Game is often accompanied by bread sauce (milk thickened with bread crumbs). To finish, consider a savory such as Welsh rarebit, soft roes, or anchovies; if that's too much, try the sherry trifle or syllabub.

We consistently find the service to be the most helpful in the West End. Since this is a bastion of traditionalism, however, don't show up wearing the latest Covent Garden fashion—you might not get in. Instead, don your oldest suit and look like you believe the Empire still exists.

MODERATE

Atlantic Bar & Grill. 20 Glasshouse St., W1. ☎ **020/7734-4888.** Reservations required. Main courses £10.50–£18 ($17.35–$29.70); fixed-price lunch £14.90 ($24.60) 3 courses. AE, DC, MC, V. Mon–Fri noon–3pm; Mon–Sat 6pm–3am, Sun 6–10:30pm. Tube: Piccadilly Circus. MODERN BRITISH.

A titanic restaurant installed in a former art deco ballroom off Piccadilly Circus, this 160-seat locale draws a trendy crowd to London's tawdry heartland. The restaurant remains cosmopolitan, and it's one of the best choices for an after-theater crowd because it closes at 3am on most nights. It doesn't attract the celebrities like Goldie Hawn as it did back in its 1994 heyday, but is still going strong nonetheless. The original chef, Richard Sawyer, is back, serving his second tour of duty and doing much to recapture the restaurant's mid-1990s chic. He is turning out a new menu that places more emphasis on organic and homegrown produce. Some dishes are quite complicated and taste as good as they sound—swordfish dumplings with a salsa of plum tomatoes, fresh cilantro, seated shiitake, soy-infused ginger, and fresh wilted spinach. The menu changes every two months, but is always strong on seafood and meats. For a starter, we recommend the Caesar club salad (the chicken is smoked on the premises). Memorable also is the loin of yellow-fin tuna served with a wild parsley and eggplant relish with a roasted red bell pepper pesto. The desserts, however, are purposefully (and inexplicably) unsophisticated: rice pudding, poire Belle Héléne (poached pear). If you're rushed, you can drop into Dick's Bar, where they serve up everything from lamb burgers sparked with yogurt and fresh mint to Cashel blue cheese and pumpkin seeds on ciabatta bread, for a quick bite.

Circus. 1 Upper James St. W1. ☎ **020/7534-4000.** Reservations required. Main courses £12.50–£17.50 ($20.65–$28.90). Fixed-price menus before 7:30pm and 10:15pm–midnight £15.75–£17.75 ($26–$29.30). AE, DC, MC, V. Daily noon–3pm and Mon–Sat 6pm–midnight. Bar menu daily noon–1:30am. Tube: Piccadilly Circus. BRITISH/INTERNATIONAL.

A minimalist haven for power design and eating in the very heart of London, this new restaurant took over the ground floor and basement of what used to be the Granada Television building at the corner of Golden Square and Beak Street. It is buzzes during pre- and post-theater times, and chef Richard Lee has already acquired a fashionable following of London foodies. The place evokes a London version of a Left Bank Parisian brasserie. For some country cousins from the north of England who missed out on the food revolution of the past decades, Lee offers braised faggot with bubble and squeak (bubble and squeak is cabbage and potatoes; and faggots aren't what you thought, but are highly seasoned squares of pig's liver, pork, onion, herbs, and nutmeg—bound with an egg and baked wrapped in a pig's caul). You might want to go on instead to taste the divine skate wing with "crushed" new potatoes accompanied by a thick pesto-like medley of rocket blended with black olives. Or else try the tasty sautéed chili-flavored squid with bok choy, made even more heavenly with the tamarind dressing. The sorbets are a nice finish to a meal, especially the delectable mango and pink grapefruit version. Of course, if you're ravenous, there's always the velvety smooth Amaretto cheesecake with a coffee sauce. Service is a delight.

Momo. 25 Heddon St., W1. ☎ **020/7434-4040.** Reservations required 2 weeks in advance. Main courses £9.50–£16.50 ($15.65–$27.20); 2-course fixed-price lunch £12.50 ($20.65), 3-course fixed-price lunch £15.50 ($25.60). AE, DC, MC, V. Mon–Fri noon–2:30pm; Mon–Sat 7–11:30pm. Tube: Piccadilly Circus. MOROCCAN/NORTH AFRICAN.

You'll be greeted by a friendly and casual staff member clad in a black-and-white T-shirt and fatigue pants. The setting is like Marrakesh, with stucco walls, a wood-and-stone floor, patterned wood window shades, burning candles, and cozy banquettes. You can fill up on the freshly baked bread, along with appetizers such as garlicky marinated olives and pickled carrots spiced with pepper and cumin. These starters are a "gift" from the chef. Other appetizers, which you'll pay for, are also tantalizing, especially the *briouat,* paper thin and very crisp triangular packets of puffed pastry that are filled with saffron-flavored chicken and other treats. One of the chef's finest specialties is *pastilla au pigeon,* a traditional poultry pie with almonds. Many diners visit for the couscous maison, among the best in London. Served in a decorative pot, this aromatic dish of raisins, meats (including merguez sausage), chicken, lamb, and chickpeas is given added flavor with that powerful hot sauce of the Middle East, marissa. After all this, the refreshing cinnamon-flavored orange slices are a tempting treat for dessert.

Teatro Club & Restaurant. 93-107 Shaftesbury Ave., W1. ☎ **020/ 7494-3040.** Reservations required. Main courses £15.50–£19.50 ($25.60– $32.15). Fixed-price menus (lunch or dinner) £16–£18 ($26.40–$29.70). AE, DC, MC, V. Mon–Fri noon–3pm and Mon–Sat 6–11:45pm. Tube: Piccadilly Circus. MODERN BRITISH.

Opening to instant glory and a lot of press hype, this restaurant burst on to the scene in 1998. It became highly acclaimed for its contemporary British fare. Having Gordon Ramsay, one of London's most acclaimed chefs, as its consultant also helped. Ramsay must have given good advice because the cuisine is quite delectable. The chef is Stuart Gillies, an artist who cooks with flavor, precision, and great skill. The cuisine is a lot richer than the minimalist interior. Starters are sweet corn ravioli with truffle oil and chanterelles, or panfried crispy pig's trotter. The crab bisque is velvety smooth, as is the foie gras du jour. Salmon appears with a lemony couscous or else you can venture into the roast fillet of cod with "crushed" potatoes, or perhaps the breast of guinea fowl with braised lettuce. The grilled halibut would put a "chippie" to shame, and it's given added zest by horseradish butter. Desserts are a journey into nostalgia—treacle tart, banana sticky toffee, and the like.

The Titanic. In the Regent Palace Hotel, 12 Sherwood St., near Piccadilly Circus, W1A. ☎ **020/7437-1912.** Reservations required. Main courses £9–£11.50 ($14.85–$18.95). Breakfast platters £7–£12.50 ($11.55–$20.65). AE, DC, MC, V. Daily noon–2:30 and 5:30–11:30pm. Breakfast daily 11:30pm–2:30am. Tube: Piccadilly. MODERN BRITISH.

Just before Christmas 1998, the most celebrated and gilt-edged of chefs (Marco Pierre White or "MPW") took a plebian plunge into the waters of middle-bracket dining with the establishment of this sought-after bistro. Despite its phone number ("1912" is the year the famous ship went down) and its name, the staff is eager to point out that the nautical art deco decor is modeled after the *Queen Mary,* not *The Titanic,* partly because they feared that there might be a public loss of appetite "because of the name's association with dead people." Expect a large, crowded venue where tables turn over several times during the course of a night, and where food items are designed for the young at heart and for palates a lot less sophisticated than those that dine in Marco Pierre's other upscale gastronomic temples. Menu items include bresaola (Scottish beef cured in the Mediterranean style with olive oil and herbs); snails in garlic butter; oysters; mussels in white wine; Caesar salads; fish 'n' chips with mushy peas; brochettes of lamb in the Provençal style, and caramelized skate. After 11:30pm, the focus moves to breakfast, presumably for night owls who have worked up an appetite at the disco, in bed, or whatever, or for any transatlantic flyer suffering from jet lag and a hankering for eggs benedict, an omelet, kippers, or shirred eggs with calves liver.

INEXPENSIVE

The Granary. 39 Albemarle St., W1. ☎ **020/7493-2978.** Main courses £7–£8.60 ($11.55–$14.20). MC, V. Mon–Fri 11:30am–8pm, Sat–Sun noon–2:30pm. Tube: Green Park. TRADITIONAL BRITISH.

This family-operated country-style restaurant has served a simple but flavorful array of home-cooked dishes, listed daily on a blackboard, since 1974. The daily specials might include lamb casserole with mint and lemon; panfried cod; or avocado stuffed with prawns, spinach, and cheese. Vegetarian meals include mushrooms stuffed with mixed vegetables, stuffed eggplant with curry sauce, and vegetarian lasagna. Tempting desserts are bread-and-butter pudding and brown

Betty (both served hot). The large portions guarantee that you won't go hungry. Cookery is standard, rather routine, but still quite good for the price.

SOHO
EXPENSIVE

Alastair Little. 49 Frith St., W1. ☎ **020/7734-5183.** Reservations recommended. Fixed-price dinner £33 ($54.45); fixed-price 3-course lunch £25 ($41.25). AE, MC, V. Mon–Fri noon–3pm; Mon–Sat 6–11pm. Tube: Leicester Sq. or Tottenham Court Rd. MODERN BRITISH/CONTINENTAL.

In a brick-fronted town house (ca. 1830)—which for a brief period supposedly housed John Constable's art studio—this informal, cozy restaurant is a pleasant place to enjoy a well-prepared lunch or dinner. Some loyal critics still claim that Alastair Little is the best chef in London, but lately he's been buried under the avalanche of new talent. Actually, Little himself is not often here; he spends a good deal of time at other enterprises and at a cooking school in Umbria. The talented James Rix is in charge. Style is now modern European with a heavy slant toward Italian. The menu still changes daily. Starters might include a salad of winter leaves with crispy pork or chicken livers in Vin Santo flavored with fresh tomatoes and basil. The terrine of wild duck and foie gras is a surefire pleaser, followed by such main-course delights as risotto with both flap and field mushrooms or home-salted cod with spicy chickpeas and greens. For dessert, you can select an array of British cheeses or else order such classics as a pear–and–red wine tart. Ever have olive oil cake? It's served here with a winter-fruit compote.

✪ **Quo Vadis.** 26–29 Dean St., W1. ☎ **020/7437-9585.** Reservations required. Main courses £13–£27.50 ($21.45–$45.40). Fixed-price lunches and pre- and post-theater £14.75–£17.95 ($24.35–$29.60). AE, MC, V. Mon–Fri noon–3pm; Mon–Sat 6–11pm, Sun 6–10:30pm. Tube: Leicester Sq. or Tottenham Court Rd. MODERN BRITISH.

This hyper-trendy restaurant occupies the former apartment house of Communist patriarch Karl Marx, who would never recognize it. It was a stodgy Italian restaurant from 1926 until the mid-1990s, when its interior was ripped apart and changed into the stylish postmodern place you'll find today. The stark street-level dining room is a showcase for the hyper-modern paintings of the controversial Damien Hirst and other contemporary artists. Many bypass the restaurant altogether for the upstairs bar, where Hirst has put a severed cow's head and a severed bull's head on display in separate aquariums. Why? They're catalysts to conversation, satirical odes to the destructive

---

👪 Frommer's Family Friendly Restaurants

- **Pizzeria Condotti,** 4 Mill St., W1 (☎ 020/7499-1308), in Mayfair, will satisfy a kid who needs a pizza fix. Pies with succulent toppings emerge bubbling hot from the oven. The "American Hot" comes with mozzarella, pepperoni, sausages, and hot peppers—and the menu isn't just confined to pizzas.

- **Deal's Restaurant and Diner** (Chelsea; *see p. 137*) After enjoying the boat ride down to Chelsea Harbour, kids will love the burgers and other American fare served here. Reduced-price children's portions are available.

- **Dickens Inn by the Tower** (Docklands; *see p. 130*) Even fussy kids will find something they like at this former spice warehouse, now a three-story restaurant with sweeping Thames and Tower Bridge views. The fare ranges from parent-pleasing modern British to yummy lasagna and pizza.

- **Ye Olde Cheshire Cheese** (The City; *see p. 148*) Fleet Street's most famous chophouse, established in 1667, is an eternal family favorite. If "ye famous pudding" turns your kids off, the sandwiches and roasts will tempt them into digging in instead.

- **Hard Rock Cafe,** 150 Old Park Lane, W1. (☎ 020/7629-0382), is the original Hard Rock, now a worldwide chain of rock-and-roll–themed American roadside diners serving up good food and service with a smile. This is a great place for older children. Teenagers like the rock 'n' roll memorabilia as well as the juicy burgers with heaps of fries and salads doused with Thousand Island dressing.

- **Porter's English Restaurant** (Covent Garden; *see p. 124*) This restaurant serves traditional English meals that most kids love—especially the pies, stews, and steamed "puds." They'll get a real kick out of ordering wonderfully named food like bubble and squeak and mushy peas.

---

effects of Mad Cow Disease, and perhaps tongue-in-cheek commentaries on the flirtatious games that patrons conduct here.

Quo Vadis is associated with Marco Pierre White, but don't expect to see the temperamental culinary superstar here; as executive chef, he only functions as a consultant. Also, don't expect that the harassed and overburdened staff will have the time to pamper you; they're too preoccupied dealing with the glare of frenetic publicity.

And the food? It's appealingly presented and very good, but not nearly as artful or innovative as the setting might lead you to believe. We suggest beginning with the tomato and red mullet broth perfumed with basil or the terrine of foie gras and duck confit before moving on to the escallop of tuna with tapenade and eggplant caviar (actually eggplant and black olives puréed and seasoned, which gives it the look of caviar) or the roast chicken a la souvaroff, truffle oil, herb dumplings, and vegetable broth.

MODERATE

✪ **The Ivy**. 1–5 West St., WC2. ☎ **020/7836-4751.** Reservations required. Main courses £8-£21.75 ($13.20-$35.90); Sat–Sun 3-course fixed price lunch £15.50 ($25.60) plus £1.50 ($2.45) cover charge. AE, DC, MC, V. Daily noon–3pm and 5:30pm–midnight (last order). Tube: Leicester Sq. MODERN BRITISH/INTERNATIONAL.

Effervescent and sophisticated, The Ivy has been intimately associated with the West End theater district since it opened in 1911. With its ersatz 1930s look and tiny bar near the entrance, this place is fun— and it hums with the energy of London's glamour scene. The menu may seem simple, but the kitchen has a solid appreciation for fresh ingredients and a talent for skillful preparation. Favorite dishes include white asparagus with sea kale and truffle butter; seared scallops with spinach, sorrel, and bacon; and salmon fish cakes. There's also Mediterranean fish soup, a great mixed grill, and such English desserts as sticky toffee and caramelized bread-and-butter pudding. Meals are served quite late to accommodate the post-theater crowd.

Mash. 19–21 Great Portland St. W1. ☎ **020/7637-5555.** Reservations required. Main courses £7.50–£13.50 ($12.40–$22.30). Set lunch Sat £16.50 ($27.20). AE, DC, MC, V. Daily Mon–Sat noon–3pm and 6–11:30pm, Sun noon–3pm and 6–10:30pm. Tube: Great Portland Street. MODERN CONTINENTAL.

What is it? you ask. A bar? A deli? A microbrewery? All of the above, and, oh, yes, a restaurant. Breakfast and weekend brunch are the highlights, but don't ignore dinner either. The novelty decor includes the likes of curvy "sci-fi" lines and "lizard-eye" lighting fixtures, but ultimately the food is the attraction. The owners of the hot Atlantic Bar & Grill and the Coast Restaurant have opened this place that invites diners to a "sunken chill out zone" created by leading designer John Currin. "The food is good," one local patron informed us, "but I really come here for the mirrored loos." He left after that enigmatic statement, allowing us to launch into suckling pig with spring cannellini stew, our companion opting for one of the terrific pizzas emerging from the wood-fired oven. On another occasion, we returned for the fish freshly grilled over wood. It was sea bass and presented enticingly with grilled artichoke. Try also the marinated quail with thin slices of crisp deep-fried taro root. Desserts are often startling, but be brave. An example is the rhubarb compote with a crisp polenta shortcake and a custard-like ice cream flavored with fresh basil.

Mezzo. 100 Wardour St., W1. ☎ **020/7314-4000.** Reservations required for Mezzonine. Mezzo 3-course dinner £35–£40 ($57.75–$66). £5 ($8.25) cover at Mezzo Wed–Sat after 10pm. Mezzonine 3-course dinner £25–£30 ($41.25–$49.50). AE, DC, MC, V. Mezzo: Mon–Fri noon–3pm; Sun noon–4pm; Mon–Thurs 6pm–1am; Fri–Sat 6pm–3am; Sun 6–11pm. Mezzonine: Mon– Fri noon–3pm; Sat noon–4pm; Mon–Thurs 5:30pm–1am; Fri–Sat 5:30pm–3am. Tube: Tottenham Court Rd. CONTINENTAL/MEDITERRANEAN.

This blockbuster 750-seat Soho restaurant—the latest creation of entrepreneur Sir Terence Conran—may be the biggest in Europe. The mammoth space, on the former site of rock's legendary Marquee club, has been split into several separate restaurants: Mezzonine upstairs, serving a Thai/Asian cuisine with European flair (deep fried salt-and-pepper squid, garlic, and coriander; roast marinated lamb with yogurt and cumin on flat bread); the swankier Mezzo downstairs offering a modern European cuisine, in an atmosphere of 1930s Hollywood (at any minute you expect Marian Davies—drunk or sober—to descend the grand staircase); and Mezzo Café, where you can stop in for a sandwich.

The food is at its most ambitious downstairs, where 100 chefs work behind glass to feed up to 400 diners at a time. This is dinner-as-theater. Not surprisingly, the cuisine tends to be uneven. We suggest the rotissere rib of beef with red wine and creamed horseradish, or the roast cod, which was crisp skinned and cooked to perfection. For dessert, you can't beat the butterscotch ice cream with a pitcher of hot fudge. A live jazz band entertains after 10pm from Wednesday to Saturday, and the world of Marlene Dietrich and Noël Coward comes alive again.

✪ **The Sugar Club.** 21 Warwick St. W1. ☎ **020/7437-7776.** Main courses £12–£18 ($19.80–$29.70). AE, DC, MC, V. Daily noon–3pm and 6–11pm. Tube: Piccadilly Circus or Oxford Circus. PACIFIC RIM.

Ashley Sumner and Vivienne Hayman originally launched their restaurant in Wellington, New Zealand in the mid-1980s. Now they have moved deep into Soho with their original chef, the talented Peter Gordon, who is known for attracting homesick Aussies with the best loin of grilled kangaroo in London (very tender with a rich piquant sauce). The setting is inviting with soft textures, colors of pale creams, bone and olive green, everything enhanced by wooden floors. The restaurant is both elegant and spacious, offering a bar waiting area for diners, a separate non-smoking floor, and a kitchen open to view. The flavors are often stunning, as evoked by the sashimi of Iki Jimi yellowtail with a black bean–and–ginger salsa. The fish tastes amazingly fresh here, and flavors are surprising at times to the palate, but only in the most exciting way. You might also dig into the duck leg braised in tamarind and star anise with coconut rice or else try the panfried turbot with spinach, sweet potato, a red-curry sauce, and onion raiata. Many of the starters are vegetarian and can be upgraded to a main course. For dessert, the blood-orange curd tart with créme fraîche is drop-dead delicious.

Villandry. 170 Great Portland St., W1. ☎ **020/7631-3131.** Reservations recommended. Main courses £11–£14 ($18.15–$23.10). AE, MC, V. Mon–Sat noon–3pm and 7–10pm. Food store Mon–Sat 8am–8pm. Tube: Great Portland Street. INTERNATIONAL/CONTINENTAL.

Food lovers and gourmands flock to this combination food store, delicatessen, and restaurant, where racks of the finest meats, cheese, and produce in the world are displayed and changed virtually every hour. Some of the best of the merchandise is quickly and almost whimsically transformed into the restaurant's menu choices. The setting—dating in this particular form only since 1997—is an oversized Edwardian-style storefront north of Oxford Circus. The inside is an artfully minimalist kind of pared-down temple to the glories of fresh produce and esoteric foodstuffs. Ingredients change here so frequently that the menu is revamped and rewritten twice a day—during our latest visit, it proposed such perfectly crafted dishes as breast of duck with fresh spinach and a gratin of baby onions; boiled haunch of pork with blood sausages, mashed potatoes, kale, and mustard sauce; and panfried turbot with deep-fried celery, artichoke hearts, and hollandaise sauce.

INEXPENSIVE

dell'Ugo. 56 Frith St., W1. ☎ **020/7734-8300.** Reservations required. Main courses £6.50–£13.50 ($10.75–$22.30). AE, DC, MC, V. Mon–Fri noon–3pm; Mon–Sat 7pm–midnight. Tube: Tottenham Court Rd. MEDITERRANEAN.

This immensely popular multistory restaurant serves very good food at affordable prices. Critics claim there's too long a wait between courses, and dishes are overly contrived. But we have to agree with its legions of (mostly young) devotees: We've found the robust Mediterranean dishes to be prepared with the finest ingredients and packed with flavor. Most everything tastes fresh and appealing. Both the restaurant and bistro change their menus frequently, but generally feature an array of pasta, meat, fish, and vegetarian dishes. If you can, start with the goat cheese in a spicy tomato vinaigrette, and follow it with the linguini with langoustines or the rosemary-skewered lamb with a charred eggplant. Fish dishes, delectably seasoned and not allowed to dry out on the grill, range from monkfish to sea bass. Not everything works out—some dishes are tough (especially the duck) and lack spice. The crème brûlée (when it *finally* arrived) was excellent. All in all, not the spot for a romantic tête-à-tête, but immensely appealing. The ground-floor "caff" offers snacks all day, from tapas to meze.

Soho Spice. 124–126 Wardour St., W1. ☎ **020/7434-0808.** Reservations recommended. Main courses £8.50–£14.50 ($14–$23.90); set lunch £8.50 ($14); set dinner £15.95–£22.95 ($26.30–$37.85). AE, DC, MC, V. Sun–Thurs noon–midnight; Fri–Sat noon–3am; Sun 12:30–10:30pm. Tube: Tottenham Court Road. SOUTH INDIAN.

One of central London's most stylish Indian restaurants combines a sense of media and fashion hip with the flavors and scents of southern India. You might opt for a drink at the cellar-level bar before heading to the large street-level dining room decorated in the saffron, cardamom, bay, and pepper hues evocative of the place's piquant cuisine. A staff member dressed in a similarly vivid uniform will propose choices from a wide array of dishes, including a range of slow-cooked Indian tikkas that feature combinations of spices with lamb, chicken, fish, or all-vegetarian. The cuisine will satisfy traditionalists, but has a modern, nouveau-Soho flair. The presentation takes it a step above typical Indian restaurants, here or elsewhere.

BLOOMSBURY & FITZROVIA
MODERATE

✪ **Nico Central.** 35 Great Portland St., W1. ☎ **020/7436-8846.** Reservations required. Fixed-price 2-course lunch £20.50 ($33.80), or £23.50 ($38.80) for a 3-course lunch; fixed-price 3-course dinner £25.50 ($42.05). AE, DC, MC, V. Mon–Fri noon–2pm; Mon–Sat 7–11pm. Tube: Oxford Circus. FRENCH/MODERN BRITISH.

This brasserie—founded and inspired by London's legendary chef, Nico Ladenis (who spends most of his time at Chez Nico at Ninety Park Lane)—delivers earthy French cuisine that's been called "haute but not haughty" and consistently praised for its "absurdly good value." Of course, everything is handled with considerable culinary urbanity. Guests sit on bentwood chairs at linen-covered tables. Nearly a dozen starters—the pride of the chef—will tempt you. The menu changes seasonally and according to the chef's inspiration, but might include grilled duck served with risotto with cèpes (flap mushrooms) and Parmesan; panfried foie gras with brioche and a caramelized orange; braised knuckle of veal; and baked fillet of brill with assorted vegetables. Save room for one of the desserts—they are, in the words of one devotee, "divine."

INEXPENSIVE

British Museum Restaurant. Great Russell St., WC1. ☎ **020/7323-8256.** Main courses £6.45–£7.45 ($10.65–$12.30); £5.45 ($9) soup & baguette special. MC, V. Mon–Sat cold food 11am–4:30pm, hot food 11:30am–3pm. Tube: Holborn or Tottenham Court Rd. TRADITIONAL BRITISH.

This is the best place for lunch if you're exploring the wonders of this world-renowned museum. It's on the lobby level of the West Wing and is decorated with full-size copies of the bas-reliefs from a temple in the town of Nereid in ancient Greece. (If you want to compare, you'll find the originals in nearby galleries.) The format is self-service. A few hot specials (including a vegetarian selection) and crisp salads are made fresh every day, and there's always a good selection of fish and cold meat dishes. Try the soup and baguette special, which is changed daily. Desserts include pastries and cakes. There's also a café offering coffee, sandwiches, pastries, and soup.

HOLBORN
INEXPENSIVE

✪ **North Sea Fish Restaurant.** 7–8 Leigh St., WC1. ☎ **020/7387-5892.** Reservations recommended. Fish platters £6–£12 ($9.90–$19.80). AE, DC, MC, V. Mon–Sat noon–2:30pm and 5:30–10:30pm. Tube: King's Cross, or Russell Sq. SEAFOOD.

The fish served in this bright and clean restaurant is purchased fresh every day; the quality is high, and the prices low. In the view of London's diehard chippie devotees, it's the best in town. The fish is most often served battered and deep-fried, but you can also order it grilled. The menu is wisely limited. Students from the Bloomsbury area flock to the place.

COVENT GARDEN & THE STRAND
EXPENSIVE

Axis. In the Hotel One Aldwych, 1 Aldwych. ☎ **020/7300-1000.** Reservations recommended. Set-price menus £14.95–£17.95 ($24.65–$29.60). Main courses £14–£25 ($23.10–$41.25). AE, DC, MC, V. Mon–Fri noon–3pm; Mon–Sat 6–11:30pm. Tube: Covent Garden or Charing Cross. MODERN BRITISH/PACIFIC RIM.

One of the newest very stylish restaurants in London occupies what was once the printing room for a now-defunct newspaper. In 1998, a team of architects and designers took advantage of its soaring, cathedral-like ceilings and installed a serpentine-shaped travertine staircase leading down from the dramatic bar upstairs. They brought in a culinary team, and opened their doors to discriminating palates across London. The result has an old-clubby feel with a dramatic mural of an "ambiguous and timeless metropolis executed in the vorticist style."

The menu manages to fuse old-fashioned English truffles and jam puddings with sushi and Pacific Rim novelties into the same, well-conceived, and almost obsessively eclectic menu. Menu items include a poached haddock–and–cheese soufflé tart; crispy duck noodle salad with watercress, spring onion, and coriander; chilled and curried apple–and–cardamon soup; grilled Scottish lobster with chicory, lemon verbena, and grapefruit salad; braised or seared breast of Norfolk duck with orange sauce, spiced red cabbage and chestnuts; and an artfully old-fashioned recipe from 1922 that features jugged hare served boneless with creamed celeriac, and a turnip and potato bake. Desserts include trifle from a recipe that originated in 1889; elderflower jelly with champagne sorbet; and roasted pineapple with cracked-pepper ice cream.

Simpson's-in-the-Strand. 100 The Strand (next to the Savoy Hotel), WC2. ☎ **020/7836-9112.** Reservations required. Main courses £15–£22 ($24.75–$36.30); fixed-price 2-course lunch and pre-theater dinner £14 ($23.10); fixed-price breakfast from £13.95 ($23). AE, DC, MC, V. Mon–Fri 7am–11am; Mon–Sat noon–2:30pm and 5:30–11pm; Sun noon–2pm and 6–9pm. Tube: Charing Cross or Embankment. TRADITIONAL BRITISH.

Simpson's is more of an institution than a restaurant—it's been in business since 1828. This very Victorian place boasts Adam paneling, crystal, and an army of grandly formal waiters to whom nouvelle cuisine means anything after Henry VIII. But most diners agree that Simpson's serves the best roasts in London, an array that includes roast sirloin of beef, roast saddle of mutton with red-currant jelly, roast Aylesbury duckling, and steak, kidney, and mushroom pie. (Remember to tip the tailcoated carver.) For a pudding, you might order the treacle roll and custard or Stilton with vintage port.

Taking advantage of the recent upsurge in popularity of traditional British cooking, Simpson's now serves traditional breakfasts. The most popular one, curiously enough, is called "The Ten Deadly Sins" for £15.95 ($26.30): a plate of sausage, fried egg, streaky and back bacon, black pudding, lamb's kidneys, bubble and squeak, baked beans, lamb's liver, and fried bread, mushrooms and tomatoes. That will certainly fortify you for the day.

Jacket and tie is no longer essential; however, we do recommend smart casual attire.

MODERATE

Belgo Centraal. 50 Earlham St., WC2. ☎ **020/7813-2233.** Reservations required for the restaurant. Main courses £8.95–£18.95 ($14.75–$31.25); fixed-price menus £6–£13 ($9.90–$21.45). AE, DC, MC, V. Mon–Sat noon–11:30pm; Sun noon–10:30pm. Closed Christmas. Tube: Covent Garden. BELGIAN.

Chaos reigns supreme in this audacious and cavernous basement, where mussels marinière with frites and 100 Belgian beers are the *raison d'être.* You'll take a freight elevator down past the busy kitchen and into a converted cellar, which has been divided into two large eating areas. One is a beer hall seating about 250; the menu here is the same as in the restaurant, but reservations aren't needed. The restaurant side has three nightly seatings: 5:30, 7:30, and 10pm. Between 5:30 and 8pm you can choose one of three fixed-price menus, and you pay based on the time of your order: the earlier you order, the less you pay. Although heaps of fresh mussels are the big attraction here, you can also opt for fresh Scottish salmon, roast chicken, a perfectly done steak, or one of the vegetarian specialties. Gargantuan plates of wild boar sausages arrive with *stoemp,* Belgian mashed spuds and cabbage. Belgian stews called *waterzooi* are also served. With waiters dressed in maroon monk's habits with black aprons, barking orders into headset microphones, it's all a bit bizarre.

✪ **Joe Allen.** 13 Exeter St., WC2. ☎ **020/7836-0651.** Reservations required. Main courses £10.50–£13.50 ($17.35–$22.30); pre-theater dinner £12–£14 ($19.80–$23.10); Sat–Sun brunch £13–£15 ($21.45–$24.75). AE, MC, V. Mon–Sat noon–12:45am; Sun noon–midnight. Tube: Covent Garden or Charing Cross. AMERICAN.

This fashionable American restaurant near the Savoy attracts primarily theater crowds. Like the New York branch, it's decorated with theater posters. The menu has grown increasingly sophisticated and might include dishes such as grilled corn-fed chicken with sunflower-seed pesto, marinated sweet peppers, and garlic roast new potatoes, as well as specialties like black-bean soup and pecan pie. The Sunday brunch is one of the best in London. You get such main dishes as a mixed grill with lamb chop, calf's liver, and Cumberland sausage, and a choice of a Bloody Mary, Bucks Fizz, or a glass of champagne. The food here has been called "unimaginative." Loyal patrons say, "Who cares? We love it!"

✪ **Porter's English Restaurant.** 17 Henrietta St., WC2. ☎ **020/ 7836-6466.** Reservations recommended. Main courses £8 ($13.20); fixed-price menu £15 ($24.75). AE, DC, MC, V. Mon–Sat noon–11:30pm; Sun noon–10:30pm. Tube: Covent Garden or Charing Cross. TRADITIONAL BRITISH.

In 1979 the 7th Earl of Bradford opened this restaurant, stating "it would serve real English food at affordable prices," and he has succeeded notably–and not just because Lady Bradford turned over her carefully guarded recipe for banana and ginger steamed pudding. A comfortable, two-storied restaurant with a friendly, informal, and lively atmosphere, Porter's specializes in classic English pies, including Old English fish pie; lamb and apricot; ham, leek, and cheese; and of course, bangers and mash. Main courses are so generous—and accompanied by vegetables and side dishes–that you hardly need appetizers. They have also added grilled English fare to the menu, with sirloin and lamb steaks, and pork chops. The puddings, including bread-and-butter pudding or steamed syrup sponge, are the real puddings (in the American sense); they're served hot or cold, with whipped cream or custard. The bar does quite a few exotic cocktails, as well as beers, wine, or English mead. A traditional English tea is also served from 2:30 to 5:30pm for £3.50 ($5.75) per person. Who knows? You may even bump into his Lordship.

WESTMINSTER/VICTORIA

Note that all the restaurants below can be found on the map "Westminster and Victoria Hotels and Restaurants" in Chapter 3.

EXPENSIVE

✪ **Rhodes in the Square.** Dolphin Square, Chichester St., SW1. ☎ **020/ 7798-6767.** Reservations required. Main courses £15.50–£23.50 ($25.60–$38.80). Set lunch £19.50 or £21.50 Sun ($32.15 or $35.50 Sun). AE, DC, MC, V. Sun–Fri noon–2:30pm, Mon–Sat 7–10pm, Sun 7–9pm. Tube: Pimlico. MODERN BRITISH.

In this discreet residential district, super-chef and media darling, Gary Rhodes has done it again. Rhodes has long been known for taking the most traditional of British cookery and giving it daring twists and adding new flavors. Count on some delightful surprises—always—from this major culinary talent. The glitterati can be seen nightly in the apartment-block-cum-hotel, sampling his offerings in an elegant high-ceilinged room done in midnight blue—it's been likened to the grand ballroom of an ocean liner. You never know what's available, perhaps his whole red mullet stuffed with a delectable medley of eggplant, anchovies, fresh garlic, and peppers, appearing with a cream-laced sauce flavored with fennel. Start, perhaps with his chicken liver parfait with foie gras, and go on to an open omelet with chunky bits of lobster topping it along with a Thermidor sauce and cheese crust. His glazed duck served with bitter orange jus is how this dish is supposed to taste and so often doesn't. For dessert, make your selection from the British "pudding plate" that ranges from lemon meringue tart to a simple seared "carpaccio" of pineapple oozing with good flavor.

MODERATE

Shepherd's. Marsham Court, Marsham St., at the corner of Page St., SW1. ☎ **020/7834-9552.** Reservations recommended. Fixed-price meals £22.95 ($37.85) for 2 courses, £24.95 ($41.15) for 3 courses. AE, DC, MC, V. Mon–Fri noon–2:30pm and 6:30–11:30pm (last order at 11pm). Tube: St. James's. TRADITIONAL BRITISH.

Some political observers claim that many of the inner workings of the British government operate from the precincts of this conservative, likable restaurant. Set in the shadow of Big Ben, two blocks north of the Tate Gallery, it enjoys a regular clientele of barristers, members of Parliament, and many of their constituents from far-flung districts of Britain. Don't imagine that the intrigue here occurs only at lunchtime; evenings seem just as ripe an hour for negotiations, particularly over the restaurant's roast rib of Scottish beef served with (what else?) Yorkshire pudding. So synchronized is this place to the goings-on at Parliament that a Division Bell rings in the dining room, calling MPs back to the House of Commons when it's time to vote. Even the decor is designed to make them feel at home, with leather banquettes, sober 19th-century accessories, and a worthy collection of English portraits and landscapes.

The menu reflects many years of British culinary tradition, and dishes are prepared intelligently and with fresh ingredients. In addition to the classic roast, they include a cream-based mussel stew, hot salmon and potato salad with dill dressing, fillet of lemon sole, roast leg of lamb with mint sauce, wild rabbit, salmon fillet with tarragon and chive butter sauce, and the English version of crème brûlée, known as "burnt Cambridge cream."

✪ **Simply Nico.** 48A Rochester Row, SW1. ☎ **020/7630-8061.** Reservations required. Fixed-price 2-course lunch £20.50 ($33.80), fixed-price 3-course lunch £23.50 ($38.80); fixed-price 3-course dinner £25.50 ($42.05). AE, DC, MC, V. Mon–Fri 12:30–2pm; Mon–Sat 7–11pm. Tube: Victoria or St. James's Park. FRENCH.

The brainchild of Nico Ladenis, of the much grander and more expensive Chez Nico at Ninety Park Lane, it's run by his sous-chef. In Nico's own words, it's "cheap and cheerful." We think it's the best value in town. The wood floors reverberate the din of contented diners, who pack in daily at snug tables to enjoy the simply prepared—and invariably French-inspired food. The fixed-price menu changes frequently, but options might include starters such as pan fried foie gras followed by shank of lamb with parsnips, or the ever-popular monkfish.

2 The City

MODERATE

✪ **Café Spice Namaste.** 16 Prescot St., E1. ☎ **020/7488-9242.** Reservations required. Main courses £8.95–£14.95 ($14.75–$24.65). AE, DC, MC, V. Mon–Fri noon–3pm and 6:15–10:30pm; Sat 6:30–10pm. Tube: Tower Hill. INDIAN.

This is our favorite Indian restaurant in London, where the competition is stiff, with Tamarind, and Bombay Brasserie also vying for top honors. It's cheerfully housed in a landmark Victorian hall near Tower Bridge, just east of the Tower of London. The chef, Cyrus Todiwala, is a Parsi and former resident of Goa, where he learned many of his culinary secrets. He concentrates on southern and northern Indian dishes with a strong Portuguese influence. Chicken and lamb are prepared a number of ways, from mild to spicy-hot. As a novelty, Todiwala occasionally even offers a menu of emu dishes; when marinated, the meat is rich and spicy and evocative of lamb. Emu is not the only dining oddity here. Ever have ostrich gizzard kebab, alligator tikka, or minced moose, bison, and blue boar? Many patrons journey here just for the complex chicken curry known as *xacutti.* Lambs' livers and kidneys are also cooked in the tandoor. A weekly specialty menu complements the long list of regional dishes. The homemade chutneys alone are worth the trip; our favorite is made with kiwi. All dishes come with fresh vegetables and Indian bread. With the exotic ingredients, the often time-consuming preparation, the impeccable service, the warm hospitality, and the spicy but subtle flavors, this is hardly a curry hash house.

✪ **Poons in the City.** 2 Minster Lane, Minster Court, Mincing Lane, EC3. ☎ **020/7626-0126.** Reservations recommended for lunch. Fixed-price lunch and dinner £22.50–£30.80 ($37.15–$50.80); main courses £6.50–£8.50 ($10.75–$14). AE, DC, MC, V. Mon–Fri noon–10:30pm. Tube: Tower Hill or Meriment. CHINESE.

In 1992, Poons opened this branch in the City, less than a 5-minute walk from the Tower of London and close to other City attractions. It's modeled on the Luk Yew Tree House in Hong Kong. Main courses feature crispy, aromatic duck; prawns with cashew nuts; and barbecued pork. Poons's famous *lap yuk soom* (like Cantonese tacos) has finely chopped wind-dried bacon. Special dishes can be ordered on 24-hour notice. At the end of the L-shaped restaurant is an 80-seat fast-food area and take-out counter that's accessible from Mark Lane. The menu changes every two weeks, and fixed-price lunches cost from £22.50 ($37.15) per person (minimum of two).

INEXPENSIVE

The George & Vulture. 3 Castle Court, Cornhill, EC3. ☎ **020/7626-9710.** Reservations accepted if you agree to arrive by 12:45pm. Main courses £6.45–£12.45 ($10.65–$20.55). AE, DC, MC, V. Mon–Fri noon–2:30pm. Tube: Bank. TRADITIONAL BRITISH.

Dickens enthusiasts should seek out this old Pickwickian place. Founded in 1660, it claims that it's "probably" the world's oldest tavern, and refers to an inn on this spot in 1175. While they no longer put up overnight guests here, English lunches are still served on the tavern's three floors. Besides the daily specials, the menu includes a mixed grill, a loin chop, and fried Dover sole fillets with tartar sauce. Potatoes and buttered cabbage are the standard vegetables, and the apple tart is always reliable. The system is to arrive and give your name, then retire to the Jamaican pub opposite for a drink; you're "fetched" when your table is ready. After, be sure to explore the mazes of pubs, shops, wine houses, and other old buildings near the tavern.

By the way, the Pickwick Club meets in this pub about six times a year for reunion dinners. This literary club is headed by Cedric Dickens, a great-great-grandson of Charles Dickens.

✪ **Fox & Anchor.** 115 Charterhouse St., EC1. ☎ **020/7253-4838.** Reservations recommended. "Full house" breakfast £7 ($11.55); steak breakfast £7–£9 ($11.55–$14.85). AE, DC, MC, V. Mon–Fri 7am–3pm. Tube: Barbican or Farringdon. TRADITIONAL BRITISH.

For British breakfast at its best, try this place, which has been serving traders from the nearby famous Smithfield meat market since the pub was built in 1898. Breakfasts are gargantuan, especially if you order the "Full House"—a plate with at least eight items, including sausage, bacon, kidneys, eggs, beans, black pudding, and a fried slice of bread, along with unlimited tea or coffee, toast, and jam. Add a Black Velvet (champagne with Guinness) and the day is yours. More fashionable is a Bucks Fizz, with orange juice and champagne (we usually call it a Mimosa). The Fox and Anchor is noted for its range of fine English ales, all available at breakfast. Butchers from the meat market, spotted with blood, still appear, as do nurses getting off their shifts and clerks and tycoons from the City who've been working at bookkeeping chores (or making millions) all night.

Restaurants in & Around the City

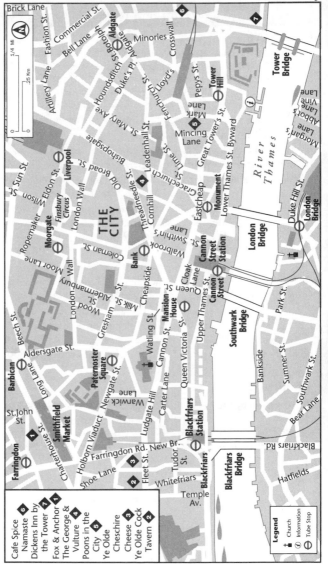

3 On the Thames: Docklands

MODERATE

Butler's Wharf Chop House. Butler's Wharf, 36E Shad Thames, SE1.
☎ **020/7403-3403.** Reservations recommended. Fixed-price 2-course lunch
£18.75 ($30.95), 3-course, fixed-price lunch £22.75 ($37.55); dinner main
courses £12–£29.50 ($19.80–$48.70). AE, DC, MC, V. Sun–Fri noon–3pm (last
order); Mon–Sat 6–11pm. Tube: Tower Hill. TRADITIONAL BRITISH.

Of the four restaurants housed in Butler's Wharf, this one is the
closest to Tower Bridge. It maintains its commitment to moderate
prices, and though there's an even cheaper restaurant, La Cantina del
Ponte, most diners consider that merely a place for pastas. The Chop
House was modeled after a large boathouse, with russet-colored banquettes, lots of exposed wood, flowers, candles, and big windows
overlooking Tower Bridge and the Thames. Lunchtime crowds include workers from the City's nearby financial district; evening
crowds are largely made up of friends dining together under less
pressing circumstances.

Dishes are largely adaptations of British recipes: fish 'n' chips with
mushy peas; steak and kidney pudding with oysters; stewed rabbit
leg with bitter leaves and mustard; roast rump of lamb, garlic mash
and rosemary; and grilled pork fillet, apples, chestnuts, and cider
sauce. To follow, there might be a dark-chocolate tart with whiskey
cream or sticky toffee pudding. The bar offers such stiff-upper-lip
choices as Theakston's best bitter, several English wines, and a half-
dozen French clarets served by the jug.

INEXPENSIVE

✪ **Dickens Inn by the Tower.** St. Katharine's Way, E1. ☎ **020/7488-2208.**
Reservations recommended. In Pickwick Grill, main courses £17.50–£35
($28.90–$57.75); in Tavern Room, snacks and platters £3.75–£6 ($6.20–$9.90);
in pizza restaurant, pizzas £9–£15 ($14.85–$24.75). AE, DC, MC, V. Restaurant
daily noon–3pm and 6:30–10pm; pizza restaurant daily noon–10pm; bar daily
11am–11pm. Tube: Tower Hill. TRADITIONAL BRITISH.

This three-floor restaurant is in an 1830 brick warehouse in St.
Katharine's Dock. Its unusual antique trusses, including a set of
massive redwood timbers, were part of the original construction.
Large windows afford a sweeping view of the nearby Thames and
Tower Bridge. On the ground level, you'll find a bar and the Tavern Room, serving sandwiches, platters of lasagna, steaming bowls
of soup and chili, bar snacks, and other foods kids love. On the floor
above is Pizza on the Dock, offering four sizes of pizzas that should
also make the kids happy when they have a craving for the familiar.

Above that, you'll find a relatively formal dining room, Wheelers Restaurant, serving more elegant modern British meals; specials include steaks, chargrilled brochette of wild mushrooms, panfried calf's kidney with tangy lime and ginger sauce, and baked fillet of cod.

4 In & Around Knightsbridge

VERY EXPENSIVE

La Tante Claire. Wilton Place, Knightsbridge, SW1. ☎ **020/7823-2003.** Reservations essential. Main courses £24–£35 ($39.60–$57.75). AE, DC, MC, V. Mon–Fri 12:30–2pm, Mon–Sat 7–11pm. Tube: Hyde Park Corner, Knightsbridge.

In swanky new digs, "Aunt Claire" has once again emerged as one of the stellar restaurants of London. Pierre Koffmann remains the chef behind this fabled place, a man more interested in turning out culinary fireworks than in creating a media feeding frenzy. The restaurant was designed by leading interior designer David Collins of Ireland. The lilac walls and the soothing green floors are a mere backdrop to the cuisine which uses only the freshest and best of produce to be found in London. The standards of Chef Koffmann are the benchmark other chefs aspire to. To sample perfection, dishes bringing out mouthwatering flavors and precise textures, try his now legendary ravioli langoustine or pig's trotters. Who would have thought that the lowly pig trotter, long a staple of the menu in Paris's Les Halles district, could be transformed into such a sublime concoction? His soup made with truffles is to make gourmands shed tears of joy. His nage de homard (lobster) with Sauterne and fresh ginger is a culinary work of skill, as is his steamed lamb with a vegetable couscous. For dessert, his hot pistachio soufflé served with its own ice cream will linger long in your memory. The service proceeds like a perfectly trained and talented orchestra.

MODERATE

Fifth Floor at Harvey Nichols. 109–125 Knightsbridge, at Sloane St., SW1. ☎ **020/7235-5250.** Reservations recommended. Fixed-price lunch £23.50 ($38.80) for 3 courses; main courses £12–£30 ($19.80–$49.50). À la carte dishes available at dinner only. AE, DC, MC, V. Mon–Fri noon–3pm, Sat and Sun noon–3:30pm; Mon–Sat 6:30–11:30pm (last order). Tube: Knightsbridge. MODERN BRITISH.

This restaurant in the Harvey Nichols flagship store is the most carefully orchestrated of London's large–department-store eateries. There's a simple café near the entrance, which tends to be the domain of package-laden shoppers looking for a quick cup of tea and

Restaurants from Knightsbridge to Kensington

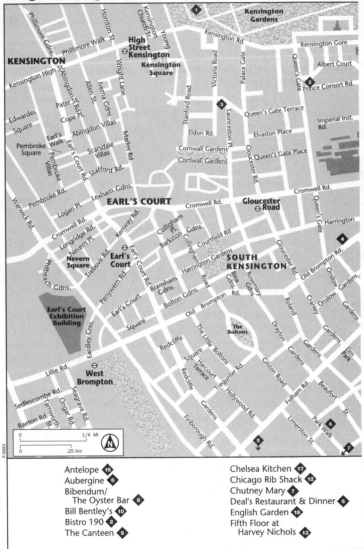

Antelope **16**
Aubergine **6**
Bibendum/
  The Oyster Bar **8**
Bill Bentley's **10**
Bistro 190 **2**
The Canteen **5**

Chelsea Kitchen **17**
Chicago Rib Shack **12**
Chutney Mary **7**
Deal's Restaurant & Dinner **5**
English Garden **18**
Fifth Floor at
  Harvey Nichols **13**

132

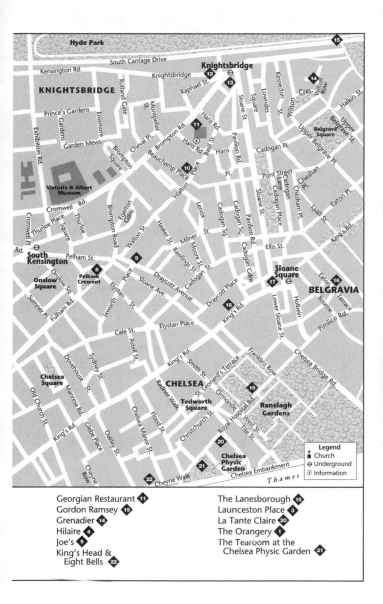

Georgian Restaurant 🔶11
Gordon Ramsey 🔶19
Grenadier 🔶14
Hilaire 🔶4
Joe's 🔶9
King's Head &
  Eight Bells 🔶22

The Lanesborough 🔶15
Launceston Place 🔶3
La Tante Claire 🔶20
The Orangery 🔶1
The Tearoom at the
  Chelsea Physic Garden 🔶21

133

a salad. Serious diners head directly to the high-ceilinged blue-and-white restaurant, where big windows overlook the red-brick Edwardian walls of the Hyde Park Hotel across the street. The menu is appropriately fashionable, and waiters imbue any meal with a polite kind of formality. Starters include goat-cheese–and–lemon risotto with deep-fried baby artichokes, and potted foie gras with orange-and-onion confit and toasted brioche. Main courses include panfried scallops in a bordelaise sauce; shredded duck confit; smoked haddock fishcakes; and a spinach, bacon, and avocado salad.

Although the department store closes at 6pm, a pair of elevators continues to haul patrons to the restaurant. There's a glamorous food emporium (open during store hours) set just outside the restaurant's entrance.

INEXPENSIVE

Chicago Rib Shack. 1 Raphael St., SW7. ☎ **020/7581-5595.** Reservations accepted, except Sat. Main courses £8–£12 ($13.20–$19.80). AE, CB, MC, V. Daily 11:45am–11:45pm. Tube: Knightsbridge. AMERICAN.

Just 100 yards from Harrods, this place specializes in real American barbecue, cooked in imported smoking ovens and marinated in a sauce made with 15 ingredients. Their decadent onion loaf is a famous treat. Visitors are encouraged to eat with their fingers, and bibs and hot towels are provided. A TV screen suspended in the bar shows American sports. The British touch is evident in an overwhelming number of Victorian architectural antiques, which have been salvaged from demolished buildings all over the country. The 45-foot–long ornate mahogany-and-mirrored bar was once part of a Glasgow pub, and eight massive stained-glass windows came from a chapel in Lancashire.

5 Chelsea

VERY EXPENSIVE

✪ **Gordon Ramsay.** 68 Royal Hospital Rd., SW3. ☎ **020/7352-4441.** Reservations essential (1 month in advance). Set lunch £28 ($46.20) for 2 courses, £50 ($82.50) for 3 courses. Set dinner £50 ($82.50) for 3 courses, £65 ($107.25) for 7 courses. Mon–Fri noon–2:30pm and 6:45–11pm. Tube: Sloane Square. FRENCH.

The buzz in London spins around one of the city's most innovative and talented chefs, Gordon Ramsay. He's taken over the premises of La Tante Claire (see above), and this genius of a chef is serving a cuisine even more innovative and exciting than the long-established "La Tante" herself. *Tout* London is rushing to sample Mr. Ramsay's viands, and he's had to turn away some big names. The Queen hasn't been denied a table yet, but that's only because she hasn't called. Already gourmand Andrew Lloyd Weber has visited, and acclaimed Ramsay as one of Europe's grandest chefs. The producer said you "can get better food here than anywhere else in London." Food critic Dominic Bradbury called Ramsay a "Captain Ahab, a dedicated monomaniac, hell-bent on cruising his kitchen until he finds his second Michelin star." Every dish from his kitchen is gratifying, reflecting subtlety and delicacy without any sacrifice to the food's natural essence. Try, for example, his celebrated cappuccino of white beans with grated truffles. His appetizers are likely to dazzle: salad of crispy pig's trotters with calf's sweetbreads, fried quail eggs, and a cream vinaigrette, or else foie gras three ways— sautéed with quince, *mi-cuit* with an Earl Grey consomme, or pressed with truffle peelings. From here, you can grandly proceed to fillet of brill poached in red wine, grilled fillet of red mullet on a bed of caramelized endives, or else caramelized Challandaise duck cooked with dates. Desserts are equally stunning, especially the pistachio soufflé with chocolate sorbet or the passion fruit and chocolate parfait.

EXPENSIVE

✪ **Aubergine.** 11 Park Walk, SW10. ☎ **020/7352-3449.** Reservations essential and accepted up to 4 weeks in advance. Fixed-price 2-course lunch £23.50 ($38.80); fixed-price 3-course dinner £39.50 ($65.20); menu gourmand £45 ($74.25). AE, DC, MC, V. Mon–Fri noon–2:30pm; Mon–Sat 6:45–11pm. Tube: South Kensington. FRENCH.

"Eggplant" is luring savvy diners down to the lower reaches of Chelsea where new chef Williams Drabble takes over from where the renowned Gordon Ramsay left off. Drabble, who earned his first Michelin star in 1998 has remained true to the style and ambience of this famous establishment. Although popular with celebrities, the restaurant remains unpretentious and refuses to pander to the special whims of the rich and famous. (When Princess Margaret complained that the air conditioning was too cold, she was lent a cardigan; and Madonna was refused a late-night booking!)

Every dish is satisfyingly flavorsome, from the warm salad of truffled vegetables with asparagus purée to the roasted monkfish served with crushed new potatoes, roasted leeks, and a red-wine sauce. Starters continue to charm and delight palates, ranging from the ravioli of crab with mussels, chili, ginger, and coriander nage, to the terrine of foie gras with confit of duck with pears poached in port. Also resting on your Villeroy or Boch aubergine plate might be mallard with a celeriac fondant or assiette of lamb with a thyme-scented jus. Another stunning (in the good sense) main course is a tranche of sea bass with bouillabaisse potatoes. A new dish likely to catch your eye is roasted veal sweetbreads with caramelized onion purée and a casserole of flap mushrooms. There are only 14 tables, so bookings are imperative.

MODERATE

English Garden. 10 Lincoln St., SW3. ☎ **020/7584-7272.** Reservations required. Main courses £9.50–£19.25 ($15.65–$31.75); fixed-price lunch £16.75 ($27.65). AE, CB, DC, MC, V. Mon–Sat 12:30–2:30pm, Sun 12:30–2pm; Mon–Sat 7:30–11:30pm, Sun 7–10:30pm. Tube: Sloane Sq. TRADITIONAL BRITISH.

This is a metropolitan restaurant par excellence. The decor is pretty and lighthearted in the historic town house: The Garden Room is white-washed brick with a domed conservatory roof; vivid florals, rattan chairs, banks of plants, and candy-pink napery complete the scene. Every component of a meal here is chopped or cooked to the right degree and well proportioned. Launch into a fine repast with a caramelized red onion–and–cheddar cheesecake or mussel-and-watercress soup. For a main course, opt for such delights as roast baron of rabbit with oven-dried tomato, prunes and olive oil mash, or saddle of venison with potted cabbage. Some of these dishes sound as if they were cloned from an English cookbook of the Middle Ages—and are they ever good. Desserts, especially the rhubarb and cinnamon ice cream or the candied orange tart with orange syrup, would've pleased Miss Marple.

INEXPENSIVE

Chelsea Kitchen. 98 King's Rd., SW3. ☎ **020/7589-1330.** Reservations recommended. Main courses £3–£5.50 ($4.95–$9.05); fixed-price menu £6 ($9.90). No credit cards. Daily 8am–11:30pm. Tube: Sloane Sq. INTERNATIONAL.

This simple restaurant feeds large numbers of Chelsea residents in a setting that's changed very little since 1961. The food and the clientele move fast, almost guaranteeing that the entire inventory of ingredients is sold out at the end of each day. Menu items usually include leek-and-potato soup, chicken Kiev, chicken parmigiana, steaks, sandwiches, and burgers. The clientele includes a broad cross-section of patrons—all having a good and cost-conscious time.

IN NEARBY CHELSEA HARBOUR
MODERATE

✪ **The Canteen.** Unit G4, Harbour Yard, Chelsea Harbour, SW10. ☎ **020/7351-7330.** Reservations recommended. Cover charge £1 ($1.65) per person. Main courses £6–£10.40 ($9.90–$17.15). AE, MC, V. Mon–Sat noon–3pm; Mon–Fri 6:30–10:30pm; Sat 6:30–11:15pm. Tube: Earl's Court, then Chelsea Harbour Hoppa Bus C3; on Sun, take a taxi. MODERN BRITISH/FRENCH.

The most viable and popular of the several restaurants in the Chelsea Harbour Complex, its whimsical setting, influenced by *Alice in Wonderland,* is very fantastical and the kind of thing that children as well as adults love. The cuisine is exceptional, too. The menu changes every two months, but may include risotto of plum tomatoes and champagne; pappardelle with field mushrooms and truffle oil; a warm salad of sea scallops, apples, and cashew nuts; sliced breast of corn-fed chicken with apple, potato-and-sage casserole, along with Spätzli, and beans; or, a real treat, seared peppered tuna with herb potatoes, a sweet shallot pickle, and crème fraîche. The chocolate soufflé is the smoothest item on the menu, and are those crêpes suzettes soufflés ever tempting. Or else you can settle for a selection of farmhouse cheeses so delectable it isn't a compromise at all to pass up all those rich desserts.

INEXPENSIVE

Deal's Restaurant and Diner. Harbour Yard, Chelsea Harbour, SW10. ☎ **020/7795-1001.** Reservations recommended. Main courses £6.75–£17 ($11.15–$28.05). AE, DC, MC, V. Mon–Thurs noon–3:30pm and 5:30–11pm; Fri–Sat noon–11:30pm; Sun noon–10pm. Tube: Earl's Court, then Chelsea Harbour Hoppa Bus C3; on Sun, take a taxi. AMERICAN/THAI.

Deal's is co-owned by Princess Margaret's son, Viscount Linley, and Lord Lichfield. As soon as the Queen Mother arrived here on a barge to order a Deal's burger, the success of this place was assured. The early-1900s atmosphere includes ceiling fans and bentwood banquettes. The food is American diner–style, with a strong Thai influence: Try a teriyaki burger, the prawn curry, spareribs, or a vegetarian dish, and finish with New England–style apple pie. We can't promise that the viscount himself is in the kitchen supervising the menu, but he is said to have tasted everything, and given it his aristocratic approval.

6 Kensington & South Kensington

KENSINGTON

MODERATE

Launceston Place. 1A Launceston Place, W8. ☎ **020/7937-6912.** Reservations required. Main courses £14.50–£16.50 ($23.90–$27.20); fixed-price menu for lunch and early dinner till 8pm, £14.50 ($23.90) for 2 courses, and £17.50 ($28.90) for 3 courses. AE, MC, V. Mon–Fri 12:30–2:30pm, Sun 12:30–3pm; Mon–Sat 7–11:30pm. Tube: Gloucester Rd. or High St. Kensington. MODERN BRITISH.

Launceston Place—sporting a new look as of 1996—is situated in an affluent, almost village-like neighborhood where many Londoners would like to live, if only they could afford it. The stylish restaurant is a series of uncluttered Victorian parlors illuminated by a rear sky-light and decorated with Victorian oils and watercolors, plus con-temporary paintings. Since its opening in spring 1986, it has been known for its new British cuisine. The menu changes every six weeks, but you're likely to be served such appetizers as smoked salmon with horseradish crème fraîche, or seared foie gras with len-tils and vanilla dressing. For a main dish, perhaps it'll be roast par-tridge with bacon, onions, and parsnip mash, or grilled sea bass with tomato and basil cream.

SOUTH KENSINGTON
EXPENSIVE

Bibendum/The Oyster Bar. 81 Fulham Rd., SW3. ☎ **020/7581-5817.** Reservations required in Bibendum; not accepted in Oyster Bar. Main courses £15–£25 ($24.75–$41.25); fixed-price 3-course lunch £28 ($46.20); cold seafood platter in Oyster Bar £45 ($74.25) for 2. AE, DC, MC, V. Bibendum Mon–Fri noon–2:30pm and 7–11:15pm, Sat 12:30–3pm and 7–11:15pm, Sun 12:30–3pm and 7–10:15pm. Oyster Bar Mon–Sat noon–11:30pm, Sun noon–3pm and 7–10:30pm. Tube: South Kensington. FRENCH/MEDITERRANEAN.

In trendy Brompton Cross, this still-fashionable restaurant occupies two floors of a garage—the former home of the Michelin tire company—that's an art deco masterpiece. Although it's still going strong, Bibendum's heyday was in the early 1990s; it no longer enjoys top berth on the lists of London's food critics. The white-tiled room, with stained-glass windows, streaming sunlight, and a chic clientele, is an extremely pleasant place to dine. The fabulously eclec-tic cuisine, known for its freshness and simplicity, is based on what's available seasonally. Dishes might include roast pigeon with celeriac purée and apple sauté; rabbit with anchovies, garlic, and rosemary; or grilled lamb cutlets with a delicate sauce. Some of the best dishes are for dining *à deux:* Bresse chicken flavored with fresh tarragon, or grilled veal chops with truffle butter.

Simpler meals and cocktails are available in the **Oyster Bar** on the building's street level. The bar-style menu stresses fresh shellfish presented in the traditional French style, on ice-covered platters occasionally adorned with strands of seaweed. It's a crustacean-lover's lair.

Hilaire. 68 Old Brompton Rd., SW7. ☎ **020/7584-8993.** Reservations recommended. 2-course fixed-price lunch £19.50 ($32.15); 3 courses £23.50 ($38.80); 3-course fixed-price dinner £34 ($56.10); 4 courses £37 ($61.05); dinner main courses £13.50–£21.50 ($22.30–$35.50). AE, DC, MC, V. Mon–Fri 12:15–2:30pm; Mon–Sat 6:30–11:30pm. Closed bank holidays. Tube: South Kensington. CONTINENTAL.

After this former Victorian storefront was refurbished following a fire, it became one classy joint, like an elegant restaurant you might find in a town in the heart of France. With its large vases of flowers and shiny mirrors, it has a fitting ambience for enjoying some of South Ken's finest food. Chef Bryan Weber prepares a mixture of classical French and *cuisine moderne,* always following his own creative impulses and good culinary sense and style. The menu reflects the best of the season's offerings. A typical lunch might begin with a red-wine risotto with radicchio and sun-dried tomato pesto, followed with sautéed scallops with creamed chicory, and ending with rhubarb sorbet. At dinner, main courses might include rack of lamb with tapenade and wild garlic, saddle of rabbit, or grilled tuna with Provençal vegetables. An aperitif bar, extra tables, and a pair of semi-private alcoves are in the lower dining room.

MODERATE

Bistro 190. In the Gore Hotel, 190 Queen's Gate, SW7. ☎ **020/7581-5666.** Reservations not accepted. Main courses £10–£15 ($16.50–$24.75). AE, DC, MC, V. Mon–Sat 7am–midnight, Sun 7:30am–11:30pm. Tube: Gloucester Rd. MEDITERRANEAN.

In the airy front room of the Gore Hotel (see chapter 4), this restaurant features a light Mediterranean cuisine much appreciated by the music and media crowd that keeps the place hopping. In an artfully simple setting of wood floors, potted plants, and framed art accented by a convivial but gossipy roar, you can dine on such dishes as lamb grilled over charcoal and served with deep-fried basil; a cassoulet of fish with chili toast; Mediterranean chowder with pesto toast; and, if available, a rhubarb crumble based loosely on an old-fashioned British dessert. Service isn't particularly fast, and the policy on reservations is confusing: Although membership is required for reservations, nonmembers may leave their name at the door and have a drink at the bar while they wait for a table. In the crush of peak dining hours, your waiter may or may not remember the nuances you expressed while placing your order, but the restaurant is nonetheless memorable. Go down to Downstairs 190 for a seafood or vegetarian meal.

Joe's. 126 Draycott Ave., SW3. ☎ **020/7225-2217.** Reservations required. Main courses £10–£17.50 ($16.50–$28.90). AE, DC, MC, V. Mon–Sat noon–3pm and 7–11pm, Sun 10:30am–4pm. Tube: South Kensington. MODERN BRITISH.

This is one of three London restaurants established by fashion designer Joseph Ettedgui. Thanks to its sense of glamour and fun, it's often filled with well-known names from the British fashion, music, and entertainment industries. You can enjoy such dishes as spiced venison strips and vegetables, roast cod in a champagne crab sauce, chargrilled swordfish with cracked wheat and salsa verde (green sauce), or fresh lobster lasagna. It's all safe, but a bit unexciting. No one will mind if your meal is composed exclusively of appetizers. There's a bar near the entrance, a cluster of tables for quick meals near the door, and more leisurely (and gossipy) dining available in an area a few steps up. Brunch is served on Sunday, which is the cheapest way to enjoy this place. The atmosphere remains laid back and unstuffy, just like trendsetters in South Ken prefer it. With a name like Joe's, what else could it be?

7 Notting Hill

MODERATE

Achy Ramp. 150 Notting Hill Gate, W11. ☎ **020/7221-2442.** Reservations required Fri–Sat; otherwise strongly recommended. Main courses £13.50–£16.50 ($22.30–$27.20). AE, DC, MC, V. Daily noon–2:45pm and 6:45–10pm. Tube: Notting Hill Gate. MODERN CONTINENTAL.

The theme of this medical-chic restaurant will remind you either of a harmless small-town pharmacy or a drug lord's secret stash of mind-altering pills. That ambiguity is richly appreciated by the arts-conscious crowd that flocks here, partly because they're interested in what Damien Hirst (*enfant terrible* of London's contemporary art world) has created, and partly because the place can be a lot of fun. You'll enter the street-level bar, where a drink menu lists lots of highly palatable martinis as well as a somewhat icky concoction known as a Cough Syrup (cherry liqueur, honey, and vodka that's shaken, not stirred, over ice). Bottles of pills; bar stools whose seats are shaped like aspirins; and painted representations of Fire, Water, Air, and Earth decorate a scene favored by minor celebs and party people. Upstairs in the restaurant, the hospital theme is a lot less pronounced, but nonetheless subtly omnipresent. Menu items include such trendy but comforting food items as carpaccio of sea bass; lamb cooked with celery, spinach, and herb juices; fisherman's pie; home-salted cod and eggplant pie; and roasted duck with white peaches and French fries.

✪ **Bali Sugar Club.** 33A All Saints Rd., W11. ☎ **020/7221-4477.** Main courses £12–£17 ($19.80–$28.05); Set lunch menu £17.50 ($28.90). AE, DC, MC, V. Daily 12:30–2:30pm and 6:30–11pm. Tube: Westbourne Park. FUSION.

The owners originally opened The Sugar Club here and achieved fame across London. But they have now moved and turned the original site into Bali Sugar, which is every bit as good as the original. They have acquired the talents of Claudio Aprile, one of Canada's most exciting and innovative young chefs, regarded as a rising star on the culinary scene. Originally from Uruguay, he trained in New York. He brings an exotic, bold, and extraordinary new look to fusion cuisine which has been labeled here "Southern Hemisphere Pacific Rim Modern Mediterranean Cosmopolitan British cookery"—whatever. Claudio has created a menu using Japanese and South American ingredients to great effect. For starters, dig into his lobster ceviche with coconut, lime, and mango, followed by rare tuna. The taste is magical. His cured salmon is perfect and wonderfully accompanied by a side order of wasabi mash. The overall effect, in the words of one diner, is the meeting of the Pacific Rim with Nuevo Latino. Try also the duck salad integrated distinctively with an irresistibly rich fufu. The two-floor eatery is a delight with a sunken garden. Chic London goes here, and there's a separate non-smoking floor.

8 Bayswater

MODERATE

✪ **Veronica's.** 3 Hereford Rd., W2. ☎ **020/7229-5079.** Reservations required. Main courses £10.50–£18.50 ($17.35–$30.55); fixed-price meals £12.50–£16.50 ($20.65–$27.20). AE, DC, MC, V. Mon–Fri noon–3pm; Mon–Sat 6pm–midnight. Tube: Bayswater or Queensway. TRADITIONAL BRITISH.

Called the "market leader in cafe salons," Veronica's offers traditional and in fact, historical fare at tabs you won't mind paying. It's a celebration of British cuisine over a 2,000 year period, with some dishes based on medieval, Tudor, and even Roman-age recipes, but all given an imaginative modern twist by owner Veronica Shaw. One month she'll focus on Scotland, another month on Victorian foods, yet another on Wales, and the next on Ireland. Your appetizer might be a salad called *salmagundy*, made with crunchy pickled vegetables, that Elizabeth I enjoyed in her day. Another concoction might be Tweed Kettle, a 19th-century recipe to improve the monotonous taste of salmon. Many dishes are vegetarian, and everything tastes better when followed with a British farmhouse cheese or a pudding. The restaurant is brightly and attractively decorated, and the service warm and ingratiating.

9　Teatime

Everyone should indulge in a formal afternoon tea at least once while in London. It's a relaxing, drawn-out, civilized affair that usually consists of three courses, all served on elegant china: first, dainty finger sandwiches; then fresh-baked scones served with jam and clotted cream (also known as Devonshire cream); and, last, an array of bite-sized sweets. All the while, an indulgent server keeps the pot of tea of your choice fresh at hand. We've listed our favorites below.

MAYFAIR

J Brown's Hotel. 29–34 Albemarle St., W1. ☎ **020/7493-6020.** Reservations not accepted. Afternoon tea £17.95 ($29.60). AE, DC, MC, V. Daily 3–5:45pm. Tube: Green Park.

Along with the Ritz, Brown's ranks as one of the most chic venues for tea in London. Tea is served in the drawing room; done in English antiques, oil paintings, and floral chintz—much like the drawing room of a country estate—it's an appropriate venue for such an affair. Give your name to the concierge upon arrival; he'll seat you at one of the clusters of sofas and settees or at low tables. There's a choice of 10 teas, plus sandwiches, scones, and pastries (all made right in the hotel kitchens) that are rolled around on a trolley for your selection.

Claridge's. Brook St., W1. ☎ **020/7629-8860.** Reservations recommended. Jacket and tie required for men. High tea £18 ($29.70). AE, DC, MC, V. Daily 3–5pm. Tube: Bond St.

Claridge's teatime rituals have managed to persevere through the years with as much pomp and circumstance as the British Empire itself. It's never stuffy, though; you'll feel very welcome. Tea is served in The Reading Room. A portrait of Lady Claridge gazes benevolently from above as a choice of 17 kinds of tea is served ever so politely. The various courses are served consecutively, including finger sandwiches with cheese savories, apple and raisin scones, and yummy pastries.

Ritz Palm Court. In The Ritz Hotel, Piccadilly, W1. ☎ **020/7493-8181.** Reservations required at least 8 weeks in advance. Jeans and sneakers not acceptable. Jacket and tie required for men. Afternoon tea £24.50 ($40.40). AE, DC, MC, V. 2 seatings daily at 3:30 and 5pm. Tube: Green Park.

This is the most fashionable place in London to order afternoon tea—and the hardest to get into without reserving way in advance. Its spectacular setting is straight out of *The Great Gatsby*, complete with marble steps and columns and a baroque fountain. You have your choice of a long list of teas, served with delectable sandwiches and luscious pastries.

COVENT GARDEN & THE STRAND

✪ **Palm Court at the Waldorf Meridien.** In the Waldorf Hotel, Aldwych, WC2. ☎ **020/7836-2400.** Reservations required for tea dance. Jacket and tie required for men at tea dance. Afternoon tea £18–£21 ($29.70–$34.65); tea dance £25–£28 ($41.25–$46.20). AE, DC, MC, V. Afternoon tea Mon–Fri 3–5:30pm; tea dance Sat 2:30–5pm; Sun 4–6:30pm. Tube: Covent Garden.

The Waldorf's Palm Court combines afternoon tea with afternoon dancing (the fox-trot, quickstep, and the waltz). The Palm Court is aptly compared to a 1920s movie set (which it has been several times in its long life). You can order tea on a terrace or in a pavilion the size of a ballroom lit by skylights. On tea-dancing days, the orchestra leader will conduct such favorites as "Ain't She Sweet" and "Yes, Sir, That's My Baby," as a butler in a cutaway asks if you want a cucumber sandwich.

KNIGHTSBRIDGE

✪ **The Georgian Restaurant.** On the 4th floor of Harrods, 87–135 Brompton Rd., SW1. ☎ **020/7225-6800.** High tea £17 ($28.05) or £23 ($37.95) with Harrods champagne per person. AE, DC, MC, V. Teatime Mon–Sat 3:30–5:15pm (last order). Tube: Knightsbridge.

As long as anyone can remember, teatime at Harrods has been one of the most distinctive features of Europe's most famous department store. A flood of visitors is somehow gracefully herded into a high-volume but nevertheless elegant room. Many come here expressly for the tea ritual, where staff haul silver pots and trolleys laden with pastries and sandwiches through the cavernous dining hall. Most exotic is Betigala tea, a rare blend from China, similar to Lapsang Souchong.

BELGRAVIA

The Lanesborough. Hyde Park Corner, SW1. ☎ **020/7259-5599.** Reservations required. High tea £19.50 ($32.15), high tea with strawberries and champagne £24.50 ($40.40); pot of tea £3.70 ($6.10). AE, DC, MC, V. Daily 3:30–6pm (last order). AE, DC, MC, V. Tube: Hyde Park Corner.

You'll suspect that many of the folks sipping exotic teas here have dropped in to inspect the public areas of one of London's most expensive hotels. The staff rises to the challenge with aplomb, offering a selection of seven teas that include the Lanesborough special blend, and such herbal esoteria as Rose Cayou. The focal point for this ritual is the Conservatory, a glass-roofed Edwardian fantasy filled with potted plants and a sense of the long-gone majesty of empire.

The finger sandwiches, scones, and sweets are all appropriately lavish and endlessly correct.

CHELSEA

The Tearoom at the Chelsea Physic Garden. 66 Royal Hospital Rd., SW3. ☎ **020/7352-5646.** Tea with cake £3.50 ($5.75). MC, V (in shop only). Wed 2:30–4:45pm; Sun 2:30–5:45pm. Closed Nov–Mar. Tube: Sloane Sq.

It encompasses only 3¹/₂ acres, crisscrossed with gravel paths and ringed with a high brick wall that shuts out the roaring traffic of Royal Hospital Road. These few spectacular acres, however, revere the memory of entire industries that were spawned from seeds developed and tested within its walls. Founded in 1673 as a botanical education center, the Chelsea Physic Garden's list of successes includes the exportation of rubber from South America to Malaysia and tea from China to India.

On the two days a week it's open, the tearoom is likely to be filled with botanical enthusiasts merrily sipping cups of tea as fortification for their garden treks. The setting is a rather banal-looking Edwardian building. Since the tearoom is only an adjunct to the glories of the garden itself, don't expect the lavish rituals of teatime venues. But you can carry your cakes and cups of tea outside into a garden that, despite meticulous care, always looks a bit unkempt. (Herbaceous plants within its hallowed precincts are left untrimmed to encourage bird life and seed production.) Botanists and flower lovers in general find the place fascinating.

KENSINGTON

✪ **The Orangery.** In the gardens of Kensington Palace, W8. ☎ **020/7376-0239.** Reservations not accepted. Pot of tea £2 ($3.30), summer cakes and puddings £1.95–£4.25 ($3.20–$7), sandwiches £6 ($9.90). MC, V. Daily 10am–6pm; closing time half an hour before gates close (usually between 4 and 5pm) in winter. Mar–Oct 10am–6pm; Nov–Mar 10am–4pm. Tube: High St. Kensington or Queensway.

In its way, the Orangery is the most amazing place for midafternoon tea in the world. Set about 50 yards north of Kensington Palace, it occupies a long and narrow garden pavilion built in 1704 by Queen Anne as a site for her tea parties. In homage to that monarch's original intentions, rows of potted orange trees bask in sunlight from soaring windows, and tea is still served amid Corinthian columns, ruddy-colored bricks, and a pair of Grinling Gibbons woodcarvings. There are even some urns and statuary that the Royal Family imported to the site from Windsor Castle. The menu includes lunchtime soups and sandwiches, which come with a salad and a portion of upscale potato chips known as "kettle chips." There's also an array of different teas, served with high style, usually accompanied by freshly baked scones with clotted cream and jam, and Belgian chocolate cake.

10 Pubs & Wine Bars

IN THE WEST END
MAYFAIR

Shepherd's Tavern. 50 Hertford St., W1. ☎ **020/7499-3017.** Reservations recommended. Main courses £7–£11 ($11.55–$18.15). AE, DC, MC, V. Restaurant daily noon–3pm; Sun–Fri 6:30–9:30pm; Sat 6:30–10:30pm. Bar Mon–Sat 11am–11pm, Sun noon–10:30pm. Tube: Green Park. BRITISH.

This pub is one of the focal points of the all-pedestrian shopping zone of Shepherd's Market. It's set amid a warren of narrow, cobble-covered streets behind Park Lane, in an 18th-century town house very similar to many of its neighbors. The street-level bar is cramped but congenial. Many of the regulars recall this tavern's popularity with the pilots of the Battle of Britain. Bar snacks include simple platters of shepherd's pie and fish-and-chips. More formal dining is available upstairs in the cozy, cedar-lined Georgian-style restaurant; the classic British menu probably hasn't changed much since the 1950s. If you're a little leery of the roast beef with Yorkshire pudding, go with the Oxford ham instead.

ST. JAMES'S

Bubbles. 41 N. Audley St., W1. ☎ **0207/491-3237.** Reservations recommended. Main courses £5.50–£11.80 ($9.05–19.45); vegetarian main courses £6–£6.25 ($9.90–$10.30). AE, DC, MC, V. Daily 11am–11pm. Tube: Bond St. BRITISH/INTERNATIONAL VEGETARIAN.

This interesting wine bar lies between Upper Brook Street and Oxford Street (in the vicinity of Selfridges). The owners attach equal importance to their food and to their impressive wine list (some wines are sold by the glass). On the ground floor, you can enjoy not only fine wines but also draft beer and liquor, along with a limited but well-chosen selection of bar food, such as smoked salmon on brown bread, or homemade steak burger with fries and salad and cheese. Downstairs, the restaurant serves both English and continental dishes, including an appealing vegetarian selection. You might begin with French onion soup, followed by bangers and mash with onion gravy, Dover sole, or grilled chicken breast with apple rice and creamed leeks.

Red Lion. 2 Duke of York St. (off Jermyn St.), SW1. ☎ **020/7930-2030.** Sandwiches £2.50 ($4.15), fish-and-chips £8 ($13.20). No credit cards. Mon–Fri 11:30am–11pm, Sat noon–11pm. Tube: Piccadilly Circus. BRITISH.

This little Victorian pub, with its early-1900s decorations and mirrors 150 years old, has been compared in spirit to Édouard Manet's painting *A Bar at the Folies-Bergère* (on display at the Courtauld Institute Galleries). You can order pre-made sandwiches, but once they're gone you're out of luck. On Saturday, homemade fish-and-chips are also served. Wash down your meal with Ind Coope's fine ales or the house's special beer, Burton's, an unusual brew made of spring water from the Midlands town of Bourton-on-Trent.

LEICESTER SQUARE

✪ **Cork & Bottle Wine Bar.** 44-46 Cranbourn St., WC2. ☎ **0207/734-7807.** Reservations not accepted after 6pm. Main courses £4.95–£11.95 ($8.15–$19.70); glass of wine from £3.45 ($5.70). AE, DC, MC, V. Mon–Sat 11am–11:30pm, Sun noon–10:30pm. Tube: Leicester Sq. INTERNATIONAL.

Don Hewitson, a connoisseur of fine wines for more than 30 years, presides over this trove of blissful fermentation. The ever-changing wine list features an excellent selection of Beaujolais crus from Alsace, 30 selections from Australia, 30 champagnes, and a good selection of California labels. If you want something to wash down, the most successful dish is a raised cheese-and-ham pie, with a cream cheese–like filling and crisp well-buttered pastry—not your typical quiche. There's also chicken and apple salad, Lancashire hot pot, Mediterranean prawns with garlic and asparagus, lamb in ale, and tandoori chicken.

Salisbury. 90 St. Martin's Lane, WC2. ☎ **020/7836-5863.** Reservations not recommended. AE, DC, MC, V. Mon–Sat 11am–11pm, Sun noon–10:30pm. Tube: Leicester Sq. BRITISH.

Salisbury's glittering cut-glass mirrors reflect the faces of English stage stars (and hopefuls) sitting around the curved buffet-style bar. A less prominent place to dine is the old-fashioned wall banquette with its copper-topped tables and art-nouveau decor. The pub's specialty—home-cooked pies set out in a buffet cabinet with salads—is really quite good and inexpensive. Both a hot and a cold food buffet is available at all times.

SOHO

Old Coffee House. 49 Beak St., W1. ☎ **020/7437-2197.** Main courses £2.50–£4.20 ($4.15–$6.95). No credit cards. Restaurant Mon–Sat noon–3pm; pub Mon–Sat 11am–11pm; Sun noon–3pm and 7–10:30pm. Tube: Oxford Circus or Piccadilly Circus. BRITISH.

Once honored as "Soho Pub of the Year" by the *Good Pub Guide*, the Old Coffee House takes its name from the coffeehouse heyday of 18th-century London, when coffee was called "the devil's brew." The pub still serves pots of filtered coffee. The place is heavily decorated with bric-a-brac, including archaic musical instruments and World War I recruiting posters. Have a drink at the long, narrow bar, or retreat to the upstairs restaurant, where you can enjoy good pub food at lunch, including steak-and-kidney pie, one of three vegetarian dishes, scampi-and-chips, or a burger and fries.

BLOOMSBURY

Museum Tavern. 49 Great Russell St., WC1. ☎ **020/7242-8987.** Bar snacks £2–£6 ($3.30–$9.90). AE, MC, V. Mon–Sat 11am–11pm, Sun noon–10:30pm. Tube: Holborn or Tottenham Court Rd. BRITISH.

Across the street from the British Museum, this pub (ca 1703) retains most of its antique trappings: velvet, oak paneling, and cut glass. It lies right in the center of the University of London area and is popular with writers, publishers, and researchers from the museum. (Supposedly, Karl Marx wrote over meals in the pub.) Traditional English food is served, with shepherd's pie, sausages cooked in English cider, and chef's specials on the hot-food menu. Cold fare includes turkey-and-ham pie, ploughman's lunch, and salads. Several English ales, cold lagers, cider, Guinness, wines, and spirits are available. Food and coffee are served all day; the pub gets crowded at lunchtime.

NEAR TRAFALGAR SQUARE (WESTMINSTER)

Sherlock Holmes. 10 Northumberland St., WC1. ☎ **020/7930-2644.** Reservations recommended for restaurant. Main courses £7.95–£12.95 ($13.10–$21.35); ground-floor snacks £2.25–£6.95 ($3.70–$11.45). AE, DC, MC, V. Restaurant Mon–Thurs noon–3pm and 5–10:45pm; Fri–Sun noon–11:45pm; pub Mon–Sat 11am–11pm; Sun noon–10:30pm. Tube: Charing Cross or Embankment. BRITISH.

It would be rather strange if the Sherlock Holmes was not the old gathering spot for the Baker Street Irregulars, a once-mighty clan of mystery lovers who met here to honor the genius of Sir Arthur Conan Doyle's most famous fictional character. Upstairs, you'll find a re-creation of the living room at 221B Baker Street and such "Holmesiana" as the serpent of *The Speckled Band* and the head of *The Hound of the Baskervilles.* In the upstairs dining room, you can order complete meals with wine. Try "Copper Beeches" (grilled butterfly chicken breasts with lemon and herbs). You select dessert from the trolley. Downstairs is mainly for drinking, but there's a good snack bar with cold meats, salads, cheeses, and wine and ales sold by the glass.

THE CITY

✪ **Ye Olde Cheshire Cheese.** Wine Office Court, 145 Fleet St., EC4.
☎ **020/7353-6170.** Main courses £8.95–£13.95 ($14.75–$23). AE, DC,
MC, V. Mon–Fri 11:30am–11pm, Sat 11:30am–2:30pm and 5:30–11pm, Sun
noon–3pm. Drinks and bar snacks daily 11:30am–11pm. Tube: St. Paul's or
Blackfriars. BRITISH.

The foundation of this carefully preserved building was laid in the
13th century, and it holds the most famous of the old City chop-
houses and pubs. Established in 1667, it claims to be the spot where
Dr. Samuel Johnson (who lived nearby) entertained admirers
with his acerbic wit. Charles Dickens and other literary lions also
patronized the place. Later, many of the ink-stained journalists and
scandalmongers of 19th- and early–20th-century Fleet Street made
it their locale. You'll find six bars and two dining rooms here. The
house specialties include "Ye Famous Pudding" (steak, kidney,
mushrooms, and game) and Scottish roast beef with Yorkshire
pudding and horseradish sauce. Sandwiches, salads, and standby
favorites like steak-and-kidney pie are also available, as are dishes like
Dover sole.

Ye Olde Cock Tavern. 22 Fleet St., EC4. ☎ **020/7353-8570.** Reservations
not required. Main courses £4.50–£6 ($7.45–$9.90). AE, DC, MC, V. Carvery
Mon–Fri noon–2:30pm; pub Mon–Fri 11am–11pm. Tube: Temple or Chancery
Lane. BRITISH.

Dating back to 1549, this tavern boasts a long line of literary patrons: Samuel Pepys mentioned the pub in his diaries; Dickens frequented it; and Tennyson referred to it in one of his poems, a copy
of which is framed and proudly displayed near the front entrance.
It's one of the few buildings in London to have survived the Great
Fire of 1666. At street level, you can order a pint as well as snackbar
food, steak-and-kidney pie, or a cold chicken-and-beef plate with
salad. At the Carvery upstairs, a meal includes a choice of appetizers, followed by lamb, pork, beef, or turkey.

KNIGHTSBRIDGE

Bill Bentley's. 31 Beauchamp Place, SW3. ☎ **020/7589-5080.** Reservations
recommended. Main courses £9–£18.95 ($14.85–$31.25). MC, V. Mon–Sat
noon–3pm and 7–11pm, Sun brunch 11am–3pm. Tube: Knightsbridge.
MODERN EUROPEAN.

Bill Bentley's, on fashionable Beauchamp Place, has a varied and
reasonable wine list with a good selection of Bordeaux. Many visitors come here just to sample the wines, including some New World
choices along with popular French selections. In summer, a garden
patio opens to patrons. If you don't prefer the formality of the

restaurant, you can order from the wine-bar menu that begins with a half-dozen oysters, or you can enjoy the chef's fish soup with croutons and *rouille*. Main dishes include the famous salmon cakes, served with tomato sauce, and daily specialties. In keeping with contemporary trends, the restaurant menu has been simplified and is rather less expensive than before. It changes frequently, but typical dishes might include avocado, crab, and prawn salad as an appetizer, followed by suprême of chicken with oyster mushrooms and a madeira jus, or else grilled rainbow trout with a petit garni and lemon sauce. A large selection of bottled beers and spirits is also available.

IN NEARBY BELGRAVIA

Antelope. 22 Eaton Terrace, SW1. ☎ **020/7730-7781.** Reservations recommended for upstairs dining room. Main courses £5.95–£6.50 ($9.80–$10.75). AE, MC, V. Mon–Sat 11:30am–11pm, Sun noon–3pm and 7–10:30pm. Tube: Sloane Sq. BRITISH.

Located on the fringe of Belgravia, at the gateway to Chelsea, the Antelope caters to a hodgepodge of clients from all classes and creeds (including English rugby aficionados). At lunchtime, the ground-floor bar provides hot and cold pub food, but in the evening, only drinks are served there. Upstairs, the lunch menu includes principally English dishes: fish 'n' chips, English roasts, and the like.

✪ **Grenadier.** 18 Wilton Row, SW1. ☎ **020/7235-3074.** Reservations recommended. Main courses £11.95–£18.95 ($19.70–$31.25). AE, DC, MC, V. Mon–Sat noon–3pm and 6–10pm, Sun noon–3:30pm and 7–10:30pm. Tube: Hyde Park Corner. BRITISH.

Tucked away in a mews, the Grenadier is one of London's reputedly haunted pubs. Aside from the poltergeist, the basement houses the original bar and skittles alley used by the Duke of Wellington's officers on leave from fighting Napoléon. The scarlet front door of the one-time officers' mess is guarded by a scarlet sentry box and shaded by a vine. The bar is nearly always crowded. Lunch and dinner are offered daily—even on Sunday, when it's a tradition to drink Bloody Marys here. In the stalls along the side, you can order good-tasting fare based on seasonal ingredients. Well-prepared dishes include pork Grenadier and chicken and Stilton roulade. Snacks like fish-and-chips are available at the bar.

CHELSEA

King's Head & Eight Bells. 50 Cheyne Walk, SW3. ☎ **020/7352-1820.** Main courses £5.25–£7.75 ($8.65–$12.80). MC, V. Mon–Sat 11am–11pm, Sun noon–10:30pm. Tube: Sloane Sq. BRITISH.

Many distinguished personalities once lived near this historic Thames-side pub; a short stroll will take you to the former homes of Carlyle, Swinburne, and George Eliot. In other days, press gangs used to roam these parts of Chelsea seeking lone travelers to abduct for a life at sea. Today, it's popular with stage and TV celebrities as well as writers. The best English beers are served here, as well as a good selection of reasonably priced wine. The menu features home-made specials of the day, such as fish-and-chips or sausage and chips, and includes at least one vegetable main dish. On Sunday, a roast of the day is served.

NOTTING HILL GATE

The Cow. 89 Westbourne Park Rd., W2 ☎ **0207/221-0021.** Main courses £12.20-£15.20 ($20.15-$25.10); fixed-price 2-course dinner £15.50 ($25.60). MC, V. Mon-Sat 7-11:30pm, Sun 12:30-3:30pm. Bar daily 11:30am-11:30pm. Tube: Westbourne Grove. MODERN EUROPEAN.

Tom Conran (son of restaurateur/entrepreneur Sir Terence Conran) holds forth nightly in this increasingly hip Notting Hill watering hole. It looks like an Irish pub, but the accents you'll hear are trustafarian rather than street-smart Dublin. With a pint of Fuller's or London Pride firmly in hand, you can linger over the modern European menu, which changes daily but is likely to include ox tongue poached in milk; a mixed grill of lamb chops, calf's liver, and sweetbreads; and steak with onion rings. The "Cow Special," a half-dozen Irish rock oysters with a pint of Guinness or a glass of wine for £8 ($13.20), is the star of the show. A raw bar downstairs serves an array of fresh choices in addition to oysters.

Exploring London

*D*r. Samuel Johnson said, "When a man is tired of London, he is tired of life, for there is in London all that life can afford." Indeed, it would take a lifetime to explore every alley, court, street, and square in this vast city (and volumes to discuss them). Since you don't have a lifetime to spend here, we've discussed the best of what London has to offer in this chapter. Still, what's included is more than enough to keep you busy on a dozen trips to the "city by the Thames."

A Note about Admission and Open Hours: In the listings below, children's prices generally apply to those 16 and under. To qualify for a senior discount, you must be 60 or older. Students must present a student ID to get discounts, where available. In addition to shutting down on bank holidays, many attractions close around Christmas and New Year's (and, in some cases, early in May), so be sure to call ahead if you're visiting in those seasons.

1 The Top Attractions

✪ **British Museum.** Great Russell St., WC1. ☎ **020/7323-8299** or 020/7636-1555 for recorded information. Free admission. Mon–Sat 10am–5pm, Sun noon–6pm. Tube: Holborn or Tottenham Court Rd.

Set in scholarly Bloomsbury, this immense museum grew out of a private collection of manuscripts purchased in 1753 with the proceeds of a lottery. It grew and grew, fed by legacies, discoveries, and purchases, until it became one of the most comprehensive collections of art and artifacts in the world. It's utterly impossible to take in this museum in a day.

The overall storehouse splits basically into the national collections of antiquities; prints and drawings; coins, medals, and banknotes; and ethnography. Even on a cursory first visit, be sure to see the Asian collections (the finest assembly of Islamic pottery outside the Islamic world), the Chinese porcelain, the Indian sculpture, and the Prehistoric and Romano-British collections. Special treasures you might want to seek out on your first visit include the **Rosetta Stone,**

Central London Sights

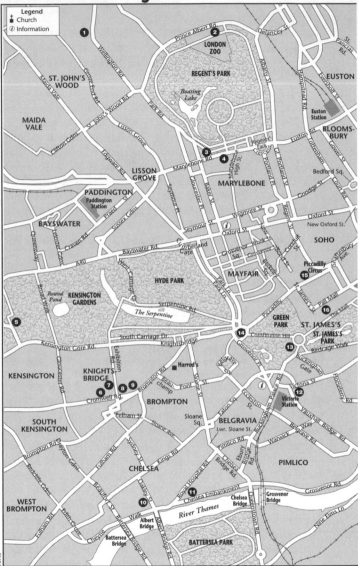

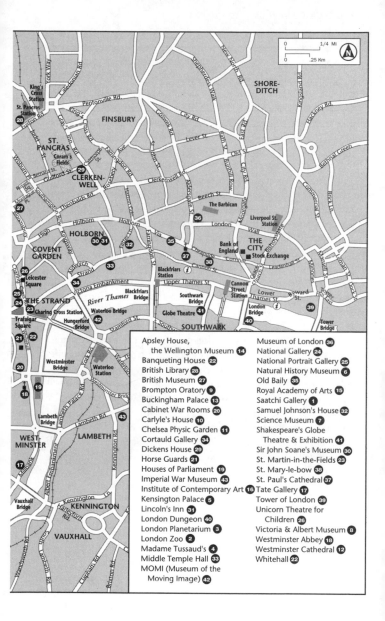

Time-Saver

With 2½ miles of galleries, the British Museum is overwhelming. To get a handle on it, we recommend taking a 1½-hour overview tour for £6 ($9.90) Monday to Saturday at 10:45am, 11:15am, 1:45pm, and 2:15pm, or Sunday at 3pm, 3:20pm, and 3:45pm. If you have only minutes to spare for the museum, concentrate on the Greek and Roman rooms (1 to 15), which hold the hoard of booty both bought and stolen from the Empire's once far-flung colonies.

---

whose discovery led to the deciphering of hieroglyphs, in the Egyptian Room; the **Elgin Marbles,** a priceless series of pediments, metopes, and friezes from the Parthenon in Athens, in the Duveen Gallery; and the legendary **Black Obelisk,** dating from around 860 B.C., in the Nimrud Gallery. Other treasures include the contents of Egyptian royal tombs (including mummies); fabulous arrays of 2,000-year-old jewelry, cosmetics, weapons, furniture, and tools; Babylonian astronomical instruments; and winged lions (in the Assyrian Transept) that once guarded Ashurnasirpal's palace at Numrud. The latest additions include a Mexican gallery, a Hellenistic gallery, and a "History of Money" exhibit. The exhibits change throughout the months, so if your heart is set on seeing a specific treasure, call ahead to make sure it's on display.

The year 2000 will see changes to the historic museum. Dubbed the "Great Court" project, the inner courtyard will be canopied by a lightweight, transparent roof transforming the area into a covered square; housing a Centre for Education, exhibition space, bookshops, and restaurants. The center of the Great Court will feature the Round Reading Room restored to its original decorative scheme.

For information on the British Library, see p. 174.

Buckingham Palace. At end of The Mall (on the road running from Trafalgar Sq.). ☎ **020/7839-1377.** Palace tours (usually offered in Aug and Sept) £10 ($16.50) adults, £7.50 ($12.40) seniors, £5 ($8.25) children under 17. Changing of the Guard free. Tube: St. James's Park, Green Park, or Victoria.

This massive, graceful building is the official residence of the queen. The red-brick palace was built as a country house for the notoriously rakish duke of Buckingham. In 1762, it was bought by King George III, who needed room for his 15 children. It didn't become the official royal residence, though, until Queen Victoria took the throne; she preferred it to St. James's Palace. From George III's time, the building was continuously expanded and remodeled, faced with Portland stone, and twice bombed (during the Blitz). Located in a 40-acre garden, it's 360 feet long and contains 600 rooms. You can tell whether the Queen is at home by the Royal Standard flying at the masthead.

For most of the year, you can't visit the palace unless you're officially invited. Since 1993, though, much of it has been open for tours during an 8-week period in August and September, when the royal family is usually vacationing outside London. Elizabeth II agreed to allow visitors to tour the State Room, the Grand Staircase, Throne Room, and other areas designed by John Nash for George IV, as well as the huge Picture Gallery, which displays masterpieces by Van Dyck, Rembrandt, Rubens, and others. The admission charges help pay for repairing Windsor Castle, badly damaged by fire in 1992.

Buckingham Palace's most famous spectacle is the **Changing of the Guard.** This ceremony begins (when it begins) after 11am and lasts for a half-hour. It's been called the finest example of military pageantry extant. The new guard, marching behind a band, comes from either the Wellington or Chelsea Barracks and takes over from the old guard in the forecourt of the palace. The changing of the guard is not always daily and varies depending on the time of year. Call ☎ **0839/123-411** to check times.

✪ **Houses of Parliament.** Westminster Palace, Old Palace Yard, SW1. House of Commons ☎ **020/7219-4272;** House of Lords ☎ **020/7219-3107.** Free admission. House of Lords open to public Mon–Wed from 2:30pm, Thurs from 3pm, and some Fridays (check by phone). House of Commons open to public Mon–Tues 2:30–10:30pm; Wed 9:30am–10:30pm, Thurs 11:30am–7:30pm, Fri call ahead—not always open. Join line at St. Stephen's entrance. Tube: Westminster.

The Houses of Parliament, along with their trademark clock tower, are the ultimate symbol of London. They're the stronghold of Britain's democracy, the assemblies that effectively trimmed the sails of royal power. Both the House of Commons and the House of

Insider Tip

You can avoid the long queues at Buckingham Palace by purchasing tickets before you go through **Edwards & Edwards,** 1270 Avenue of the Americas, Suite 2414, New York, NY 10020 (☎ **800/ 223-6108** or 212/332-2435). Visitors with disabilities can reserve tickets directly through the palace by calling ☎ **020/7930-5526.**

Warning

Buckingham Palace does not reveal its plans in advance, which poses a dilemma for guidebook writers. In theory, the guard is changed daily from some time in April to mid-July, at which time it goes on its "winter" schedule—that is, every other day. Always check locally with the tourist office to see if it's likely to be staged at the time of your visit. The ceremony has been cut at the last minute, leaving thousands of tourists feeling they have missed out on a London must-see.

Lords are in the former royal Palace of Westminster, the king's residence until Henry VIII moved to Whitehall. The current Gothic Revival buildings date from 1840 and were designed by Charles Barry. (The earlier buildings were destroyed by fire in 1834.) Assisting Barry was Augustus Welby Pugin, who designed the paneled ceilings, tiled floors, stained glass, clocks, fireplaces, umbrella stands, and even the inkwells. There are more than 1,000 rooms and 2 miles of corridors.

The clock tower at the eastern end houses the world's most famous timepiece. **"Big Ben"** refers not to the clock tower itself, but to the largest bell in the chime, which weighs close to 14 tons and is named for the first commissioner of works. At night a light shines in the tower whenever Parliament is in session.

You may observe parliamentary debates from the **Stranger's Galleries** in both houses. Sessions usually begin in mid-October and run to the end of July, with recesses at Christmas and Easter. Although we can't promise you the oratory of a Charles James Fox or a William Pitt the Elder, the debates in the House of Commons are often lively and controversial (seats are at a premium during crises). The chances of getting into the House of Lords when it's in session are generally better than for the more popular House of Commons, where even the queen isn't allowed. Many political observers maintain that the peerage speak their minds more freely and are less likely to adhere to the party line than their counterparts in the Commons; they do behave, however, in a much more civilized fashion, without the yelling that sometimes accompanies Commons debates.

The general public is admitted to the Strangers' Galleries on "sitting days." You have to join a public line outside the St. Stephen's entrance on the day in question, and there's often considerable delay before the public is admitted. The line forms on the left for the House of Commons, on the right for the Lords. You can speed matters up somewhat by applying at the American Embassy or the Canadian High Commission for a special pass, which should be issued well in advance of your trip, but this is too cumbersome for many people. Besides, the embassy has only four tickets for daily distribution, so you might as well stand in line. It's usually easier to get in after about 5:30pm; debates often continue until about 11pm. To arrange a tour before you leave home, you can write **House of Commons Information Office,** 1 Derby Gate, Westminster, London SW1A 2TT. Tours are usually conducted on Friday.

Stay tuned for developments surrounding the House of Lords, which London's tabloid newspaper portray as a bunch of "Monty Pythonesque upper-class twits." For years this house has given Britain its wit and wisdom, including a 1992 remark by the earl of Longford, "A girl is not ruined for life by being seduced—a young fellow is." Today, under Tony Blair's Labour government, the Houses of Parliament are facing radical reforms. In 1999, more than 600 of the 752 hereditary peers, often descendants of royal mistresses and ancient landowners, have been fired from the upper chamber. By 2000 a parliamentary commission will report who will replace them. Britain's foreign secretary has already called the House of Lords "medieval lumber."

The right of the dukes, the marquesses, the earls, the viscounts, and the barons to sit in the House of Lords has been granted to them for centuries. But as long as it's still there, the House of Lords is busy, often voting down measures passed by the House of Commons. For example, it defeated a measure that would have lowered the age of consent for homosexual sex to 16 from 18. The measure had passed in Commons with a wide majority. The House of Lords, obviously, is overwhelmingly conservative. Recent debates have ranged from outlawing spitting by sports figures to banning chewing gum altogether. Lord Dean, a life peer, defended his colleagues. "Life peers aren't overburdened with geniuses any more than any other group."

Kensington Palace. The Broad Walk, Kensington Gardens, W8. ☎ **020/ 7937-9561.** Admission £8.50 ($14) adults, £6.70 ($11.05) seniors/students, £6.10 ($10.05) children, family £26.10 ($43.05). June–Sept daily 10am–5pm; off-season Wed–Sun 10am–3pm. Tube: Queensway or Bayswater on north side of gardens; High St. Kensington on south side.

Once the residence of British monarchs, Kensington Palace hasn't been the official home of reigning kings since George II. It was acquired in 1689 by joint monarchs William III and Mary II as an escape from the damp royal rooms along the Thames. Since the end of the 18th century, the palace has been home to various members of the royal family, and the State Apartments are open for tours.

It was here in 1837 that a young Victoria was roused from her sleep with the news that her uncle, William IV, had died and that she was now queen of England. You can view a nostalgic collection of Victoriana, including some of her memorabilia. In the apartments of Queen Mary II, is a striking 17th-century writing cabinet inlaid with tortoiseshell. Paintings from the Royal Collection line the walls of the apartments. A rare 1750 lady's court dress and splendid examples of male court dress from the 18th century are on display in rooms adjacent to the State Apartments.

Kensington Palace is now the London home of Princess Margaret as well as the duke and duchess of Kent. Of course, it was once the home of Diana, Princess of Wales, and her two sons. (Harry and William now live with their father at St. James's Palace, where Diana's body lay in the Chapel Royal during the week prior to her funeral.) The palace is probably best known for the millions of flowers that were placed in front of it during the days following Diana's death.

Kensington Gardens are open daily to the public for leisurely strolls through the manicured grounds and around the Round Pond. One of the most famous sights here is the controversial Albert Memorial, a lasting tribute not only to Victoria's consort but also to the questionable artistic taste of the Victorian era. There's a wonderful afternoon tea offered in The Orangery; see "Teatime" in chapter 5.

Madame Tussaud's. Marylebone Rd., NW1. ☎ **020/7935-6861.** Admission £10 ($16.50) adults, £7.50 ($12.40) seniors, £6.50 ($10.75) children under 16, free for children under 5. Combination tickets including the new planetarium £12.25 ($20.20) adults, £9.30 ($15.35) seniors, £8 ($13.20) children under 16. Mon–Fri 10am–5:30pm, Sat–Sun 9:30am–5:30pm. Tube: Baker St.

Madame Tussaud's is not so much a wax museum as an enclosed amusement park. A weird, moving, sometimes terrifying collage of exhibitions, panoramas, and stage settings, it manages to be most things to most people, most of the time.

Madame Tussaud attended the court of Versailles and learned her craft in France. She personally took the death masks from the guillotined heads of Louis XVI and Marie Antoinette (which you'll find among the exhibits). She moved her original museum from Paris to England in 1802. Her exhibition has been imitated in every part of the world, but never with the realism and imagination on hand here.

Madame herself molded the features of Benjamin Franklin, whom she met in Paris. All the rest—from George Washington to John F. Kennedy, Mary Queen of Scots to Sylvester Stallone—have been subjects for the same painstaking (and breathtaking) replication.

In the well-known Chamber of Horrors there are all kinds of instruments of death, along with figures of their victims. The shadowy presence of Jack the Ripper lurks in the gloom as you walk through a Victorian London street. Present-day criminals are portrayed within the confines of prison. The latest attraction to open here is "The Spirit of London," a musical ride that depicts 400 years of London's history, using audio-animatronic figures that move and speak. Visitors take "time-taxis" that allow them to see and hear "Shakespeare" as he writes and speaks lines, and feel and smell the Great Fire of 1666 that destroyed London.

✪ **National Gallery.** Northwest side of Trafalgar Sq., WC2. ☎ **020/ 7747-2885.** Free admission. Thurs–Tues 10am–6pm; Wed 10am–9pm. Tube: Charing Cross, Embankment, or Leicester Square.

This stately neoclassical building contains an unrivaled collection of Western art that spans seven centuries—from the late 13th to the early 20th—and covers every great European school. For sheer skill of display and arrangement, it surpasses its counterparts in Paris, New York, Madrid, and Amsterdam.

The largest part of the collection is devoted to the Italians, including the Sienese, Venetian, and Florentine masters. They're now housed in the Sainsbury Wing, which was designed by noted Philadelphia architects Robert Venturi and Denise Scott Brown and opened by Elizabeth II in 1991. On display are such works as Leonardo's *Virgin of the Rocks;* Titian's *Bacchus and Ariadne;* Giorgione's *Adoration of the Magi;* and unforgettable canvases by Bellini, Veronese, Botticelli, and Tintoretto. Botticelli's *Venus and Mars* is eternally enchanting. (The Sainsbury Wing is also used for large temporary exhibits.)

Of the early-Gothic works, the *Wilton Diptych* (French or English school, late 14th century) is the rarest treasure; it depicts Richard II being introduced to the Madonna and Child by John the Baptist and the Saxon kings, Edmund and Edward the Confessor.

Then there are the Spanish giants: El Greco's *Agony in the Garden,* and portraits by Goya and Velázquez. The Flemish-Dutch school is represented by Brueghel, Jan van Eyck, Vermeer, Rubens, and de Hooch; the Rembrandts include two of his immortal self-portraits. There's also an immense French impressionist and postimpressionist collection that includes works by Manet, Monet, Degas, Renoir, and Cézanne. Particularly charming is the peep-show cabinet by Hoogstraten in one of the Dutch rooms: It's like spying through a keyhole.

British and modern art are the specialties of the Tate Gallery (see below), but the National Gallery does have some fine 18th-century British masterpieces, including works by Hogarth, Gainsborough, Reynolds, Constable, and Turner.

Insider Tip: The National Gallery has a computer information center where you can design your own personal tour map. The computer room, located in the Micro Gallery, includes a dozen hands-on workstations. The on-line system lists 2,200 paintings and has background notes for each artwork. The program includes four indexes that are cross referenced for your convenience. Using a touch-screen computer, you design your own personalized tour by selecting a maximum of 10 paintings that you would like to view. Once you have made your choices, you print a personal tour map with your selections; this mapping service is free.

✪ **St. Paul's Cathedral.** St. Paul's Churchyard, EC4. ☎ **020/7236-4128.** Cathedral £4 ($6.60) adults, £2 ($3.30) children 6–16. Galleries £3.50 ($5.75) adults, £1.50 ($2.45) children. Guided tours £2 ($3.30); recorded tours £3 ($4.95). Free for children 5 and under. Sightseeing Mon–Sat 8:30am–4pm; galleries Mon–Sat 9:30am–4pm. No sightseeing Sun (services only). Tube: St. Paul's.

During World War II, newsreel footage reaching America showed St. Paul's Cathedral standing virtually alone among the rubble of the City, its dome lit by fires caused by bombings all around it. That it survived at all is a miracle, since it was badly hit twice during the early years of the bombardment of London in World War II. But St. Paul's is accustomed to calamity, having been burned down three times and destroyed once by invading Norsemen. It was during the Great Fire of 1666 that the old St. Paul's was razed, making way for a new structure designed by Sir Christopher Wren and built between 1675 and 1710. It's the architectural genius's ultimate masterpiece.

The classical dome of St. Paul's dominates the City's square mile. The golden cross surmounting it is 365 feet above the ground; the golden ball on which the cross rests measures 6 feet in diameter yet looks like a marble from below. Surrounding the interior of the dome is the Whispering Gallery, an acoustic marvel in which the faintest whisper can be heard clearly on the opposite side—so be careful of what you say. You can climb to the top of the dome for a spectacular 360° view of London.

Although the interior looks almost bare, it houses a vast number of monuments. The duke of Wellington (of Waterloo fame) is entombed here, as are Lord Nelson and Sir Christopher Wren himself. At the east end of the cathedral is the American Memorial Chapel, honoring the 28,000 U.S. service personnel who lost their lives while stationed in Britain in World War II.

Guided tours last 1¹/₂ hours and include parts of the cathedral not open to the general public. They take place Monday to Saturday at 11am, 11:30am, 1:30pm, and 2pm. Recorded tours lasting 45 minutes are available throughout the day.

St. Paul's is an Anglican cathedral with daily services at the following times: matins at 7:30am Monday to Friday, 8:30am on Saturday; Holy Communion Monday to Saturday at 8am and 12:30pm; and evensong Monday to Saturday at 5pm. On Sunday, there's Holy Communion at 8am and again at 11:30am, matins at 10:15am, and evensong at 3:15pm. Admission charges don't apply if you're attending a service.

Tate Gallery. Millbank, SW1. ☎ **020/7887-8000.** Free admission; special exhibitions sometimes incur a charge. Daily 10am–5:50pm. Tube: Pimlico. Bus: 77A, 88, or C10.

Fronting the Thames near Vauxhall Bridge in Pimlico, the Tate looks like a smaller and more graceful relation of the British Museum. The most prestigious gallery in Britain, it houses the national collections covering British art from the 16th century on, as well as an international array of moderns. The Tate's holdings are split between the traditional and the contemporary. Since only a portion of the collections can be displayed at any one time, the works on view change from time to time. Because it's difficult to take in all the exhibits, we suggest that you try to schedule two visits—the first to see the classic British works, the second to take in the modern collection—or concentrate on whichever section interests you more, if your time is limited.

The older works include some of the best of Gainsborough, Reynolds, Stubbs, Blake, and Constable. William Hogarth is well-represented, particularly by his satirical *O the Roast Beef of Old England* (known as *The Gate of Calais*). The illustrations of William Blake, the incomparable mystical poet for such works as *The Book of Job, The Divine Comedy,* and *Paradise Lost* are here. The collection of works by J.M.W. Turner is its largest collection of works by a single artist; Turner himself willed most of the paintings and watercolors here to the nation.

Also on display are the works of many major 19th- and 20th-century painters, including Paul Nash. In the modern collections are works by Matisse, Dalí, Modigliani, Munch, Bonnard, and Picasso. Truly remarkable are the several enormous abstract canvases by Mark Rothko, the group of paintings and sculptures by Giacometti, and the paintings of one of England's best-known modern artists, the late Francis Bacon. Sculptures by Henry Moore and Barbara Hepworth are also occasionally displayed.

Plans call for the Tate Gallery to split into two separate galleries, the original to be known as the Tate Gallery of British Art. The modern international collection will move across the Thames and will become the new Tate Gallery of Modern Art. The galleries will be linked by a pedestrian bridge across the river. Dates of this transfer and split have not been announced. Stay tuned.

Downstairs is the internationally renowned **Tate Gallery Restaurant** with murals by Whistler, as well as a coffee shop.

✪ **Tower of London.** Tower Hill, EC3. ☎ **020/7709-0765.** Admission £10.50 ($17.35) adults, £7.90 ($13.05) students and seniors, £6.90 ($11.40) children, free for children under 5; £31 ($51.15) family ticket for 5 (but no more than 2 adults). Mar–Oct Mon–Sat 9am–5pm, Sun 10am–5pm; off-season Tues–Sat 9am–4pm, Mon and Sun 10am–4pm. Tube: Tower Hill.

This ancient fortress continues to pack in the crowds, largely because of its macabre associations with all the legendary figures who were imprisoned and/or executed here. James Street once wrote, "There are more spooks to the square foot than in any other building in the whole of haunted Britain. Headless bodies, bodiless heads, phantom soldiers, icy blasts, clanking chains—you name them, the Tower's got them." Even today, centuries after the last head rolled on Tower Hill, a shivery atmosphere of impending doom lingers over the mighty walls. Plan on spending a lot of time here.

The Tower is actually an intricately patterned compound of structures built throughout the ages for varying purposes, mostly as expressions of royal power. The oldest is the **White Tower,** begun by William the Conqueror in 1078 to keep London's native Saxon population in check. Later rulers added other towers, more walls, and fortified gates, until the building became something like a small town within a city. Until the reign of James I, the Tower was also one of the royal residences. But above all, it was a prison for distinguished captives.

Every stone of the Tower tells a story—usually a gory one. In the **Bloody Tower,** according to Shakespeare, the two little princes (the sons of Edward IV) were murdered by henchmen of Richard III.

Tower of London

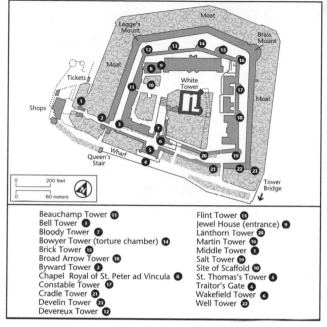

Beauchamp Tower **11**
Bell Tower **3**
Bloody Tower **7**
Bowyer Tower (torture chamber) **14**
Brick Tower **15**
Broad Arrow Tower **18**
Byward Tower **2**
Chapel Royal of St. Peter ad Vincula **8**
Constable Tower **17**
Cradle Tower **21**
Develin Tower **23**
Devereux Tower **12**

Flint Tower **13**
Jewel House (entrance) **9**
Lanthorn Tower **20**
Martin Tower **16**
Middle Tower **1**
Salt Tower **19**
Site of Scaffold **10**
St. Thomas's Tower **5**
Traitor's Gate **4**
Wakefield Tower **6**
Well Tower **22**

(Modern historians, however, tend to think that Richard may not have been the guilty party.) Here, too, Sir Walter Raleigh spent 13 years before his date with the executioner. On the walls of the **Beauchamp Tower,** you can actually read the last messages scratched by despairing prisoners. Through **Traitors' Gate** passed such ill-fated, romantic figures as Robert Devereux, the second earl of Essex, a favorite of Elizabeth I. A plaque marks the eerie place at **Tower Green** where two wives of Henry VIII, Anne Boleyn and Catherine Howard, Sir Thomas More, and the 4-day queen, Lady Jane Grey, all lost their lives.

The Tower, besides being a royal palace, a fortress, and a prison, was also an armory, a treasury, a menagerie, and in 1675 an astronomical observatory. Reopened in 1999, the White Tower holds the **Armouries,** which date from the reign of Henry VIII. In the Jewel House, you'll find the tower's greatest attraction, the **Crown Jewels.** Here, some of the world's most precious stones are set into the robes, swords, scepters, and crowns. The Imperial State Crown, the most famous, was made for Victoria in 1837, it's worn today by

Queen Elizabeth when she opens Parliament. Studded with some 3,000 jewels (principally diamonds), it includes the Black Prince's Ruby, worn by Henry V at Agincourt. The 530-carat Star of Africa, a cut diamond on the Royal Sceptre, would make Harry Winston turn over in his grave. You'll have to stand in long lines to catch just a glimpse of the jewels as you and hundreds of others scroll by on moving sidewalks, but the wait is worth it.

A **palace** once inhabited by King Edward I in the late 1200s stands above Traitors' Gate. It's the only surviving medieval palace in Britain. Guides are dressed in period costumes. Reproductions of furniture and fittings, including Edward's throne, evoke the era, along with burning incense and candles.

Oh, yes—and don't forget to look for the ravens. Six of them (plus two spares) are all registered as official Tower residents. According to a legend, the Tower of London will stand as long as those black, ominous birds remain; so, to be on the safe side, one of the wings of each raven is clipped.

One-hour guided tours of the entire compound are given by the Yeoman Warders (also known as "Beefeaters") every half-hour, starting at 9:25am from the Middle Tower near the main entrance. The last guided walk starts about 3:25pm in summer, 2:25pm in winter, weather permitting, of course.

You can attend the nightly **Ceremony of the Keys,** the ceremonial locking-up of the Tower by the Yeoman Warders. For free tickets, write to the Ceremony of the Keys, Waterloo Block, Tower of London, London EC3N 4AB, and request a specific date, but also list alternative dates. At least 6 weeks' notice is required. All requests must be accompanied by a stamped, self-addressed envelope (British stamps only) or two International Reply Coupons. With ticket in hand, you'll be admitted by a Yeoman Warder at 9:35pm.

Victoria and Albert Museum. Cromwell Rd., SW7. ☎ **020/7938-8500.** Admission £5 ($8.25) adults, £3 ($4.95) seniors, free for children under 18 and persons with disabilities. Daily 10am–5:45pm. Tube: South Kensington. Bus: C1, 14, or 74.

The Victoria and Albert is the greatest museum of the decorative arts in the world. It's also one of the liveliest and most imaginative museums in London—where else would you find the quintessential "little black dress" in the permanent collection?

The medieval holdings include such treasures as the early-English Gloucester Candlestick; the Byzantine Veroli Casket, with its ivory panels based on Greek plays; and the Syon Cope, a highly valued embroidery made in England in the early 14th century. An area devoted to Islamic art houses the Ardabil Carpet from 16th-century Persia.

The V&A houses the largest collection of Renaissance sculpture outside Italy. A highlight of the 16th-century collection is the marble group *Neptune with Triton* by Bernini. The cartoons by Raphael, which were conceived as designs for tapestries for the Sistine Chapel, are owned by the queen and on display here. A most unusual, huge, and impressive exhibit is the Cast Courts, life-size plaster models of ancient and medieval statuary and architecture.

The museum has an important collection of Indian art, plus Chinese and Japanese galleries. In complete contrast are suites of English furniture, metalwork, and ceramics, and a superb collection of portrait miniatures, including the one Hans Holbein the Younger made of Anne of Cleves for the benefit of Henry VIII. The Dress Collection includes a collection of corsetry through the ages that's sure to make you wince. There's also a remarkable collection of musical instruments.

Because of redevelopment, the entire run of British Galleries won't be fully open until 2001. But the museum has a lively program of changing exhibitions and displays, so there's always something new to see.

Insider Tip: The museum hosts a jazz brunch on Sunday from 11am to 3pm. You can hear some of the hottest jazz in the city, accompanied by a full English brunch for only £8.50 ($14). And don't miss the V&A's most bizarre gallery, "Fakes and Forgeries." The impostors here are amazingly authentic—in fact, we'd judge some of them as better than the old masters themselves.

✪ **Westminster Abbey.** Broad Sanctuary, SW1. ☎ **020/7222-7110** or 020/ 7222-5897. Admission £5 ($8.25) adults, £3 ($4.95) for students and seniors, £2 ($3.30) children 11–18, under 11 free, family ticket £16 ($26.40). Mon–Fri 9:15am–3:45pm, Sat 9:15am–1:45pm. Tube: Westminster or St. James's Park.

With its square twin towers and superb archways, this early-English Gothic abbey is one of the greatest examples of ecclesiastical architecture on earth. But it's far more than that: It's the shrine of a nation, the symbol of everything Britain has stood for and stands for, the place in which most of its rulers were crowned and where many lie buried.

Nearly every figure in English history has left his or her mark on Westminster Abbey. Edward the Confessor founded the Benedictine abbey in 1065 on this spot, overlooking Parliament Square. The first

English king crowned in the abbey was Harold in 1066. The man who defeated him at the Battle of Hastings the next year, William the Conqueror, was also crowned here. The coronation tradition has continued to the present day, broken only twice (Edward V and Edward VIII). The essentially early–English Gothic structure existing today owes more to Henry III's plans than to those of any other sovereign, although many architects, including Wren, have contributed to the abbey.

Built on the site of the ancient lady chapel in the early 16th century, the **Henry VII Chapel** is one of the loveliest in Europe, with its fan vaulting, Knights of Bath banners, and Torrigiani-designed tomb of the king himself, over which hangs a 15th-century Vivarini painting, *Madonna and Child.* Also here, ironically buried in the same tomb, are Catholic Mary I and Protestant Elizabeth I (whose archrival, Mary Queen of Scots, is entombed on the other side of the Henry VII Chapel). In one end of the chapel, you can stand on Cromwell's memorial stone and view the **Royal Air Force chapel** and its Battle of Britain memorial window, unveiled in 1947 to honor the RAF.

You can also visit the most hallowed spot in the abbey, the **shrine of Edward the Confessor** (canonized in the 12th century). In the chapel is the Coronation Chair, made at the command of Edward I in 1300 to display the Stone of Scone. Scottish kings were once crowned on it (it has since been returned to Scotland).

When you enter the transept on the south side of the nave and see a statue of the Bard with one arm resting on a stack of books, you've arrived at **Poets' Corner.** Shakespeare himself is buried at Stratford-upon-Avon, but resting here are Chaucer, Ben Jonson, Milton, Shelley, and many others; there's even an American, Henry Wadsworth Longfellow, as well as monuments to just about everybody: Chaucer, Shakespeare, "O Rare Ben Johnson" (his name misspelled), Samuel Johnson, George Eliot, Dickens, and others. The most stylized monument is Sir Jacob Epstein's sculptured bust of William Blake. More recent tablets commemorate poet Dylan Thomas and Lord Olivier.

Statesmen and men of science—such as Disraeli, Newton, Charles Darwin—are also interred in the abbey or honored by monuments. Near the west door is the 1965 memorial to Sir Winston Churchill. In the vicinity of this memorial is the tomb of the **Unknown Soldier,** commemorating the British dead in World War I.

Off the Cloisters, the **College Garden** is the oldest garden in England, under cultivation for more than 900 years. Surrounded by

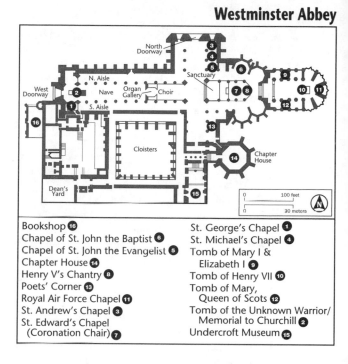

Bookshop **16**

Chapel of St. John the Baptist **6**

Chapel of St. John the Evangelist **5**

Chapter House **14**

Henry V's Chantry **8**

Poets' Corner **13**

Royal Air Force Chapel **11**

St. Andrew's Chapel **3**

St. Edward's Chapel
(Coronation Chair) **7**

St. George's Chapel **1**

St. Michael's Chapel **4**

Tomb of Mary I &
Elizabeth I **9**

Tomb of Henry VII **10**

Tomb of Mary,
Queen of Scots **12**

Tomb of the Unknown Warrior/
Memorial to Churchill **2**

Undercroft Museum **15**

high walls, flowering trees dot the lawns and park benches provide comfort where you can hardly hear the roar of passing traffic. It's open only on Tuesday and Thursday. In the Cloisters, you can make a rubbing at the **Brass Rubbing Centre** (☎ 020/7222-2085).

The only time photography is allowed in the abbey is Wednesday evening from 6 to 7:45pm. On Sunday, the Royal Chapels are closed, but the rest of the church is open unless a service is being conducted. For times of services, phone the **Chapter Office** (☎ 020/7222-5152). Up to six supertours of the abbey are conducted by the vergers Monday to Saturday, beginning at 10am and costing £3 ($4.95) per person.

2 More Central London Attractions

CHURCHES & CATHEDRALS

Many of London's churches offer free lunchtime concerts; a full list is available from the London Tourist Board. It's customary to leave a small donation.

⭐ **Brompton Oratory.** Brompton Rd., SW7. ☎ **020/7589-4811.** Free admission. Daily 6:30am–8pm. Tube: South Kensington.

A group of Victorian intellectuals turned Catholic, the Oxford Movement, certainly didn't go halfway when they created this church in 1884. Done in the Italian Renaissance style, this dramatic Roman Catholic church is famous for its musical services, and its organ with nearly 4,000 pipes. After Westminster Cathedral and York Minster, it has the widest nave in England.

St. Martin-in-the-Fields. Trafalgar Sq., WC2. ☎ **020/7930-0089.** Mon–Sat 10am–8pm, Sun noon–8pm as long as there is no service taking place. Tube: Charing Cross.

Designed by James Gibbs, a disciple of Christopher Wren, and completed in 1726, this classical temple stands at the northeast corner of Trafalgar Square, opposite the National Gallery. Its spire, added in 1824, towers 185 feet (taller than Nelson's Column, which also rises on the square). The steeple became the paradigm for many churches in colonial America. Since the first year of World War I (1914), the homeless have sought "soup and shelter" at St. Martin, a tradition that continues.

At one time the crypt held the remains of Charles II (he's in Westminster Abbey now), who was christened here, giving St. Martin a claim as a royal parish church. His mistress, Nell Gwynne, was also interred here, as was the notorious highwayman Jack Sheppard (both still here). The little restaurant, **Café in the Crypt,** is still called "Field's" by its devotees. Also in the crypt is The London Brass Rubbing Centre (☎ **020/7930-9306**) with 88 exact copies of bronze portraits ready for use. Paper, rubbing materials, and instructions on how to begin are furnished; charges range from £2.50 to £15 ($4.15 to $24.75), the latter price for the largest, a life-size Crusader knight. There's also a gift shop with brass-rubbing kits for children, budget-priced ready-made rubbings, Celtic jewelry, miniature brasses, and model knights. The center is open Monday to Saturday 11am to 4pm and Sunday 1 to 4pm.

Insider's Tip: In back of the church is a crafts market. Lunchtime and evening concerts are staged Monday, Tuesday, and Friday at 1:05pm, and Thursday to Saturday at 7:30pm. Tickets cost £6 to £15 ($9.90 to $24.75).

St. Mary-le-Bow. Cheapside, EC2. ☎ **020/7248-5139.** Free admission. Mon–Wed 6:30am–6pm, Thurs 6:30am–6:30pm, Fri 6:30am–4pm. Tube: St. Paul's or Bank or Mansion House.

A true Cockney is said to be born within hearing distance of this church's famous Bow bells. The church certainly hasn't been blessed by the series of disasters that mark its sometimes gruesome history: In 1091, its roof was ripped off in a storm; the church tower collapsed in 1271 and 20 people were killed; in 1331, Queen Philippa and her ladies-in-waiting fell to the ground when a balcony collapsed during a joust celebrating the birth of the Black Prince; it was rebuilt by Wren after being engulfed by the Great Fire; and the original "Cockney" Bow bells were destroyed in the Blitz, but have been replaced. The church was rededicated in 1964 after extensive restoration work.

Westminster Cathedral. Ashley Place, SW1. ☎ **020/7798-9055.** Cathedral free, audio tours £2.50 ($4.15). Tower, £2 ($3.30). Cathedral, daily 7am–7pm. Tower, Apr–Nov daily 9am–1pm and 2–5pm; otherwise Thurs–Sun only. Tube: Victoria.

This spectacular brick-and-stone church (1903) is the headquarters of the Roman Catholic Church in Britain. Adorned in early-Byzantine style, it is massive: 360 feet long and 156 feet wide. Its interior is lavishly decorated with marble columns and mosaics. If you take the elevator to the top of the 273-foot-tall campanile, you're rewarded with sweeping views that take in Buckingham Palace, Westminster Abbey, and St. Paul's Cathedral. There is a café serving light snacks and soft drinks from 9am to 5pm and a gift shop open from 9:30am to 5:15pm.

HISTORIC BUILDINGS & LANDMARKS

Banqueting House. Whitehall Palace, Horse Guards Ave., SW1. ☎ **020/ 7930-4179.** Admission £3.50 ($5.75) adults, £2.70 ($4.45) seniors and students, £2.30 ($3.80) children. Mon–Sat 10am–5pm (last admission 4:30pm). Tube: Westminster, Charing Cross, or Embankment.

The feasting chamber in Whitehall Palace is probably the most sumptuous dining hall on earth. Designed by Inigo Jones and decorated with, among other things, original ceiling paintings by Rubens, the hall is dazzling enough to make you forget food altogether. Among the historic events that took place here were the beheading of King Charles I, who stepped through a window onto the scaffold outside, and the restoration ceremony of Charles II, marking the return of monarchy after Cromwell's brief Puritan Commonwealth.

Cabinet War Rooms. Clive Steps, at end of King Charles St. (off Whitehall near Big Ben), SW1. ☎ **020/7930-6961.** Admission £4.80 ($7.90) adults, £3.50 ($5.75) seniors and students, £2.40 ($3.95) children. Apr–Sept daily 9:30am–6pm (last admission at 5:15pm); Oct–Mar daily 10am–5:30pm. Tube: Westminster or St. James's.

This is the bombproof bunker from which Sir Winston Churchill and his government ran the nation during World War II. Many of

The Great Millennium Wheel

The world's largest observation wheel is now rising on the South Bank and should be luring thousands of visitors to London at the millennium. Called the **British Airways London Eye,** at 450 feet the Eye will be the capital's fourth tallest structure when it opens in 2000 on the South Bank of the Thames.

From 32 fully enclosed, high-tech capsules, each accommodating 25 people, its gradual 30-minute, 360-degree rotation will provide passengers with a bird's-eye view usually accessible only by aircraft or helicopter of London's famous landmarks. More than two million visitors are expected to ride the eye in the first year alone.

It lies close to Westminster Bridge (you can hardly miss it). Tickets for the attraction cost £6.95 ($11.45) for adults and £4.80 ($7.90) for children. When the Eye opens, tickets will be sold on site, and there will be a telephone box-office number to call. Before heading here check with one of the local British tourist information centers for full details.

the rooms are exactly as they were in September 1945: Imperial War Museum curators studied photographs to put notepads, files, typewriters, even pencils, pins, and clips, in their correct places.

Along the tour, you'll have a step-by-step personal sound guide that provides a detailed account of the function and history of each room of this World War II nerve center. They include the Map Room, with its huge wall maps. Next door is Churchill's bedroom-cum-office; it has a very basic bed and a desk with two BBC microphones for those famous broadcasts that stirred the nation. The Transatlantic Telephone Room is little more than a broom closet, but it held the extension linked to the special scrambler phone (called "Sig-Saly"), that allowed Churchill to confer with Roosevelt. (The scrambler equipment itself was actually too large to house in the bunker, so it was placed in the basement of Selfridges department store on Oxford Street.)

✪ **Horse Guards.** Whitehall, SW1. ☎ **020/7414-2396.**

North of Downing Street, on the west side of Whitehall, is the building of the Horse Guards, designed by William Kent, chief architect to George II, as the headquarters of the British Army. The real draw here is the Horse Guards themselves: Their unit is the

Household Cavalry Mounted Regiment, which is a union of the two oldest and most senior regiments in the British Army: The Life Guards and the Blues and Royals. In theory, their duty is to protect the sovereign. "Life Guards" wear red tunics and white plumes and the "Blues and Royals" are attired in blue tunics with red plumes. Two much-photographed mounted members of the Household Cavalry keep watch daily from 10am to 5pm. The mounted sentries change duty every hour as a benefit to the horses. Foot sentries change every two hours. The chief guard rather grandly inspects the troops here daily at 4pm. The guard, with flair and fanfare, dismounts at 5pm.

Some visitors prefer the **changing of the guards** here to the more famous ceremony at Buckingham Palace. Beginning around 11am Monday to Saturday and 10:30am on Sunday, a new guard leaves the Hyde Park Barracks, rides down Pall Mall, and arrives at the Horse Guards building, all in about 30 minutes. The old guard then returns to the barracks.

If you pass through the arch at Horse Guards, you'll find yourself at the **Horse Guards Parade,** which opens onto St. James's Park. This spacious court provides the best view of the various architectural styles that make up Whitehall. Regrettably, the parade ground itself is now a parking lot.

The military pageant—the most famous in Britain—known as **Trooping the Colour,** which celebrates the queen's birthday, takes place in June at the Horse Guards Parade. For devotees of pomp and circumstance, "Beating the Retreat" is staged here 3 or 4 evenings a week during the first 2 weeks of June.

LEGAL LONDON

The smallest borough in London, bustling **Holborn** (*ho*-burn) is often referred to as "Legal London"; it's home to the majority of the city's barristers, solicitors, and law clerks (Tube: Holborn, Chancery Lane). All barristers (litigators) must belong to one of the Inns of Court: **Gray's Inn, Lincoln's Inn,** and **the Middle** and **Inner Temple.**

Lincoln's Inn. Carey St., WC1. ☎ **020/7405-1393.** Free admission. Mon–Fri 7am–7pm. Tube: Holborn or Chancery Lane.

Lincoln's Inn is the oldest of the four Inns of Court and the best preserved. It comprises 11 acres, including lawns, squares, gardens, a 17th-century chapel (open Monday to Friday 12:30 to 2pm), a library, and two halls. One of these, Old Hall, dates from 1490 and has remained almost unaltered with its linenfold paneling, stained glass, and wooden screen by Inigo Jones. It was once the home of Sir Thomas More, and it was where barristers met, ate, and debated 150 years before the *Mayflower* sailed on its epic voyage. Old Hall set the scene for the opening chapter of Charles Dickens's *Bleak House.* The other hall, Great Hall, remains one of the finest Tudor Revival buildings in London.

Middle Temple Hall. Middle Temple Lane, EC4. ☎ **020/7427-4800.** Free admission. Mon–Fri 10–11:30am and 3–4pm. Tube: Temple.

From the Victoria Embankment, Middle Temple Lane runs between Middle and Inner Temple Gardens to the area known as The Temple, named after the medieval order of the Knights Templar (originally formed by the Crusaders in Jerusalem in the 12th century). It was in the Middle Temple Garden that Henry VI's barons are supposed to have picked the blooms of red and white roses and started the War of the Roses in 1430; today only members of the Temple and their guests are allowed to enter the gardens. But the Middle Temple contains a Tudor hall, completed in 1570, that's open to the public. It's believed that Shakespeare's troupe played *Twelfth Night* here for the first time in 1602. A table on view is said to have been built from timber from Sir Francis Drake's *The Golden Hind.*

Old Bailey. Newgate St., EC4. ☎ **020/7248-3277.** Free admission. Court in session Mon–Fri 10:30am–1pm and 2–4:30pm. Children under 14 not admitted; those 14–16 must be accompanied by a responsible adult. No cameras, tape recorders, or cell phones (and there are no checking facilities). Tube: St. Paul's. To get here from the Temple, travel east on Fleet St., which becomes Ludgate Hill; cross Ludgate Circus and turn left at the Old Bailey, a domed structure with the figure of *Justice* atop it.

This courthouse replaced the infamous Newgate Prison, once the scene of hangings and other forms of "public entertainment." It's fascinating to watch the bewigged barristers presenting their cases to the high-court judges. Entry is strictly on a first-arrival basis, and guests line up outside; security will then direct you to one of the rooms where cases are being tried. You enter courts 1 to 4, 17, and 18 from Newgate Street, and the balance from Old Bailey (the street).

LITERARY LANDMARKS

Dickens House. 48 Doughty St., WC1. ☎ **020/7405-2127.** Admission £3.50 ($5.75) adults, £2.50 ($4.15) students, £1.50 ($2.45) children, £7 ($11.55) families. Mon–Fri 9:45am–5:30pm, Sat 10am–5pm. Tube: Russell Sq.

Here in Bloomsbury stands the simple abode in which Charles Dickens wrote *Oliver Twist* and finished *The Pickwick Papers* (his American readers actually waited at the dock for the ship that brought in each new installment). The place is almost a shrine: It contains his study, manuscripts, and personal relics, as well as reconstructed interiors.

Samuel Johnson's House. 17 Gough Sq., EC4. ☎ **020/7353-3745.** Admission £3 ($4.95) adults, £2 ($3.30) students and seniors, £1 ($1.65) children, free for children 10 and under. Apr–Sept Mon–Sat 11am–5:30pm; Oct–Mar Mon–Sat 11am–5pm. Tube: Blackfriars or Temple. Bus from Trafalgar: 11, 15, or 23. Walk up New Bridge St. and turn left onto Fleet; Gough Sq. is tiny and hidden, north of Fleet St.

Dr. Johnson and his copyists compiled his famous dictionary in this Queen Anne house, where the lexicographer, poet, essayist, and fiction writer lived from 1748 to 1759. Although Johnson also lived at Staple Inn in Holborn and at a number of other places, the Gough Square house is the only one of his residences remaining in London. The 17th-century building has been painstakingly restored, and it's well worth a visit.

MUSEUMS & GALLERIES

Apsley House, the Wellington Museum. 149 Piccadilly, Hyde Park Corner, SW1. ☎ **020/7499-5676.** Admission £4.50 ($7.45) adults, £3 ($4.95) seniors and children 12–17, free for children under 12. Tues–Sun 11am–5pm. Tube: Hyde Park Corner.

This was the mansion of the duke of Wellington, one of Britain's greatest generals. The "Iron Duke" defeated Napoléon at Waterloo, but later, for a short period while prime minister, he had to have iron shutters fitted to his windows to protect him from the mob outraged by his autocratic opposition to reform. (His unpopularity soon passed, however.)

The house is crammed with art treasures, including three original Velázquez paintings, and military mementos that include the duke's medals and battlefield orders. Apsley House also holds some of the finest silver and porcelain pieces in Europe in the Plate and China Room. Grateful to Wellington for saving their thrones, European monarchs endowed him with treasures. The collection includes a Sèvres Egyptian service that was intended as a divorce present from Napoléon to Josephine (but she refused it); Louis XVIII eventually presented it to Wellington. The Portuguese Silver Service, created between 1812 and 1816, has been hailed as the single greatest artifact of Portuguese neoclassical silver.

⊙ **British Library.** 96 Euston Rd., NW1. ☎ **020/7412-7000.** Free admission. Mon, Wed–Fri 9:30am–6pm, Tues 9:30am–8pm, Sat 9:30am–5pm, Sun 11am–5pm. Tube: King's Cross/St. Pancras.

One of the world's greatest libraries is no longer at the British Museum but has moved to St. Pancras. The bright, roomy interior is far more inviting than the rather dull red-brick exterior suggests (it earned the condemnation of Prince Charles). The most spectacular room is the Humanities Reading Room, constructed on three levels and with daylight filtered through the ceiling.

The fascinating collection includes such items of historical and literary interest as two of the four surviving copies of King John's Magna Carta (1215), a Gutenberg Bible, Nelson's last letter to Lady Hamilton, and the journals of Captain Cook. Almost every major author—Dickens, Jane Austen, Charlotte Brontë, Keats, hundreds of others—is represented in the section devoted to English literature. Beneath Roubiliac's 1758 statue of Shakespeare stands a case of documents relating to the Bard, including a mortgage bearing his signature and a copy of the First Folio of 1623. There's also an unrivaled collection of philatelic items.

Visitors can also view the Diamond Sutra, dating from 868, said to be the oldest surviving printed book. Using headphones set up around the room, you can also hear thrilling audio snippets, even James Joyce reading a passage from *Finnegans Wake.* There is a copy of the *Canterbury Tales* from 1410, even manuscripts from *Beowulf* (ca. 1000). In the Historical Documents section are epistles by everybody from Henry VIII to Napoléon, from Elizabeth I to Churchill. In the music displays, you can seek out works by

An Open Sesame to Viewing

If you're coming to London as a serious museum-goer, you can save money by purchasing the **London White Card.** Available to individuals or families, it's a saver pass including some of the major attractions of London: the Museum of Moving Image, the Victoria and Albert Museum, and the Science Museum, plus a lot more. An adult three-day costs £16 ($26.40), a 7-day card £26 ($42.90). Families of two adults and up to four children can purchase a 3-day card for £32 ($52.80) or a 7-day card for £50 ($82.50). Cards are sold at British tourist information centers, London Transport centers, airports, and various attractions. For more details, call ☎ **020/7923-0807.**

Beethoven, Handel, and Stravinsky, even lyric drafts by Paul McCartney and John Lennon.

Walking tours of the library (£4 ($6.60) for adults or £3 ($4.95) for seniors, students and children) are conducted Wednesday to Monday at 3pm, Tuesday at 6:30pm, with an extra tour on Saturday at 10:30am. Reservations are advised three weeks in advance.

✪ **Courtauld Gallery.** Somerset House, The Strand, WC2. ☎ **020/7873-2526.** Admission £4 ($6.60) adults, £2 ($3.30) students, free for children under 18. Mon–Sat 10am–6pm, Sun noon–6pm; last admission 5:15pm. Tube: Temple or Covent Garden.

Although surprisingly little-known, the Courtauld contains a fabulous wealth of paintings. It has one of the world's greatest collections of Impressionist works outside of Paris. There are French Impressionists and post-Impressionists, with masterpieces by Monet, Manet, Degas, Renoir, Cézanne, Van Gogh, and Gauguin. The gallery also has a superb collection of Old-Master paintings and drawings, including works by Rubens, Michelangelo, and Tiepolo; early-Italian paintings, ivories, and majolica; the Lee collection of old masters; early-20th-century English and French paintings, as well as 20th-century British paintings.

Like the Frick Collection in New York, it's a superb display, a visual feast in a jewel-like setting. We come here at least once every season to revisit one painting in particular: Manet's *A Bar at the Folies-Bergère*—exquisite. Many of the paintings are displayed without glass, giving the gallery a more intimate feeling than most.

Imperial War Museum. Lambeth Rd., SE1. ☎ **020/7416-5321.** Admission £5 ($8.25) adults, £4 ($6.60) seniors and students, £2.50 ($4.15) children; free daily 4:30–6pm. Daily 10am–6pm. Tube: Lambeth North or Elephant and Castle.

One of the few major sights south of the Thames, this museum occupies one city block the size of an army barracks, greeting you with 15-inch guns from the battleships *Resolution* and *Ramillies.* The large domed building, constructed in 1815, was the former Bethlehem Royal Hospital for the insane, known as "Bedlam."

A wide range of weapons and equipment is on display, along with models, decorations, uniforms, posters, photographs, and paintings. You can see a Mark V tank, a Battle of Britain Spitfire, and a German one-man submarine, as well as a rifle carried by Lawrence of Arabia. In the Documents Room, you can view the self-styled "political testament" that Hitler dictated in the chancellery bunker in the closing days of World War II, witnessed by henchmen Joseph

Goebbels and Martin Bormann, as well as the famous "peace in our time" agreement that Neville Chamberlain brought back from Munich in 1938. (Of his signing the agreement, Hitler later said, "[Chamberlain] was a nice old man, so I decided to give him my autograph.") It's a world of espionage and clandestine warfare in the major new permanent exhibit known as the "Secret War Exhibition," where you can discover the truth behind the image of James Bond—and find out why the real secret war is even stranger and more fascinating than fiction. Displays include many items never before seen in public: coded messages, forged documents, secret wirelesses, and equipment used by spies from World War I to the present day.

Public film shows take place on weekends at 3pm and on certain weekdays during school holidays and on public holidays.

Institute of Contemporary Arts. The Mall, SW1. ☎ **020/7930-3647.** Admission £1.50 ($2.45) Mon–Fri, £2.50 ($4.15) Sat–Sun adults; £1 ($1.65) Mon–Fri, £1.50 ($2.45) Sat–Sun students. Galleries daily noon–7:30pm. Bookstore daily noon–9pm. Three film screenings daily. Tube: Piccadilly Circus or Charing Cross.

London's liveliest cultural program takes place in this temple to the avant-garde, launched in 1947. It keeps Londoners and others up to date on the latest in the worlds of cinema, theater, photography, painting, sculpture, and other performing and visual arts media. Technically you have to be a member to visit, but membership is immediately granted. Foreign or experimental movies are shown, and special tributes—perhaps a retrospective of the films of Rainer Werner Fassbinder—are often the order of the day. The classics are frequently dusted off, along with cult favorites. On Saturday and Sunday at 3pm, the cinémathèque offers screenings for the kids. Sometimes well-known writers and artists speak here, which makes the low cost of membership even more enticing. Experimental plays are also presented. The American computer company that wrote the computer language that helped spawn the Internet, Sun Microsystems, donated £2 million to build a state-of-the-art New Media Centre in 1998.

✪ **Museum of London.** 150 London Wall, EC2. ☎ **020/7600-3699.** Admission £5 ($8.25) adults, £3 ($4.95) children, students, and seniors, £12 ($19.80) family ticket. Tues–Sat 10am–5:50pm, Sun noon–5:50pm. Tube: St. Paul's or Barbican.

In London's Barbican district near St. Paul's Cathedral, overlooking the city's Roman and medieval walls, the museum traces the history of London from prehistoric times to the 20th century through archeological finds; paintings and prints; social, industrial, and historical artifacts; and costumes, maps, and models. Exhibits are arranged so that you can begin and end your chronological stroll through 250,000 years at the main entrance to the museum. The museum's pièce de résistance is the Lord Mayor's Coach, a gilt-and-scarlet fairy-tale coach built in 1757 and weighing in at 3 tons, but you can also see the Great Fire of London in living color and sound; the death mask of Oliver Cromwell; cell doors from Newgate Prison, made famous by Charles Dickens; and most amazing of all, a shop counter showing pre–World War II prices.

Museum of the Moving Image. South Bank (underneath Waterloo Bridge), SE1. ☎ **020/7401-2636.** Admission £6.25 ($10.30) adults, £5.25 ($8.65) students, £4.50 ($7.45) children and seniors, £17 ($28.05) family ticket (up to 2 adults and 2 children). Daily 10am–6pm (last admission 5pm). Tube: Waterloo or Embankment.

MOMI, part of the South Bank complex, traces the history of cinema and TV, taking you on an incredible journey from cinema's earliest experiments to modern animation, from Charlie Chaplin to the operation of a TV studio. There are artifacts to handle, buttons to push, and a cast of actors to tell visitors more. Three to four changing exhibitions are presented yearly; it's wise to allow 2 hours for a visit.

✪ **National Portrait Gallery.** St. Martin's Place, WC2. ☎ **020/7306-0055.** Free admission; fee charged for certain temporary exhibitions. Mon–Sat 10am–6pm, Sun noon–6pm. Tube: Charing Cross.

In a gallery of remarkable and unremarkable pictures (they're collected here for their notable subjects rather than their artistic quality), a few paintings tower over the rest, including Sir Joshua Reynolds's first portrait of Samuel Johnson ("a man of most dreadful appearance"). Among the best are Nicholas Hilliard's miniature of a handsome Sir Walter Raleigh and a full-length Elizabeth I, along with the Holbein cartoon of Henry VIII. There's also a portrait of William Shakespeare (with a gold earring, no less) by an unknown artist that bears the claim of being the "most authentic contemporary likeness" of its subject. One of the most famous pictures in the gallery is the group portrait of the Brontë sisters (Charlotte, Emily, and Anne) painted by their brother, Bramwell. An idealized portrait of Lord Byron by Thomas Phillips is also on display.

The galleries of Victorian and early-20th-century portraits were radically redesigned recently. Occupying the whole of the first floor, they display portraits from 1837 (when Victoria took the throne) to present day; later 20th-century portraiture includes major works by such artists as Warhol and Hambling. Some of the more flamboyant personalities of the last two centuries are on show: T. S. Eliot, Disraeli, Macmillan, Sir Richard Burton, Elizabeth Taylor, Baroness Thatcher, and our two favorites: G. F. Watts' famous portrait of his great actress wife, Ellen Terry, and Vanessa Bell's portrait of her sister, Virginia Woolf. The late Princess Diana is on the Royal Landing. The Gallery has recently opened a new café and art bookshop.

Natural History Museum. Cromwell Rd., SW7. ☎ **020/7938-9123.** Admission £6 ($9.90) adults, £3.20 ($5.30) seniors and students, £3 ($4.95) children 5–17, free for children 4 and under, £16 ($26.40) family ticket; free to everyone Mon–Fri after 4:30pm and Sat–Sun after 5pm. Mon–Sat 10am–5:50pm, Sun 11am–5:50pm. Tube: South Kensington.

This is the home of the national collections of living and fossil plants, animals, and minerals, with many magnificent specimens on display. Exciting exhibits designed to encourage people of all ages to learn about natural history include "Human Biology—An Exhibition of Ourselves," "Our Place in Evolution," "Origin of the Species," "Creepy Crawlies," and "Discovering Mammals." The Mineral Gallery displays marvelous examples of crystals and gemstones. Also in the museum is the Meteorite Pavilion, which exhibits fragments of rock that have crashed into the earth, some from the farthest reaches of the galaxy. What attracts the most attention is the huge dinosaur exhibit, displaying 14 complete skeletons. The center of the show depicts a trio of full-size robotic Deinonychus enjoying a freshly killed Tenontosaurus for lunch. The latest addition is "Earth Galleries," an exhibition outlining humankind's relationship with planet Earth. Here in the exhibition "Earth Today and Tomorrow," visitors are invited to explore the planet's dramatic history from the big bang to its inevitable death.

✪ **The Saatchi Gallery.** 98A Boundary Rd., NW8. ☎ **020/7624-8299.** Admission £4 ($6.60), free for children under 12. Thurs–Sun 12–6pm. Tube: St. John's Wood or Swiss Cottage.

In the world of contemporary art, this collection is unparalleled. Charles Saatchi is one of Britain's greatest private collectors, and this personal museum features rotating displays from his vast holdings. Enter through the unmarked metal gateway of a former paint warehouse. The aim, as set forth by Saatchi, is to introduce new and unfamiliar art to a wider audience. The collection comprises more than 1,000 paintings and sculptures. Works which are not on display at the gallery are frequently on loan to museums around the world.

The main focus is works by young British artists, including such controversial ones as Damien Hirst's 14-foot tiger shark preserved in a formaldehyde-filled tank. Also on occasional exhibit is Marc Quinn's frozen "head" cast from nine pints of plasma taken from the artist over several months. Art critics were shocked at Richard Wilson's art when it was introduced: 2,500 gallons of used sump oil that flooded through an entire gallery. Young American and European artists are also represented, their work often controversial as well. Regardless of the exhibition on display at the time of your visit, it's almost guaranteed to be fascinating. And if you've ever wondered what many British people think American tourists look like, catch Duane Hanson's *Tourists II* (1988). It's devastating!

Science Museum. Exhibition Rd., SW7. ☎ **020/7938-8000.** Admission £6.50 ($10.75) adults, £3.50 ($5.75) children 5–17, free for children under 5. Free to all after 4:30pm. Daily 10am–6pm. Tube: South Kensington.

This museum traces the development of science and industry and their influence on everyday life. These are among the largest, most comprehensive, and most significant scientific collections anywhere. On display is Stephenson's original rocket, the tiny prototype railroad engine; you can also see Whittle's original jet engine and the Apollo 10 space module. The King George III Collection of scientific instruments is the highlight of a gallery on science in the 18th century. Health Matters is a permanent gallery on modern medicine. The museum has two hands-on galleries, as well as working models and video displays.

Shakespeare's Globe Theatre & Exhibition. New Globe Walk, Southwork, SE1. ☎ **020/7902-1500.** Exhibition and tour admission £6 ($9.90) adults, £4 ($6.60) children 15 and under, £5 ($8.25) seniors and students. Guided tours £5 ($8.25) adults, £4 ($6.60) students and seniors, £3 ($4.95) children 15 and under. May–Sept daily 9:30am–2pm, Oct–Apr daily 10am–5pm (guided tours every 30 minutes or so). Tube: Mansion House or London Bridge.

This is a recent re-creation of what was probably the most important public theater ever built, on the exact site where many of Shakespeare's plays opened. The late American filmmaker, Sam Wanamaker, worked for some 20 years to raise funds to re-create the theater as it existed in Elizabethan times, thatched roof and all. A fascinating exhibit tells the story of the Globe's construction, using the material (including goat hair in the plaster), techniques, and craftsmanship of 400 years ago. The new Globe isn't an exact replica: It seats 1,500 patrons, not the 3,000 that regularly squeezed in during the early 1600s; and *this* thatched roof has been specially treated with a fire retardant. Guided tours of the facility are offered throughout the day.

✪ **Sir John Soane's Museum.** 13 Lincoln's Inn Fields, WC2. ☎ **020/ 7430-0175.** Free admission (donations invited). Tues–Sat 10am–5pm; first Tues of each month 6–9pm. Tours given Sat at 2:30pm; £3 ($4.95) tickets distributed at 2pm on a first-come, first-served basis (group tours by appointment only; call **020/7405-2107**). Tube: Holborn.

This is the former home of Sir John Soane (1753–1837), an architect who rebuilt the Bank of England (not the present structure). With his multiple levels, fool-the-eye mirrors, flying arches, and domes, Soane was a master of perspective and a genius of interior space (his picture gallery, for example, is filled with three times the number of paintings that a room of similar dimensions would be likely to hold). One prize of the collection is William Hogarth's satirical series *The Rake's Progress,* which includes his much-reproduced *Orgy* and *The Election,* a satire on mid–18th-century politics. Soane also filled his house with classical sculpture. The sarcophagus of Pharaoh Seti I was found in a burial chamber in the Valley of the Kings. Also on display are architectural drawings from Soane's collection of 30,000.

PARKS & GARDENS

The largest of the central London parks is **Hyde Park** (Tube: Marble Arch, Hyde Park Corner, or Lancaster Gate), once a favorite deer-hunting ground of Henry VIII. With the adjoining Kensington Gardens (see below), it covers 615 acres of central London with velvety lawns interspersed with ponds, flowerbeds, and trees. Running through its width is a 41-acre lake known as the Serpentine, where you can row, sail model boats, or swim (provided you don't mind sub-Florida water temperatures). Rotten Row, a 1 1/2-mile sand horseback riding track, attracts some skilled equestrians on Sunday. At the northeastern tip, near Marble Arch, is Speakers' Corner.

Blending with Hyde Park and bordering on the grounds of Kensington Palace, well-manicured **Kensington Gardens** (Tube: High Street Kensington or Queensway) contains the famous statue of Peter Pan, with the bronze rabbits that toddlers are always trying to kidnap. It's also home to that Victorian extravaganza, the Albert Memorial. The Orangery is an ideal place to take afternoon tea (see "Teatime" in chapter 5).

East of Hyde Park, across Piccadilly, stretch **Green Park** (Tube: Green Park) and **St. James's Park** (Tube: St. James's Park), forming an almost unbroken chain of landscaped beauty. This is an ideal area for picnics; you'll find it hard to believe that this was once a festering swamp near a leper hospital. There's a romantic lake stocked with a variety of ducks and some surprising pelicans, descendants of the pair that the Russian ambassador presented to Charles II back in 1662.

Regent's Park (Tube: Regent's Park or Baker Street), covers most of the district of that name, north of Baker Street and Marylebone Road. Designed by the 18th-century genius John Nash to surround a palace for the prince regent that never materialized, this is the most classically beautiful of London's parks. Its core is a rose garden planted around a small lake alive with waterfowl and spanned by Japanese bridges; in early summer, the rose perfume in the air is as heady as wine. The park is home to the Open-Air Theatre (see chapter 8) and the London Zoo (see "Especially for Kids," below). As at all the local parks, hundreds of deck chairs are scattered around the lawns, just waiting for sunbathers. The deck-chair attendants, who collect a small fee, are mostly college students on break.

Chelsea Physic Garden, 66 Royal Hospital Rd., SW3 (☎ 020/ 7352-5646; Tube: Sloane Square), founded in 1673 by the Worshipful Society of Apothecaries, is the second-oldest surviving botanical garden in England. Sir Hans Sloane, doctor to George II, required the apothecaries of the empire to develop 50 plant species a year for presentation to the Royal Society. The objective was to grow plants for medicinal study; plant specimens and even trees arrived at the gardens by barge, many to grow in English soil for the first time. Cottonseed from this garden launched an industry in the new colony of Georgia. Some 7,000 plants still grow here, everything from the pomegranate to the willow Pattern tree; there's even exotic cork oak, as well as England's earliest rock garden. The garden is open April to November, Wednesday from noon to 5pm and Sunday from 2 to 6pm. Admission is £4 ($6.60) for adults, £2 ($3.30) for children 5 to 15 and students. The garden is also the setting for a well-recommended afternoon tea, where you can carry your cuppas on promenades through the garden (see "Teatime," in chapter 5).

The hub of England's—and perhaps the world's—horticulture are the ✪ **Royal Botanic Gardens** (☎ **020/8940-1171**) at **Kew**, near Richmond, 9 miles southwest of central London. The famous Kew Gardens are perhaps the best-known botanic gardens in Europe. Kew is not only a pleasure garden—it's essentially a vast

The World's Biggest Dome for the Millennium

Mired in controversy, with four out of five Brits opposed to it according to polls, the **Greenwich Millennium Dome** should be open to the world by the time you read this. A multimedia extravaganza that mixes education and entertainment, as of this writing, it's still not known what the dome will contain, only a vague theme called "Time." The 181-acre site for the Dome lies on a north-Greenwich peninsula, bounded on three sides by the River Thames.

Greenwich Mean Time is the basis of standard time through-out most of the world, and Greenwich is the zero point used in the reckoning of terrestrial longitudes. Greenwich is the official "start-point" of the millennium. In 1884 an international confer-ence in Washington, D.C., agreed to have a "Universal Day," that date to begin at the prime meridian of the world (that is, zero lon-gitude). Hence, each and every day since begins in Greenwich, in-cluding, of course, January 1, 2000. (Of course, the millennium and the 21st century don't officially start until January 2, 2001.) But the party begins in 2000, and Britain is planning to put on quite a show for its visitors. The prime meridian cuts across the north of the site of the Dome.

Prime minister Tony Blair has declared that the Dome will "open a window to the future." From agriculture to automobiles, Britain is developing ground-breaking products, and the Millennium Dome showcases these breakthroughs. Some of the exhibits for the Millennium Dome have already been announced: a state-of-the-art life-raft system for ships (no more *Titanics*), an artificial heart for training surgeons, and a more environmentally friendly passenger jet engine, a 150-foot androgynous human figure with working ar-teries and veins. The Dome's performance area is the setting for shows with live performers and stunning visual effects.

scientific research center that happens to be beautiful. The gardens, on a 300-acre site, encompass lakes, greenhouses, walks, pavilions, and museums. Among the 50,000 plant species are notable collec-tions of ferns, orchids, aquatic plants, cacti, mountain plants, palms, and tropical water lilies. No matter what season you visit Kew, there's always something to see. Gigantic hothouses grow species of

Historic Greenwich, about a mile from the Dome, also has other sights. The **Cutty Sark** (☎ **020/8858-3445**), docked now at Greenwich Pier, was the greatest of the clipper ships that carried tea from China and wool from Australia. The **National Maritime Museum** illustrates the glory that was Britain at sea, and the **Old Royal Observatory** is the original home of Greenwich Mean Time. The **Queen's House** (1616), designed by Inigo Jones, is a fine example of this architect's innovative style. All are open daily from 10am to 5pm. For more information, contact the **Greenwich Tourist Information Centre** at 46 Greenwich Church St. (☎ **020/8858- 6376**, or call ☎ 0181 /858-4422).

GETTING THERE The London Underground is extending the Jubilee Line from Green Park to North Greenwich. You can also take the train from Charing Cross Station; call **Rail Europe** (☎ **0345/484950** in London or 800/848-7245 in the U.S.). Trains take about 15 minutes to reach Greenwich from Charing Cross, costing between £1.90 to £2.90 ($3.15 to $4.80) round-trip.

If you'd like to go to Greenwich the way Henry VIII did, you can board any of the frequent ferryboats that cruise along the Thames. Boats depart from Westminster Pier every half-hour in summer and every 45 minutes in winter (Tube: Westminster). Call **Westminster Passenger Services, Ltd.** (☎ **020/7930-4097**). Boats that leave from Charing Cross Pier (Tube: Embankment) and Tower Pier (Tube: Tower Hill) are run by **Catamaran Cruises, Ltd.** (☎ **020/7987-1185**). Travel time varies from 50 to 75 minutes each way. Passage is £7.25 to £7.30 ($11.95 to $12.05) round-trip for adults, £3.70 to £3.95 ($6.10 to $6.50) for children 5 to 12, free for those under 5.

shrubs, blooms, and trees from every part of the globe, from the Arctic Circle to tropical rain forests. The gardens are open daily from 9:30am to 5pm. Admission is £5 ($8.25) for adults, £3.50 ($5.75) students and seniors, £2.50 ($4.15) children;a family ticket is £13 ($21.45) There are a number of restaurants and cafes in the gardens. Tube: Kew Gardens.

3 Sightseeing & Boat Tours Along the Thames

A trip up or down the river will give you an entirely different view of London from the one you get from dry land. You'll see exactly how the city grew along and around the Thames and how many of its landmarks turn their faces toward the water. Several companies operate motor launches from the Westminster piers (Tube: Westminster), offering panoramic views of one of Europe's most historic waterways en route.

Westminster-Greenwich Thames Passenger Boat Service, Westminster Pier, Victoria Embankment, SW1 (☎ **020/ 7930-4097**), concerns itself only with downriver traffic from Westminster Pier. The most popular excursion departs for Greenwich (a 50-minute ride) at half-hour intervals between 10am and 4pm April to October, and between 10:30am and 5pm from June to August; from November to March, boats depart from Westminster Pier at 40-minute intervals daily from 10:40am to 3:20pm. One-way fares are £6 ($9.90) for adults, £3.20 ($5.30) for children under 16. Round-trip fares are £7.30 ($12.05) for adults, £3.70 ($6.10) for children. A family ticket for two adults and up to three children under 15 costs £16.20 ($26.75) one-way, £19.20 ($31.70) round-trip.

Westminster Passenger Association (Upriver) Ltd., Westminster Pier, Victoria Embankment, SW1 (☎ **020/7930-2062** or 020/ 7930-4721), offers the only riverboat service upstream from Westminster Bridge to Kew, Richmond, and Hampton Court. There are regular daily sailings from the Monday before Easter until the end of October, on traditional riverboats, all with licensed bars. Trip time, one-way, can be as little as $1^{1}/_{2}$ hours to Kew and between $2^{1}/_{2}$ to 4 hours to Hampton Court, depending on the tide. Cruises from Westminster Pier to Hampton Court via Kew Gardens leave daily at 10:30am, 11:15am, and noon. Round-trip tickets are £9 to £13.50 ($14.85 to $22.30) adults, £6.50 to £11 ($10.75 to $18.15) seniors, and £4.50 to £8 ($7.45 to $13.20) children 4 to 14; one child under 4 accompanied by an adult goes free. Evening cruises from May to September are also available departing Westminster Pier at 7:30pm and 8:30pm (9:30pm on demand) for £5.50 ($9.05) adults and £4 ($6.60) children.

THE THAMES BRIDGES Some of the Thames bridges are household names. **London Bridge,** contrary to the nursery rhyme, never fell down, but it has been replaced a number of times, and is vastly different from the original London Bridge, which was lined with houses and shops. The one that you see now is the ugliest of the bunch; the previous incarnation was dismantled and shipped to Lake Havasu, Arizona, in the 1960s.

Its neighbor to the east is the more interesting **Tower Bridge** (SE1; ☎ 020/7403-3761; Tube: Tower Hill), one of the city's most celebrated landmarks and possibly the most photographed and painted bridge on earth. Its outward appearance is familiar to Londoners and visitors alike. (This is the one that a certain American thought he'd purchased instead of the one farther up the river that really ended up in the middle of the desert.) In spite of its medieval appearance, Tower Bridge was actually built in 1894.

In 1993 an exhibition opened inside the bridge to commemorate its century-old history; it takes you up the north tower to high-level walkways between the two towers with spectacular views of St. Paul's, the Tower of London, and the Houses of Parliament—a photographer's dream. You're then led down the south tower and on to the bridge's original engine room, with its Victorian boilers and steam-pumping engines that used to raise and lower the bridge for ships to pass. Exhibits housed in the bridge's towers use advanced technology, including animatronic characters, video, and computers to illustrate the history of the bridge. Admission to the **Tower Bridge Experience** (☎ 020/7403-3761) is £6.15 ($10.15) for adults and £4.15 ($6.85) for children 5 to 15, students, and seniors; it's free for children 4 and under. Open April to October daily 10am to 6:30pm, November to March daily 9:30am to 6pm; last entry is 1¼ hours before closing. Closed Good Friday and January 1 to 28 as well as a few days around Christmas.

4 Especially for Kids

The attractions below are fun places for kids of all ages. In addition to what's listed below, kids love **Madame Tussaud's, the Science Museum, the Natural History Museum, the Tower of London,** and **the National Maritime Museum in Greenwich,** all discussed above. **Kidsline** (☎ 020/7222-8070) offers computerized information about current events that might interest kids. The line is open from 4 to 6pm during school-term time, 9am to 4pm on holidays. Only problem is, when every parent in London is calling for information, it's almost impossible to get through.

The London Dungeon. 28–34 Tooley St., SE1. ☎ **020/7403-0606** or 020/7403-7221. Admission £9.50 ($15.65) adults, £7.50 ($12.40) students and seniors, £6.50 ($10.75) children under 15. Admission includes Judgment Day boat ride. Daily 10:30am–5pm. Tube: London Bridge

This ghoulish place was deliberately designed to chill the blood. Set under the arches of London Bridge Station, the dungeon is a series of tableaux that are more grisly than the ones in Madame Tussaud's. The rumble of trains overhead adds to the atmosphere, and tolling bells bring a constant note of melancholy; dripping water and caged rats make for even more atmosphere. Naturally, there's a burning at the stake as well as a torture chamber, and a spine-chilling "Jack the Ripper Experience." The special effects were originally conceived for major film and TV productions.

London Planetarium. Marylebone Rd., NW1. ☎ **020/7935-6861.** £6 ($9.90) adults, £4.60 ($7.60) seniors, £4 ($6.60) children 5–17. Weekdays daily from 10am, Sat–Sun 9:30am with shows beginning at 12:20pm (10:20am on weekends) and last show at 5pm. Tube: Baker St.

Next door to Madame Tussaud's, the planetarium explores the mysteries of the stars and the night sky. The most recent star show starts with a spaceship of travelers forced to desert their planet when a neighboring star explodes; accompanying them on their journey, the audience travels through the solar system, visiting its major landmarks and witnessing spectacular cosmic activity. There are also several hands-on exhibits that relate to planets and space; for example, you can see what shape or weight you'd be on other planets. You can also hear Stephen Hawking talk about mysterious black holes.

✪ **London Zoo.** Regent's Park, NW1. ☎ **020/7722-3333.** Admission £8.50 ($14) adults, £6.50 ($10.75) children, free for children under 4. Mar–Oct daily 10am–5:30pm; Nov–Feb daily 10am–4pm. Tube: Regent's Park or Camden Town, then bus C2 or 274.

One of the world's great zoos, the London Zoo is more than a century and a half old. This 36-acre garden houses about 8,000 animals, including some of the rarest species on earth. There's an insect house (incredible bird-eating spiders); a reptile house (huge dragon-like monitor lizards and a fantastic 15-foot python); and others, such as the Sobell Pavilion for Apes and Monkeys and the Lion Terraces. In the Moonlight World, special lighting effects simulate night for the nocturnal beasties, while rendering them clearly visible to onlookers, so you can see all the night rovers in action.

In 1999 a new building opened, the Millennium Conservation Centre, combining animals, visuals, and interactive displays to demonstrate the diverse nature of life on this planet. Many families budget almost an entire day here, watching the penguins being fed, enjoying an animal ride in summer, and meeting elephants on their walks around the zoo.

Unicorn Theatre for Children. The Arts Theatre, 6–7 Great Newport St., WC2. ☎ **020/7379-3280;** box office 020/7836-3334. Admission £10 ($16.50), £7.50 ($12.40), £5 ($8.25) depending on seat locations. Show times Sept–June daily 11am and/or 2:30pm (times may vary). Tube: Leicester Sq.

The Unicorn is the only children's theater in London's West End theater district. Founded in 1947 and going stronger than ever, it presents a season of plays for 4- to 12-year-olds from September to June. The schedule includes specially commissioned plays and adaptations of old favorites, all performed by adult actors. You can also become a temporary member while you're in London and join in an exciting program of weekend workshops.

5 Organized Tours

For the first-timer, the quickest and most economical way to bring the big city into focus is to take a bus tour. **The Original London Sightseeing Tour** passes by all the major sights in about 1$^{1}/_{2}$ hours. The tour, which uses a traditional double-decker bus with live commentary by a guide, costs £12 ($19.80) for adults, £6 ($9.90) for children under 16, free for those under 5. You can hop off or hop on the bus at any point in the tour at no extra charge. Departures are from convenient points within the city; you can choose your departure point when you purchase your ticket. Tickets can be purchased on the bus or at a discount from any London Transport or London Tourist Board Information Centre. For information or phone purchases, call ☎ **020/8877-1722.**

A double-decker air-conditioned coach in the distinctive green-and-gold livery of **Harrods,** 87–135 Brompton Rd. (☎ **020/ 7581-3603;** Tube: Knightsbridge), offers sightseeing tours around London. The first departure from Door 8 of Harrods is at 10:30am; afternoon tours begin at 1:30 and 4pm. Tea, coffee, and orange juice are served on board. It's £20 ($33) for adults, £10 ($16.50) for children under 14, free for those under 5. All-day excursions to Blenheim Palace, Windsor, Stratford-upon-Avon, and outlying areas of London are available. You can purchase tickets at Harrods, Sightseeing Department, lower-ground floor.

Big Bus Company Ltd., Waterside Way, London SW17 (☎ **020/8944-7810**), operates a 2-hour tour in summer, departing from 8:30am to 6 or 7pm daily (depending on time of year; in winter, 9am to 4:30pm) from Marble Arch by Speakers Corner, Green Park by the Ritz Hotel, and Victoria Station (Buckingham Palace Road by the Royal Westminster Hotel).

Tours cover the highlights—18 in all—ranging from the Houses of Parliament and Westminster Abbey to the Tower of London and Buckingham Palace (exterior looks only), accompanied by live commentary. The cost is £12 ($19.80) for adults, £6 ($9.90) for children. There's also a 1-hour tour that follows the same route, but covers only 13 sights. Tickets are valid all day; you can hop on and off the bus as you wish.

7

Shopping

*A*lthough London is one of the world's best shopping cities, it often seems made for visitors who sleep by a pot of gold at the end of the rainbow; locals are far more careful with their hard-earned pounds. To find real values, you'll have to do what most Londoners do: wait for sales or search out specialty finds.

American-style shopping has taken Britain by storm, both in concept—warehouse stores and outlet malls—and in actual name: One block from Hamley's, you'll find the Disney Store. The Gap is everywhere; Tiffany sells more wedding gifts than Asprey these days. Your best bet is to ignore anything American and to concentrate on British goods. You can also do well with French products; values are almost as good as those you'd find in Paris.

TAXES Value-Added Tax (VAT) is the British version of sales tax. VAT is a whopping 17.5% on most goods, but it's already included in the price, so the number you see on the price tag is exactly what you'll pay at the register. Non-EU residents can get back much of the tax they pay by applying for a VAT refund.

In Britain, the minimum expenditure needed to qualify for a refund on Value-Added Tax is £50. Not every single store honors this minimum (it's £100 at Harrods; £75 at Selfridges; £62 at Hermès), but it's far easier to qualify for a tax refund in Britain than almost any other country in the European Union.

Vendors at flea markets might not be equipped to provide the paperwork for a refund, so if you're contemplating a major purchase and really want that refund, ask before you buy. Be suspicious of any dealer who tells you there's no VAT on antiques. Once this was true, but things have changed—the European Union has made the British add VAT to antiques. Since dealers still have mixed stock, pricing should reflect this fact. So ask if it's included—before you bargain on a price. Get to the price you're comfortable with first, then ask for the VAT refund.

VAT is not charged on goods shipped out of the country, whether you spend £50 or not. Many London shops will help you beat the VAT rap by shipping for you. But watch out: Shipping can double

How to Get Your VAT Refund

You *must* get your VAT refund form from the retailer. Several readers have reported that merchants have told them that they can get refund forms at the airport on their way out of the country. *This is not true.* Don't leave the store without a form—it must be completed by the retailer on the spot. After you have asked if the store does VAT refunds and determined their minimum, request the paperwork.

Fill out your portion of the form and then present it—along with the goods—at the Customs office in the airport. Allow a half hour to stand in line. Remember: You're required to show the goods at your time of departure, so put them in your carry-on.

Once the paperwork has been stamped by the officials, you have two choices: You can mail the papers (remember to bring a stamp) and receive your refund either as a British check (no!) or a credit-card refund (yes!), or you can go directly to the Cash VAT Refund desk at the airport and get your refund in cash. The bad news: If you accept cash other than sterling, you will lose money on the conversion rate.

Be advised that many stores charge a flat fee for processing your refund, so £3 to £5 may be automatically deducted from the total that you receive. But since the VAT in Britain is 17.5%, if you get back 15%, you're doing fine.

Note: If you're traveling to other countries within the European Union, you go through this at your final destination in the EU, filing all your VAT refunds at one time.

the cost of your purchase. Also expect to pay U.S. duties when the goods get to you at home.

You can ship on your flight home by paying for excess baggage (rates vary with the airline), or can have your packages shipped independently. Independent operators are generally less expensive than the airlines. Try **London Baggage,** London Air Terminal, Victoria Place, SW1 (☎ 020/7828-2400; Tube: Victoria), or **Burns International Facilities,** at Heathrow Airport Terminal 1 (☎ 020/8745-5301) and Terminal 4 (☎ 020/8745-7460). But remember, you can only avoid the VAT up front if you have the store ship directly for you. If you ship via excess baggage or London Baggage, you'll still have to pay the VAT up front, and apply for a refund.

HOURS   London keeps fairly uniform store hours, mostly shorter than American equivalents. The norm is 10am opening and 5:30pm closing, with a late Wednesday or Thursday night until 7pm, maybe 8pm. Some stores in districts such as Chelsea and Covent Garden tend to keep slightly later hours.

Sunday shopping is now legal. Stores may be open for six hours; usually they choose 11am to 5pm. Stores in designated tourist areas and flea markets are exempt from this law and may stay open all day on Sunday. Therefore, Covent Garden, Greenwich, and Hampstead are big Sunday destinations for shoppers.

1 The Top Shopping Streets & Neighborhoods

There are several key streets that offer some of London's best retail stores—or simply one of everything—compactly located in a niche or neighborhood so you can just stroll and shop.

THE WEST END   The West End is home to the core of London's big-name shopping. Most of the department stores, designer shops, and multiples (chain stores) have their flagships in this area.

The key streets are **Oxford Street** for affordable shopping (start at Marble Arch Tube station if you're ambitious, or Bond Street station if you just want to see some of it); and **Regent Street,** which intersects Oxford Street at Oxford Circus (Tube: Oxford Circus). The Oxford Street flagship (at Marble Arch) of the private-label department store **Marks & Spencer** is worth visiting for high-quality goods. Regent Street has fancier shops—more upscale department stores (including the famed **Liberty of London**), multiples (**Laura Ashley**), and specialty dealers—and leads all the way to Piccadilly.

Parallel to Regent Street, **Bond Street** (Tube: Bond Street) connects Piccadilly with Oxford Street and is synonymous with the luxury trade. Divided into New and Old, it has experienced a recent revival and is the hot address for all the international designers; **Donna Karan** has not one but two shops here. A slew of international hotshots from **Chanel** to **Ferragamo** to **Versace** have digs nearby.

Burlington Arcade (Tube: Piccadilly Circus), the famous glass-roofed, Regency-style passage leading off Piccadilly, looks like a period exhibition and is lined with intriguing shops and boutiques. Lit by wrought-iron lamps and decorated with clusters of ferns and flowers, its small, smart stores specialize in fashion, jewelry, Irish linen, cashmere, and more. If you linger there until 5:30pm, you can watch the beadles, those ever-present attendants in their black-and-yellow livery and top hats, ceremoniously put in place the iron grills that block off the arcade until 9am the next morning, at which time they just as ceremoniously remove them to mark the start of a new business day. (There are only three beadles remaining; they're the last London representatives of Britain's oldest police force.) Also at 5:30pm, a hand bell called the Burlington Bell is sounded, signaling the end of trading.

Tucked right behind Regent Street is **Carnaby Street** (Tube: Oxford Circus). While it no longer dominates the world of pacesetting fashion as it did in the 1960s, it's become a comeback street for cheap souvenirs, a purple wig, or a little something in leather. There's also a convenient branch of **Boots** here.

For a total contrast, check out **Jermyn Street** (Tube: Piccadilly Circus), on the far side of Piccadilly, a tiny 2-block–long street devoted to high-end men's haberdasher's and toiletries shops; many have been doing business for centuries. Several hold royal warrants, including **Turnbull & Asser,** where HRH Prince Charles has his pjs made.

The West End theater district borders two more shopping areas: the still-not-ready-for-prime-time **Soho** (Tube: Tottenham Court Road), where the sex shops are slowly converting into cutting-edge designer shops; and **Covent Garden** (Tube: Covent Garden), which is a masterpiece unto itself. The original marketplace has overflowed its boundaries and eaten up the surrounding neighborhood; it's fun to wander the narrow streets and shop. Covent Garden is mobbed on Sundays.

KNIGHTSBRIDGE & CHELSEA The home of **Harrods, Knightsbridge** (Tube: Knightsbridge) is the second-most famous of London's retail districts. (Oxford Street edges it out.) Nearby **Sloane Street** is chock-a-block with designer shops; in the opposite direction, **Cheval Place** is lined with designer resale shops.

Walk toward Museum Row and you'll soon find **Beauchamp** (*Bee*-cham) **Place.** It's only 1 block long, but it's very "Sloane Ranger or Sloanie," (as the Brits would say) featuring the kinds of shops where young British aristos buy their clothing for "The Season."

King's Road (Tube: Sloane Square), the main street of Chelsea, will forever remain a symbol of the Swinging Sixties. Today, it's still popular with the young crowd, but there are fewer Mohawk haircuts, Bovver boots, and Edwardian ballgowns than before. More and more, King's Road is a lineup of markets and "multistores," large or small conglomerations of indoor stands, stalls, and booths within one building or enclosure. About a third of King's Road is devoted to these kinds of antiques markets; another third houses design-trade showrooms and stores of household wares for British yuppies; and the remaining third is faithful to the area's teenybopper roots.

If you walk west from Harrods along Brompton Road, you connect to **Brompton Cross,** another hip area for designer shops made popular when Michelin House was rehabbed by Sir Terence Conran for **The Conran Shop.**

Also seek out **Walton Street,** a tiny little snake of a street running from Brompton Cross back toward the museums. Most of the street is devoted to fairytale shops for m'lady where you can buy aromatherapy from **Jo Malone,** needlepoint, or costume jewelry.

Finally, don't forget all those museums in nearby South Kensington—they all have great gift shops.

KENSINGTON, NOTTING HILL & BAYSWATER   Kensington High Street (Tube: High Street Kensington) is the hangout of the classier breed of teen, one who has graduated from Carnaby Street and is ready for street chic. While there are a few staples of basic British fashion on this strip, most of the stores feature items that stretch, are very, very short, very, very tight, and very, very black.

From Kensington High Street, you can walk up **Kensington Church Street,** which, like Portobello Road, is one of the city's main shopping avenues for antiques, selling everything from antique furniture to Impressionist paintings.

Kensington Church Street dead-ends at the Notting Hill Gate Tube station, jumping-off point for **Portobello Road;** the dealers and weekend market are 2 blocks beyond.

Not far from Notting Hill Gate is **Whiteleys of Bayswater,** Queensway, W2 (☎ 020/7229-8844; Tube: Bayswater or Queensway), an Edwardian mall whose chief tenant is Marks & Spencer. There are also 75 to 85 shops (the number varies from year to year), mostly specialty outlets, and an array of restaurants, cafés, and bars as well as an eight-screen movie theater.

2 Street & Flea Markets

THE WEST END   ✪ Covent Garden Market (☎ 020/ 7836-9136; Tube: Covent Garden), the most famous market in all of England—possibly all of Europe—offers several different markets daily from 9am to 6:30pm (we think it's most fun to come on Sunday). It can be a little confusing until you dive in and explore it all. Apple Market is the fun, bustling market in the courtyard, where traders sell…well, everything. Many of the items are what the English call collectible nostalgia; they include a wide array of glassware and ceramics, leather goods, toys, clothes, hats, and jewelry. Some of the merchandise is truly unusual. Many items are handmade, with some of the craftspeople selling their own wares—except on Mondays, when antiques dealers take over. Out back is Jubilee Market (☎ 020/7836-2139), also an antiques market on Mondays. Every other day, it's sort of a fancy hippie-ish market with cheap clothes and books. Out front there are a few tents of cheap stuff, except again on Monday.

The market itself (in the superbly restored hall) is one of the best shopping opportunities in London. Specialty shops sell fashions and herbs, gifts and toys, books and personalized dollhouses, hand-rolled cigars, automata, and much, much more. There are bookshops and branches of famous stores (**Hamley's, The Body Shop**), and prices are kept moderate.

St. Martin-in-the-Fields Market (Tube: Charing Cross) is good for teens and hipsters who don't want to trek all the way to Camden Market (see "North London," below) and can make due with imports from India and South America, crafts, and some local football souvenirs. Located near Trafalgar Square and Covent Garden; hours are Monday to Saturday 11am to 5pm, and Sundays noon to 5pm.

Berwick Street Market (Tube: Oxford Circus or Tottenham Court Road) may be the only street market in the world that's flanked by two rows of strip clubs, porno stores, and adult-movie dens. Don't let that put you off, however. Humming 6 days a week in the scarlet heart of Soho, this array of stalls and booths sells probably the best and cheapest fruit and vegetables in town. It also hawks ancient records, tapes, books, and old magazines, all which may turn out to be collectors' items one day. It's open Monday to Saturday from 8am to 5pm.

On Sunday mornings along **Bayswater Road,** artists hang pictures, collages, and crafts on the railings along the edge of Hyde Park and Kensington Gardens for more than a mile. If the weather's right, start at Marble Arch and walk. You'll see much of the same thing by walking along the railings of **Green Park** along Piccadilly on Saturday afternoon.

NOTTING HILL   **Portobello Market** (Tube: Notting Hill Gate) is a magnet for collectors of virtually anything. It's mainly a Saturday happening, from 6am to 5pm. You needn't be here at the crack of dawn; 9am is fine. Once known mainly for fruit and vegetables (still sold here throughout the week), in the past 4 decades Portobello has become synonymous with antiques. But don't take the stallholder's word for it that the fiddle he's holding is a genuine Stradivarius left to him in the will of his Italian great-uncle; it might just as well have been "nicked" from an East End pawnshop.

The market is divided into three major sections. The most crowded is the antiques section, running between Colville Road and Chepstow Villas to the south. (Warning: There's a great concentration of pickpockets in this area.) The second section (and the oldest part) is the "fruit and veg" market, lying between Westway and Colville Road. In the third and final section, there's a flea market, where Londoners sell bric-a-brac and lots of secondhand goods they didn't really want in the first place. But looking around still makes for interesting fun.

The serious collector can pick up a copy of a helpful official guide, *Saturday Antique Market: Portobello Road & Westbourne Grove,* published by the Portobello Antique Dealers Association. It lists where to find what, ranging from music boxes to militaria, lace to 19th-century photographs.

NORTH LONDON   If it's Wednesday, it's time for Camden Passage (☎ **020/7359-9969;** Tube: Angel) in Islington, where each Wednesday and Saturday there's a very upscale antiques market. It starts in Camden Passage and then sprawls into the streets behind. It's on Wednesdays from 8am to 4pm, and Saturdays from 9am to 5pm.

Don't confuse Camden Passage with Camden Market (very, very downtown). **Camden Market** (Tube: Camden Town) is for teens and others into body piercing, blue hair (yes, still), and vintage clothing. Serious collectors of vintage may want to explore during the week, when the teen scene isn't quite so overwhelming. Market hours are 9:30am to 5:30pm daily, with some parts opening at 10am.

3 The Department Stores

Contrary to popular belief, Harrods is not the only department store in London. The British invented the department store, and they have lots of them—mostly in Mayfair, and each with its own customer profile.

Daks Simpson Piccadilly. 34 Jermyn St., W1. ☎ **020/7734-2002.** Tube: Piccadilly Circus.

Opened in 1936 as the home of DAKS clothing, Simpson's has been going strong ever since. It's known for menswear—its basement-level men's shoe department is a model of the way quality shoes should be fitted—as well as women's fashions, perfume, jewelry, and lingerie. Many of the clothes are lighthearted, carefully made, and well suited to casual elegance. Its Simpson Collection rubs shoulders with international designer names such as Armani and Yves Saint Laurent.

✪ **Fortnum & Mason.** 181 Piccadilly, W1. ☎ **020/7734-8040.** Tube: Piccadilly Circus.

The world's most elegant grocery store is a British tradition dating back to 1707. Down the street from the Ritz, it draws the carriage trade, those from Mayfair to Belgravia who come seeking such tinned treasures as pâté de foie gras or a boar's head. This store exemplifies the elegance and style you would expect from an establishment with three royal warrants. Enter and be transported to another world of deep-red carpets, crystal chandeliers, spiraling wooden staircases, and unobtrusive, tailcoated assistants.

The grocery department is renowned for its impressive selection of the finest foods from around the world—the best champagne, the most scrumptious Belgian chocolates, and succulent Scottish smoked salmon. You can wander through the four floors and inspect the bone china and crystal cut glass, find the perfect gift in the leather or stationery departments, or reflect on the changing history of furniture and ornaments in the antiques department. Dining choices include the **Patio,** the recently refurbished **St. James Restaurant, The Fountain Restaurant,** and the brand new **Salmon and Champagne Bar** (for details on taking afternoon tea here, see "Teatime" in chapter 5). After a £14 million development, Fortnum & Mason now offer exclusive and specialty ranges for the home, beauty, and fashions for both women and men.

✪ **Harrods.** 87–135 Brompton Rd., Knightsbridge, SW1. ☎ **020/ 7730-1234.** Tube: Knightsbridge.

Harrods is an institution. As firmly entrenched in English life as Buckingham Palace and the Ascot Races, it's an elaborate emporium, at times as fascinating as a museum. Some of the goods displayed for sale are works of art, and so are the 300 departments displaying them. The sheer range, variety, and quality of merchandise are dazzling. The motto remains, "If you can eat or drink it, you'll find it at Harrods."

The whole fifth floor is devoted to sports and leisure, with a wide range of equipment and attire. Toy Kingdom is on the fourth floor, along with children's wear. The Egyptian Hall, on the ground floor, sells crystal from Lalique and Baccarat, plus porcelain. There's also a men's grooming room, an enormous jewelry department, and a fashion-forward department for younger customers. Along with the beauty of the bounty, check out the tiles and architectural touches. When you're ready for a break, you have a choice of 18 restaurants and bars. Best of all are the Food Halls, stocked with a huge variety of foods and several cafés. Harrods began as a grocer in 1849, and that's still the heart of the business.

In the basement you'll find a bank, a theater-booking service, and a travel bureau. Harrods Shop for logo gifts is on the ground floor.

Harvey Nichols. 109–125 Knightsbridge, SW1. ☎ **020/7235-5000.** Tube: Knightsbridge.

Locals call it Harvey Nicks. Once a favorite of the late Princess Di, the store is large, but doesn't compete with Harrods because it has a much more upmarket, fashionable image. Harvey Nicks has its own gourmet food hall and fancy restaurant, The Fifth Floor (see chapter 5), and a huge store crammed with the best designer home furnishings, gifts, and fashions for all, although women's clothing is the largest segment of its business. The store carries many American designer brands; avoid them, as they're more expensive in London.

Liberty. 214–220 Regent St., W1. ☎ **020/7734-1234.** Tube: Oxford Circus.

This major British department store is celebrated for its Liberty Prints, top-echelon, carriage-trade fabrics, often in floral patterns, that are prized by decorators for the way they add a sense of English tradition to a room. The front part of the store on Regent Street isn't particularly distinctive, but don't be fooled: Some parts of the place have been restored to Tudor-style splendor that includes half-timbering and lots of interior paneling. There are six floors of fashion, china, and home furnishings, as well as the famous Liberty Print fashion fabrics, upholstery fabrics, scarves, ties, luggage, and gifts.

Peter Jones. Sloane Sq., SW1. ☎ **020/7730-3434.** Tube: Sloane Sq.

Founded in 1877 and rebuilt in 1936, Peter Jones is known for household goods, household fabrics and trims, china, glass, soft furnishings, and linens. The linen department is one of the best in London.

4 Goods A to Z

ANTIQUES

Alfie's Antique Market. 13–25 Church St., NW8. ☎ **020/7723-6066.**
Tube: Marylebone or Edgware Rd.

This is the biggest and one of the best-stocked conglomerates of antiques dealers in London, all crammed into the premises of what was
built before 1880 as a department store. It has more than 370 stalls,
showrooms, and workshops scattered over 35,000 square feet of
floor space. You'll find the biggest Susie Cooper collection in
Europe here (Susie Cooper was a well-known designer of tableware
and ceramics for Wedgwood). A whole antique district has grown
up around Alfie's along Church Street.

Grays & Grays in the Mews. 58 Davies St., and 1–7 Davies Mews, W1.
☎ **020/7629-7034.** Tube: Bond St.

These antiques markets have been converted into walk-in stands
with independent dealers. The term "antique" here covers items
from oil paintings to, say, the 1894 edition of the *Encyclopaedia
Britannica.* Also sold here are exquisite antique jewelry; silver; gold;
maps and prints; bronzes and ivories; arms and armor; Victorian and
Edwardian toys; furniture; art-nouveau and art-deco items; antique
lace; scientific instruments; craft tools; and Asian, Persian, and Islamic pottery, porcelain, miniatures, and antiquities. There's a café
in each building. Check out the 1950s-style **Victory Café** on Davies
Street for the delectable homemade cakes.

ART & CRAFTS

ACAVA (☎ **020/7603-3039**) represents about 250 artists located
in West London. Call for individual open-studio schedules, as well
as dates for the annual Open Studios weekend.

Contemporary Applied Arts. 2 Percy St., W1. ☎ **020/7436-2344.** Tube:
Goodge St.

This association encourages both traditional and progressive contemporary artwork. Many of Britain's best-established craftspeople, as
well as lesser-known but promising talents, are represented in galleries that house a diverse retail display of glass, ceramics, textiles,
wood, furniture, jewelry, and metalwork—all by outstanding arti-
sans currently producing in the country, ranging in price from £12
to £10,000 ($19.80 to $16,500). A program of special exhibitions,
including solo and small-group shows, focuses on innovations in
craftwork. There are new exhibitions every 6 weeks.

Crafts Council Gallery. 44A Pentonville Rd., Islington, N1. ☎ **020/ 7278-7700.** Tube: Angel.

The largest crafts gallery is run by the Crafts Council, the national body for promoting contemporary crafts. You'll discover some of today's most creative work here. There's also a shop specializing in craft objects and publications, a picture library, a reference library, and a café. The gallery is closed on Mondays.

✪ **Whitechapel Art Gallery.** 80–82 Whitechapel High St., E1. ☎ **020/ 7522-7888** or 7878 (recorded). Tube: Aldgate East.

Since it opened its art-nouveau doors in 1901, savvy collectors have been heading to this East End gallery to find out what's hot and happening in the art world. It still maintains its cutting edge; to some, it's the incubation chamber for some of the most talented of East London's artists. The collections are fun, hip, often sexy, and definitely in your face.

BATH & BODY

The Body Shop. 375 Oxford St., W1. ☎ **020/7409-7868.** Tube: Bond St. Other locations throughout London.

There's a branch of The Body Shop in every trading area and tourist zone in London. Some stores are bigger than others, but all are filled with politically and environmentally correct beauty, bath, and aromatherapy products. Prices are drastically lower in the United Kingdom than they are in the United States. There's an entire children's line, a men's line, and lots of travel sizes and travel products. You won't have as much fun in a candy store.

Boots The Chemist. 72 Brompton Rd., SW3. ☎ **020/7589-6557.** Tube: Knightsbridge. Other locations throughout London.

This store has a million branches; we like the one across the street from Harrods for convenience and size. The house brands of beauty products are usually the best, be they Boots products (try the cucumber facial scrub), Boot's versions of The Body Shop (two lines, Global and Naturalistic), or Boot's versions of Chanel makeup (called No. 7). They also sell film, pantyhose (called tights), sandwiches, and all of life's little necessities.

✪ **Floris.** 89 Jermyn St., SW1. ☎ **020/7930-2885.** Tube: Piccadilly Circus.

A variety of toilet articles and fragrances fill Floris's floor-to-ceiling mahogany cabinets, which are architectural curiosities in their own right. They were installed relatively late in the establishment's history—that is, 1851—long after the shop had received its royal warrants as suppliers of toilet articles to the king and queen.

○ **Penhaligon's.** 41 Wellington St., WC2. ☎ **020/7836-2150,** or 800/ 588-1992 in the U.S. for mail order. Tube: Covent Garden.

This Victorian perfumery, established in 1870, holds royal warrants to HRH Duke of Edinburgh and HRH Prince of Wales. All items sold are exclusive to Penhaligon's. It offers a large selection of perfume, aftershave, soap, and bath oils for women and men. Gifts include antique-silver scent bottles, grooming accessories, and leather traveling requisites. Penhaligon's is now in more than 20 Saks Fifth Avenue stores across the United States.

BOOKS, MAPS, & ENGRAVINGS

In addition to the specialty bookstores listed below, you'll also find well-stocked branches of the **Dillon's** chain around town, including one at 82 Gower St. (Tube: Euston Square).

Children's Book Centre. 237 Kensington High St., W8. ☎ **020/7937-7497.** Tube: High St. Kensington.

With thousands of titles, this is the best place to go for children's books. Fiction is arranged according to age, up to 16. There are also videos and toys for kids.

Gay's The Word. 66 Marchmont St., WC1. ☎ **020/7278-7654.** Tube: Russell Sq.

Britain's leading gay and lesbian bookstore offers a large collection as well as a selection of magazines, cards, and guides. There's also a used-books section.

Murder One. 71–73 Charing Cross Rd., WC2. ☎ **020/7734-3483.** Tube: Leicester Sq.

Maxim Jakubowski's bookshop is dedicated to the genres of crime, romance, science fiction, and horror. Crime and science fiction magazines, some of them obscure, are also available.

Stanfords. 12–14 Long Acre, WC2. ☎ **020/7836-1321.** Tube: Leicester Sq. or Covent Garden.

Established in 1852, Stanfords is the world's largest map shop. Many of its maps, which include worldwide touring and survey maps, are unavailable elsewhere. It's also London's best travel bookstore (with a complete selection of Frommer's guides!).

W & G Foyle, Ltd. 113–119 Charing Cross Rd., WC2. ☎ **020/7439-8501.** Tube: Tottenham Court Rd.

Claiming to be the world's largest bookstore, W & G Foyle has an impressive array of hardcovers and paperbacks, as well as travel maps, records, videotapes, and sheet music.

CASHMERE & WOOLENS

London Store. Ritz Hotel, 150 Piccadilly, London W1. ☎ **020/7404-2606.** Tube: Green Park or Piccadilly Circus.

Here you'll find woolens from all over the British Islands, including the Scottish Shetlands. Some are handmade; many of the designers are well known. Some have a tweedy English look, while others are more high fashion.

Scotch House. 84–86 Regent St., W1. ☎ **020/7734-0203.** Tube: Piccadilly Circus.

For top-quality woolen fabrics and garments, go to Scotch House, renowned worldwide for its comprehensive selection of cashmere and wool knitwear for men, women, and children. Also available is a wide range of tartan garments and accessories, as well as Scottish tweed classics.

Westaway & Westaway. 64–65 and 92–93 Great Russell St. (opposite the British Museum), WC1. ☎ **020/7405-4479.** Tube: Tottenham Court Rd.

Stopping in here is a substitute for a shopping trip to Scotland. You'll find a large range of kilts, scarves, waistcoats, capes, dressing gowns, and rugs in authentic clan tartans. The staff is knowledgeable about the intricate clan symbols. They also sell cashmere, camelhair, and Shetland knitwear, plus Harris tweed jackets, Burberry raincoats, and cashmere overcoats for men.

CHINA, GLASS & SILVER

London Silver Vaults. Chancery House, 53–63 Chancery Lane, WC2. ☎ **020/7242-3844.** Tube: Chancery Lane.

Don't let the slightly out-of-the-way location, or the facade's lack of charm, slow you down. Downstairs, you go into real vaults—40 in all—that are filled with tons of silver and silverplate, plus a collection of jewelry. It's a staggering selection of old to new, with excellent prices and friendly dealers.

Reject China Shop. 183 Brompton Rd., SW3. ☎ **020/7581-0739.** Tube: Knightsbridge. Other locations throughout London.

Don't expect too many rejects or too many bargains, despite the name. This shop sells seconds (sometimes) along with first-quality pieces of china with such names as Royal Doulton, Spode, and Wedgwood. You also can find a variety of crystal, glassware, and flatware. If you'd like to have your purchases shipped home for you, the shop can do it for a fee.

Thomas Goode. 19 S. Audley St., W1. ☎ **020/7499-2823.** Tube: Bond St. or Green Park.

This is one of the most famous emporiums in Britain; it's worth visiting for its architectural interest and nostalgic allure alone. Originally built in 1876, Goode's has 14 rooms loaded with porcelain, gifts, candles, silver, tableware, and even a private museum. There's also a tearoom-cum-restaurant tucked into the corner.

FASHION

Austin Reed. 103–113 Regent St., W1. ☎ **020/7734-6789.** Tube: Piccadilly Circus.

Austin Reed has long stood for superior-quality clothing and excellent tailoring. The suits of Chester Barrie, for example, are said to fit like bespoke (custom-made) clothing. The polite employees are unusually honest about telling you what looks good. The store always has a wide variety of top-notch jackets and suits, and men can outfit themselves from dressing gowns to overcoats. For women, there are carefully selected suits, separates, coats, shirts, knitwear, and accessories.

✪ **Burberry.** 18–22 Haymarket, SW1. ☎ **020/7930-3343.** Tube: Piccadilly Circus.

The name has been synonymous with raincoats ever since Edward VII publicly ordered his valet to "bring my Burberry" when the skies threatened. An impeccably trained staff sells the famous raincoats, plus excellent men's shirts, sportswear, knitwear, and accessories. Raincoats are available in women's sizes and styles as well. Prices are high, but you get quality and prestige.

Dr. Marten's Department Store. 1–4 King St., WC2. ☎ **020/7497-1460.** Tube: Covent Garden.

Dr. Marten (called Doc Marten) makes a brand of shoe that has become so popular internationally that now there's an entire department store selling them in a huge variety of styles, plus accessories, gifts, and even an ever-expanding range of clothes. Teens come to worship here because ugly is beautiful, and because the prices are far better than they are in the United States or elsewhere in Europe.

Gieves & Hawkes. 1 Savile Row, W1. ☎ **020/7434-2001.** Tube: Piccadilly Circus or Green Park.

This place has a prestigious address and a list of clients that includes the Prince of Wales, yet its prices aren't as lethal as others on this street. They're high, but you get good quality. Cotton shirts, silk ties, Shetland sweaters, and exceptional ready-to-wear and tailor-made (bespoke) suits are sold.

Hilditch & Key. 37 and 73 Jermyn St., SW1. ☎ **020/7734-4707.** Tube: Piccadilly Circus or Green Park.

The finest name in men's shirts, Hilditch & Key has been in business since 1899. The two shops on this street both offer men's clothing (including a bespoke shirt service) and women's ready-made shirts. There's also an outstanding tie collection. Shirts go for half price during the twice-yearly sales; men fly in from all over the world for them.

Jigsaw. 21 Long Acre, WC2. ☎ **020/7240-3855.** Tube: Covent Garden. Also at 9–10 Floral St., WC2 (☎ **020/7240/5651**) and other locations throughout London.

Branches of this fashion chain are too numerous to mention here, but the Long Acre shop features safely trendy, middle-market womenswear and children's clothing. Around the corner, the Floral Street shop carries menswear, including a wide range of colored moleskin items.

✪ **Thomas Pink.** 85 Jermyn St., SW1. ☎ **020/7930-6364.** Tube: Green Park.

This Jermyn Street shirtmaker, named after an 18th-century Mayfair tailor, gave the world the phrases "hunting pink" and "in the pink." It has a prestigious reputation for well-made cotton shirts, for both men and women. The shirts are created from the finest two-fold Egyptian and Sea Island pure-cotton poplin. Some patterns are classic, others new and unusual. All are generously cut, with extra-long tails and finished with a choice of double cuffs or single-button cuffs. A small pink square in the tail tells all.

CUTTING-EDGE DESIGNERS

Anya Hindmarch. 91 Walton St., SW3. ☎ **020/7584-7644.** Tube: South Kensington.

Although her fashionable bags are sold at Harvey Nichols, Liberty, Harrods, and in the United States and Europe, this is the only place to see the complete range of Anya Hindmarch's designs. Featuring handbags, wash bags, wallets, purses, and key holders, smaller items range in price from £42 ($69.30) whereas handbag prices stretch from £150 ($247.50) and up, with alligator being the most expensive. There's a limited bespoke service, and you may bring in your fabric to be matched.

✪ **Browns.** 23–27 S. Molton St., W1. ☎ **020/7491-7833.** Tube: Bond St.

This is the only place in London to find the designs of Alexander McQueen, now head of the House of Givenchy in Paris, and one of the fashion industry's major stars. Producing his own cottons, silks, and plastics, McQueen creates revealing and feminine women's couture and ready-to-wear, and has recently started marketing a well-received menswear line. McQueen made his reputation creating shock-value apparel more eagerly photographed than worn. But recently his outfits have been called more "consumer friendly" by fashion critics. Browns have recently introduced "Browns Living" which is an eclectic array of lifestyle products.

Egg. 36 Kinnerton St., SW1. ☎ **020/7235-9315.** Tube: Hyde Park Corner or Knightsbridge.

This shop is hot, hot, hot with fashionistas. It features imaginatively designed, contemporary clothing by Indian textile designer Asha Sarabhai and knitwear by Eskandar. Designs created from handmade textiles from a workshop in India range from everyday dresses and coats to hand-embroidered silk coats. Prices begin at £60 ($96). Crafts and ceramics are also available. Closed Sunday and Monday.

Hennes. 261–271 Regent St., W1. ☎ **020/7493-4004.** Tube: Oxford Circus.

Here are copies of hot-off-the-catwalk fashions at affordable prices. While the quality isn't much to brag about, the prices are. For disposable cutting-edge fashion, you can't beat it.

Joseph. 23 Old Bond St., W1. ☎ **020/7629-3713.** Tube: Green Park. Also at 16 Sloane St., SW1 (☎ 020/7235-1991; Tube: Sloane Sq.); 26 Sloane St., SW1 (☎ 020/7235-5470; Tube: Sloane Sq.); and 77 Fulham Rd., SW3 (☎ 020/7823-9500; Tube: South Kensington).

Joseph Ettedgui, a fashion retailer born in Casablanca, is a maverick in the fashion world—he's known for his daring designs and his ability to attract some of the most talented designers in the business to work with him. This is the flagship store among five London branches, and it carries the Ettedgui collection of suits, knitwear, suede, and leather clothing for men and women. The stretch jeans with flair ankles are the label's best-selling items.

The 16 Sloane St. branch carries only the label's womenswear; the 26 Sloane St. shop displays all Joseph products and stocks the complete menswear line. The Fulham Road store showcases mens- and womenswear collections by other designers, including Prada, Gucci, Marni, Misoni, and Anne Deimunister.

Katharine Hamnett. 20 Sloane St., SW1. ☎ **020/7823-1002.** Tube: Knightsbridge.

One of Britain's big-name designers—her so-called slut dresses earned her the title of the bad girl of Brit fashion—Katharine

Hamnett is best known for her slogan T-shirts. Recent collections, although greeted with a media feeding frenzy, continue to receive mixed reviews. You can judge for yourself while browsing through her complete line of men's and women's day and evening wear. She's also a strong environmental activist and is known for using "nature friendly" fabrics.

✪ **Vivienne Westwood.** 6 Davies St., W1. ☎ **020/7629-3757.** Tube: Bond St. Branches: World's End, 430 King's Rd., SW3 (☎ 020/7352-6551; Tube: Sloane Sq.); and Vivienne Westwood, 44 Conduit St., W1 (☎ 020/7439-1109; Tube: Oxford Circus).

No one in British fashion is hotter than the unstoppable Vivienne Westwood. While it's possible to purchase select Westwood pieces around the world, her U.K. shops are the best places to find her full range of fashion designs. The flagship location concentrates on her couture line, or The Gold Label, as it's known. Using a wide range of uniquely British resources, Westwood creates jackets, skirts, trousers, blouses, dresses, and evening dresses. Her latest line features taffeta ballgowns, made-to-measure tailored shirts, even some Highland plaids. If all this weren't enough, she came out with her own perfume in 1997 (who hasn't?).

The World's End branch carries casual designs, including T-shirts, jeans, and other sportswear. The sale shop on Conduit Street has a bit of everything: The Gold Label; her second women's line, The Red Label; and The Man Label, her menswear collection. Accessories available include women's and men's shoes, belts, and jewelry.

VINTAGE & SECONDHAND

Note that there's no VAT refund on used clothing.

Annie's Vintage Costume and Textiles. 10 Camden Passage, N1. ☎ **020/7359-0796.** Tube: Angel.

The shop concentrates on carefully preserved dresses from the 1920s and 1930s, but has a range of clothing and textiles from the 1880s through the 1960s. A 1920s fully beaded dress will run you about £400 ($640), but there are scarves for £10 ($16.50), camisoles for £20 ($33), and a range of exceptional pieces priced between £50 and £60 ($82.50 and $99). Clothing is located on the main floor; textiles, including old lace, bed linens, and tapestries, are upstairs.

Pandora. 16 Cheval Place, SW7. ☎ **020/7589-5289.** Tube: Knightsbridge.

A London institution since the 1940s, Pandora stands in fashionable Knightsbridge, a stone's throw from Harrods. Several times a week, chauffeurs will drive up with bundles packed anonymously by

England's gentry. One woman voted best-dressed at Ascot several years ago was wearing a secondhand dress acquired here. Prices are generally one-third to one-half the retail value. Chanel and Anne Klein are among the designers represented. Outfits are usually no more than two seasons old.

FOOD

English food has come a long way lately; it's worth enjoying and bringing home. Don't pass up the Food Halls in Harrods; consider the Fifth Floor at Harvey Nicks if Harrods is crammed with too many tourists—it isn't the same, but it'll do. Also, **Fortnum & Mason** is internationally famous as a food emporium. See "The Department Stores," above.

Charbonnel et Walker. 1 The Royal Arcade, 28 Old Bond St., W1. ☎ **020/ 7491-0939.** Tube: Green Park.

Charbonnel et Walker is famous for its hot chocolate in winter (buy it by the tin) and their strawberries-and-cream chocolates during "The Season." The firm will send messages of thanks or love spelled out on the chocolates themselves. Ready-made presentation boxes are also available.

HOME DESIGN & HOUSEWARES

The Conran Shop. Michelin House, 81 Fulham Rd., SW3. ☎ **020/ 7589-7401.** Tube: South Kensington.

You'll find high style at reasonable prices from the man who invented it all for Britain: Sir Terance Conran. It's great for gifts, home furnishings, and table top—or just for gawking.

✪ **Designers Guild.** 267–271 and 275–277 King's Rd., SW3. ☎ **020/ 7351-5775.** Tube: Sloane Sq.

Often copied but never outdone—after more than 26 years in business, creative director Tricia Guild and her young designers still lead the pack in all that's bright and whimsical. There's an exclusive line of handmade furniture and accessories at the no. 267–271 location, and wallpaper and more than 2,000 fabrics at the neighboring no. 275–277 shop. The colors remain forever vivid, and the designs always irreverent. Also available are children's accessories, toys, crockery, and cutlery.

Irish Linen Company. 35–36 Burlington Arcade, W1. ☎ **020/7493-8949.** Tube: Green Park or Piccadilly Circus.

This royal-warrant boutique carries items crafted of Irish linen, including hand-embroidered handkerchiefs and bed and table linens.

Purves & Purves. 80–81 and 83 Tottenham Court Rd., W1. ☎ **020/ 7580-8223.** Tube: Tottenham Court Rd. or Goodge St.

This store has a varied collection of modern furniture from Britain and the Continent. Many pieces are individually made by the designers themselves. The light and airy interior holds an eye-catching display of furniture, lighting, fabrics, rugs, and beds. Two doors up is an accessory shop with everything from clocks to cufflinks.

JEWELRY

Asprey & Garrard. 167 New Bond St., W1. ☎ **020/7493-6767.** Tube: Green Park.

Previously known as Garrard & Co., this recently merged jeweler specializes in both antique and modern jewelry and silverware. The in-house designers also produce pieces to order and do repairs. You can have a pair of pearl earrings or silver cufflinks for a mere £60 ($99)—but the prices go nowhere but up from there.

Lesley Craze Gallery/Craze 2/C2 Plus. 33–35 Clerkenwell Green, EC1. ☎ **020/7608-0393** (Gallery), 020/7251-0381 (Craze 2), 020/7251-9200 (C2 Plus). Tube: Farringdon.

This complex has developed a reputation as a showcase of the best contemporary British jewelry and textile design. The gallery shop focuses on precious metals, and includes pieces by such renowned designers as Wendy Ramshaw. Prices start at £50 ($82.50). Craze 2 features costume jewelry in materials ranging from bronze to paper, with prices starting at £12 ($19.80). C2 Plus features contemporary textile designs, including wall hangings, scarves, and ties by artists such as Jo Barker, Dawn DuPree, and Victoria Richards. C2 Plus has recently added a hanging gallery to display their textiles and wall hangings. The store is now billing itself as "London's only contemporary textile gallery."

MUSEUM SHOPS

London Transport Museum Shop. Covent Garden, WC2. ☎ **020/ 7379-6344.** Tube: Covent Garden.

This museum shop carries a wide range of reasonably priced repro and antique travel posters as well as tons of fun gifts and souvenirs. Those great London Underground maps that you see at every Tube station can be purchased here.

Victoria & Albert Gift Shop. Cromwell Rd., SW7. ☎ **020/7938-8500.** Tube: South Kensington.

Run by the Craft Council, this is the best museum shop in London—indeed, one of the best in the world. It sells cards, a fabulous selection of art books, and the usual items, along with reproductions from the museum archives.

MUSIC

Collectors should browse Notting Hill; there's a handful of good shops near the Notting Hill Gate Tube stop. Also browse Soho in the Wardour Street area, near the Tottenham Court Road Tube stop. Sometimes dealers show up at Covent Garden on the weekends.

In addition to the two listed below, also worth checking out is the ubiquitous **Our Price** chain, which offers only the current chart-toppers, but usually at great prices.

Virgin Megastore. 14–16 Oxford St., W1. ☎ **020/7631-1234.** Tube: Tottenham Court Rd. Also at Kings Walk Shopping Centre, Kings Rd., Chelsea SW3 (☎ 020/7591-0957). Tube: Sloane Sq.

If a record has just been released—and if it's worth hearing in the first place—chances are this store carries it. It's like a giant musical grocery store, and you get to hear the release on headphones at listening stations before making a purchase. Even visiting rock stars come here to pick up new releases. A large selection of classical and jazz recordings is sold, as are computer software and video games. In between selecting your favorites, you can enjoy a coffee at the café, or purchase an airline ticket from the Virgin Atlantic office.

SHOES

Also see **Dr. Marten's Department Store** in "Fashion," above.

Church's. 1–4 King St., WC2. ☎ **020/7497-1460.** Tube: Covent Garden.

Well-made shoes, the status symbol of well-heeled executives in financial districts around the world, have been turned out by Church's since 1873. These are said to be recognizable to all the maîtres d'hôtel in London, who have always been suspected of appraising the wealth of their clients by their footwear.

Shelly's. 266–270 Regent St., W1. ☎ **020/7287-0939.** Tube: Oxford Circus. Other locations throughout London.

Warning

Americans should beware of buying videotapes in the United Kingdom; the British standard is PAL, which is incompatible with the U.S. standard NTSC. Even if a tape says VHS, it won't play in your machine at home.

This is the flagship of the mother of all London shoe shops, where they sell everything from tiny-tot hip shoes to grown-up hip shoes and boots at affordable prices. They're famous for their Dr. Martens, but there's much more—and none of it traditional.

TEA

Of course, don't forget to visit Fortnum & Mason as well (see "The Department Stores," above).

The Tea House. 15 Neal St., WC2. ☎ **020/7240-7539.** Tube: Covent Garden.

This shop sells everything associated with tea, tea drinking, and tea-time. It boasts more than 70 quality teas and tisanes, including whole-fruit blends, the best tea of China (Gunpowder, jasmine with flowers), India (Assam leaf, choice Darjeeling), Japan (Genmaicha green), and Sri Lanka (pure Ceylon), plus such longtime favorite English blended teas as Earl Grey. The shop also offers novelty tea-pots and mugs, among other items.

TOYS

✪ **Hamleys.** 188–196 Regent St., W1. ☎ **020/7494-2000.** Tube: Oxford Circus. Also at Covent Garden and Heathrow Airport.

This flagship is the finest toy shop in the world—more than 35,000 toys and games on seven floors of fun and magic. The huge selection includes soft, cuddly stuffed animals as well as dolls, radio-controlled cars, train sets, model kits, board games, outdoor toys, and computer games.

8

London After Dark

*L*ondon's pulsating scene is the most vibrant in Europe. Although pubs still close at 11pm, the city is staying up later. More and more clubs extend partying into the wee hours. London nightlife, of course, abounds with the world's best live theater scene, as well as classical music and dance.

London is on a real high right now in terms of pop culture. Much of the current techno and electronica (including the hip-hop, tribal, and drum-and-bass styles that aging rockers like Bowie and U2 have appropriated) originated in London clubs. Sounds made hip by Tricky and Aphex Twin reverberate not only throughout the city, but across the Continent and the Atlantic as well. Youth culture prevails; downtown denizens flock to the latest clubs where pop-culture superstars are routinely spotted.

HOW TO FIND OUT WHAT'S GOING ON   Weekly publications such as *Time Out and Where* provide the most complete up-to-the-minute entertainment listings. They contain information on live music and dance clubs as well as London's diverse theater scene, which includes everything from big-budget West End shows to fringe productions. Daily newspapers, notably *The Times* and the *Daily Telegraph*, also provide listings. The arts section of the weekend *Independent* is also a good reference.

If you really want to take full advantage of London's arts scene, your best bet is to do a bit of research before you leave home—even a few months in advance. To get a good idea of what's going on, check out ***Time Out*'s World Wide Web page** at **www.timeout.co.uk**. If you're not online, *Time Out* is available at many international newsstands in the United States and Canada. In London, it can be picked up almost anywhere.

1   The Play's the Thing: The London Theater

London is the theater capital of the world; the number and variety of productions, as well as high standards of acting and directing, are unrivaled. The London stage accommodates both the traditional and the avant-garde and is uniquely accessible and affordable.

GETTING TICKETS   Prices for London shows usually vary from £18 to £60 ($29.70 to $99), depending on the theater and the seat. Matinees, performed Tuesday to Saturday, are cheaper than evening performances, but London theater tickets are no longer the bargain they used to be.

Evening performances begin between 7:30 and 8:30pm, midweek matinees at 2:30 or 3pm, and Saturday matinees at 5:45pm. West End theaters are closed Sundays. Many theaters offer the bonus of licensed bars on the premises and coffee at intermissions (which Londoners call "intervals").

Many theaters accept telephone bookings at regular prices with a credit card. They'll hold your tickets for you at the box office, where you pick them up at show time with a credit card.

TICKET AGENCIES   If you want to see one of the big hits, you'll have to reserve through one of the many London ticket agencies. For tickets and information before you go, try **Edwards & Edwards,** 1270 Ave. of the Americas, Suite 2414, New York, NY 10020 (☎ 800/223-6108 or 914/328-2150; fax 914/328-2752). Their offices in London are at the **Palace Theatre,** Shaftesbury Avenue, W1 8AY (☎ 020/7734-4555) or at the **Harrods** ticket desk, 87–135 Brompton Rd. (☎ 020/7589-9109), located on the lower-ground floor opposite the British Airways desk. A booking and handling fee of up to 20% is added to the ticket price.

You might also try calling **Keith Prowse/First Call** (☎ 0129/343-3600). This agency's office in the United States is at: Suite 1000, 234 W. 44th St., New York, NY 10036 (☎ 800/669-8687 or 212/398-1430). Various locations exist in London. The fee for booking a ticket is 20% in London and 35% in the United States. **Theatre Direct International (TDI)** (☎ 800/334-8457, U.S.

Warning

Beware of unlicensed ticket agencies in London. You could end up paying £28 ($46.20) for a ticket worth only £16 ($26.40). The **Society of London Theatre** (☎ 020/7557-6700) reports that it receives complaints of overcharging on a frequent basis. The society advises that you book your ticket at the theater box office by telephone or in person. Beware also of **scalpers** who hang out in front of hit shows at London theaters. Even if the tickets they're selling are valid—there are many reports of forged tickets—scalpers charge very high prices.

only), specializes in providing London theater and fringe production tickets, but also has tickets to the Royal National Theatre and the Barbican.

GALLERY & DISCOUNT TICKETS   Sometimes gallery seats (the cheapest) are sold only on the day of the performance; you'll need to head to the box office early in the day and, since these are not reserved seats, return an hour before the performance to queue up. Many major theaters offer reduced-price tickets to students on a standby basis. When available, they are sold 30 minutes prior to curtain—of course, you'll need a valid student ID.

The **Society of London Theatre** (☎ **020/7557-6700**) operates a **discount ticket booth** in Leicester Square, where tickets for many shows are sold at half price, plus a £2 ($3.30) service charge, for cash only, and only on the day of performance.

MAJOR THEATERS & COMPANIES

Barbican Theatre—Royal Shakespeare Company. In the Barbican Centre, Silk St., Barbican, EC2. ☎ **020/7638-8891.** Barbican Theatre £5–£26 ($8.25–$42.90). The Pit £11–£18.50 ($18.15–$30.55) matinees and evening performances. Box office daily 9am–8pm. Tube: Barbican or Moorgate.

The Barbican is the London home of the Royal Shakespeare Company, one of the world's finest theater companies. The core of its repertoire remains, of course, the plays of William Shakespeare. It also presents a wide-ranging program in its two theaters. There are three productions in repertory each week in the Barbican Theatre— a 2,000-seat main auditorium with excellent sight lines throughout, thanks to a raked orchestra. The Pit, a small studio space, is where the company's new writing is presented. The Royal Shakespeare Company performs both here and at Stratford-upon-Avon. It is in residence in London during the winter months; in the summer, it tours in England and abroad.

Open-Air Theatre. Inner Circle, Regent's Park, NW1. ☎ **020/7486-2431.** Tickets £8–£21 ($13.20–$34.65). Tube: Baker St.

False Discounts

Many less-than-scrupulous agents near Leicester Square offer "discounted" tickets that are nothing of the kind. Out-of-towners could pay $30 to $35 for a "discount" ticket only to find them available at the box office for $25.

This outdoor theater is in Regent's Park; the setting is idyllic, and both seating and acoustics are excellent. Presentations are mainly of Shakespeare, usually in period costume. Its theater bar, the longest in London, serves both drink and food. In the case of a rained-out performance, tickets are given for another date. The season runs from the end of May to mid-September, Monday to Saturday at 8pm, plus Wednesday, Thursday, and Saturday matinees at 2:30pm.

Royal Court Theatre. Sloane Square, SW1. ☎ **020/7565-5000.** Tube: Sloane Sq.

This theater, always a leader in producing provocative, cutting-edge new drama, was still closed at press time, with opening slated for the autumn of 1999. In the 1950s, it staged the plays of the angry young men, notably John Osborne's then-sensational *Look Back in Anger;* earlier it debuted the plays of George Bernard Shaw. A recent work was *The Beauty Queen of Leenane,* which won a Tony on Broadway. The theater is home to the English Stage Company, formed to promote serious stage writing. Tickets generally range in price from £5 to £19.50 ($8.25–$32.20); call for the latest information.

✪ **Royal National Theatre.** South Bank, SE1. ☎ **020/7452-3400.** Tickets £9–£27 ($14.85–$44.55); midweek matinees, Sat matinees, and previews cost less. Tube: Waterloo, Embankment, or Charing Cross.

Home to one of the world's greatest stage companies, the Royal National Theatre is not one but three theaters—the Olivier, reminiscent of a Greek amphitheater with its open stage; the more traditional Lyttelton; and the Cottesloe, with its flexible stage and seating. The National presents the finest in world theater, from classic drama to award-winning new plays, including comedies, musicals, and shows for young people. There is a choice of at least six plays at any one time. It's also a full-time theater center, with an amazing selection of bars, cafés, restaurants, free foyer music and exhibitions, short early-evening performances, bookshops, backstage tours, riverside walks, and terraces. You can have a three-course meal in Mezzanine, the National's restaurant; enjoy a light meal in the brasserie-style Terrace café; or have a snack in one of the coffee bars.

Shakespeare's Globe Theatre. New Globe Walk, Bankside, SE1. ☎ **020/7902-1500.** Box office: 020/7401-9919. Tickets £5 ($8.25) for groundlings, £5–£25 ($8.25–$41.25) for gallery seats. Tube: Mansion House.

Productions in this replica of the Elizabethan original, vary in style and setting; not all are performed in Elizabethan costume. In keeping with the historic setting, there's no lighting focused just on the stage, but floodlighting is used during evening performances to replicate daylight in the theater—Elizabethan performances took place in the afternoon. Theatergoers sit on wooden benches of yore—in thatch-roofed galleries, no less—but these days you can rent a cushion to make yourself more comfortable. About 500 "groundlings" can stand in the uncovered yard around the stage, just as they did when the Bard was here.

From May to September, performances are Tuesday to Saturday at 3pm and 7pm, and Sunday at 4pm. There is a limited winter schedule. In any season, the schedule may be affected by the weather, since this is an outdoor theater. Performances last $2^{1}/_{2}$ to 4 hours, depending on the play.

Also in the works is a second theater, the **Inigo Jones Theatre,** based on the architect's designs from the 1600s, where plays will be staged year round. For details on the exhibition that tells the story of the painstaking re-creation of the Globe, as well as guided tours of the theatre, see "More Central London Attractions" in chapter 5.

Theatre Royal Drury Lane. Catherine St., Covent Garden, WC2. ☎ **020/7494-5060.** Tickets £8–£35 ($13.20–$57.75). Box office Mon–Sat 10am–8pm. Evening performances Mon–Sat 7:45pm; matinees Wed and Sat 3pm. Tube: Covent Garden.

Drury Lane is one of London's oldest and most prestigious theaters, crammed with tradition—not all of it respectable. This, the fourth theater on this site, dates from 1812; the first was built in 1663. Nell Gwynne, the rough-tongued cockney lass who became Charles II's mistress, used to sell oranges under the long colonnade in front. Nearly every star of London theater has taken the stage here at some time. It has a wide-open repertoire but leans toward musicals, especially long-running hits. Guided tours of the backstage area and the front of the house are given most days at 10:30am and 12:30pm. Call ☎ **020/7494-5091** for more information.

2 London's Classical Music & Dance Scene

Currently, London supports five major orchestras—the **London Symphony,** the **Royal Philharmonic,** the **Philharmonia Orchestra,** the **BBC Symphony,** and the **BBC Philharmonic**—several choirs, and many smaller chamber groups and historic-instrument ensembles. Look for the **London Sinfonietta,** the **English Chamber Orchestra,** and of course the **Academy of St. Martin in the Fields.** Performances are in the South Banks Arts Centre and the Barbican. For smaller recitals, there's Wigmore Hall and St. John's Smith Square.

British Music Information Centre, 10 Stratford Place, W1 (☎ **020/7499-8567**), is the city's clearinghouse and resource center for serious music. The center is open Monday to Friday noon to 5pm, and provides free telephone and walk-in information on current and upcoming events. Recitals featuring 20th-century British classical compositions cost up to £5 ($8.25) and are offered here weekly, usually on Tuesday and Thursday at 7:30pm; call ahead for day and time. Since capacity is limited to 40, you may want to check early. Take the tube to Bond Street.

✪ **Barbican Centre—London Symphony Orchestra (& more).** Silk St., the City, EC2. ☎ **020/7638-8891.** Tickets £6.50–£32 ($10.75–$52.80). Box office daily 9am–8pm. Tube: Barbican or Moorgate.

The largest art and exhibition center in Western Europe, the roomy and comfortable Barbican complex is a perfect setting for enjoying music and theater. Barbican Hall is the permanent home address of the **London Symphony Orchestra** as well as host to visiting orchestras and performers, from classical to jazz, folk, and world music.

In addition to the hall and the two theaters of the Royal Shakespeare Company, Barbican Centre includes: The Barbican Art Gallery, a showcase for visual arts; the Concourse Gallery and foyer exhibition spaces; Cinemas One and Two, which show recently released mainstream films and film series; the Barbican Library, a general lending library that places a strong emphasis on the arts; the Conservatory, one of London's largest plant houses; and restaurants, cafés, and bars.

English National Opera. London Coliseum, St. Martin's Lane, WC2. ☎ **020/7632-8300.** Tickets £5–£10 ($8.25–$16.50) balcony, £12.50–£55 ($20.65–$90.75) upper or dress circle or stalls; about 100 discount balcony tickets sold on the day of performance from 10am. Tube: Charing Cross or Leicester Sq.

Built in 1904 as a variety theater and converted into an opera house in 1968, the London Coliseum is the city's largest theater. One of two national opera companies, the English National Opera performs a wide range of works from classics to Gilbert and Sullivan to new and experimental works, staged with flair and imagination. All performances are in English. A repertory of 18 to 20 productions is presented 5 or 6 nights a week for 11 months of the year (dark in July). Although balcony seats are cheaper, many visitors seem to prefer the upper circle or dress circle.

Royal Albert Hall. Kensington Gore, SW7. ☎ **020/7589-8212.** Tickets £3–£130 ($4.95–$214.50), depending on the event. Box office daily 9am–9pm. Tube: South Kensington.

Opened in 1871 and dedicated to the memory of Victoria's consort, Prince Albert, the circular building holds one of the world's most famous auditoriums. With a seating capacity of 5,200, it's a popular place to hear music by stars like Eric Clapton and Shirley Bassey.

The hall has been the setting for the BBC Henry Wood Promenade Concerts, known as **"The Proms,"** a concert series that lasts for 8 weeks between mid-July and mid-September. The Proms have been a British tradition since 1895—the final evening is the most traditional when rousing favorites like "Jerusalem" or "Land of Hope and Glory" echo through the hall. For tickets, call Ticketmaster (☎ **020/7344-4444**) directly.

✪ **Royal Festival Hall.** On the South Bank, SE1. ☎ **020/7960-4242.** Tickets £5–£50 ($8.25–$82.50). Box office daily 9am–9pm. Tube: Waterloo or Embankment.

Three of the most acoustically perfect concert halls in the world are here. They include Royal Festival Hall, the Queen Elizabeth Hall, and the Purcell Room. Together they hold more than 1,200 performances a year, including classical music, ballet, jazz, popular music, and contemporary dance. The Royal Festival Hall, which opens daily at 10am, in addition to concerts, offers free lunchtime music at 12:30pm. On Friday, Commuter Jazz in the foyer from 5:15 to 6:45pm is free. The Poetry Library is open from 11am to 8pm. The Festival Buffet has food at reasonable prices, and the People's Palace offers lunch and dinner with a panoramic view of the River Thames. Reservations by calling ☎ **020/7928-9999** are recommended.

✪ **The Royal Opera House—The Royal Ballet & the Royal Opera.** Bow St., Covent Garden, WC2. Closed for redevelopment. For information on Royal Opera and Royal Ballet performances, in other venues, call ☎ **020/ 7212-9123.**

The two world-famous companies, the Royal Opera and the great Royal Ballet were temporarily dislodged from the Royal Opera House, their Covent Garden home, because of its ongoing renovation, but they'll be back on their home stage in the autumn of 1999. In the meantime, they will be appearing at a number of venues around London. Performances of the Royal Opera are usually sung in the original language, but supertitles are projected, translating the libretto for the audience. The Royal Ballet, that ranks with top companies such as the Kirov and the Paris Opera Ballet, performs a repertory with a tilt toward the classics, including works by its earlier choreographer-directors Sir Frederick Ashton and Sir Kenneth MacMillan.

3   The Club, Music & Bar Scene

It's the nature of live music and dance clubs to come and go with alarming speed, or shift violently from one trend to another. *Time Out* is the best way to keep current.

LIVE MUSIC

Bagley's Studios. King's Cross Freigh Depot, off York Way, N1. ☎ **020/7278-2777**. Cover £10–£20 ($16.50–$33). Guaranteed openings Fri–Sun 10pm–7am. Otherwise, openings depend on whatever promoter wants to book the space. Tube: King's Cross.

The premises of this place are vast, echoing, a bit grimy, and warehouse-like. Set in the bleak industrial landscapes behind King's Cross Station, its interior is radically transformed three nights a week into an animated rave event. Its two floors, each the size of an American football field, are divided into trios of individual rooms, with their own ambience and sound system. You'll be happiest here if you wander from room to room, searching out the site that best corresponds to your energy level at the moment. Choices will probably include sites devoted to garage, club classics as promoted by AM/FM radio, "banging" (hard house) music, and "bubbly" upbeat dance music. If you happen to be in London on a weeknight, don't assume that the place will be dark, as various social groups, including lots of East Indian social clubs, rent the place for gatherings, some of which might be open to the public. Saturday night "Freedom" parties are more fun.

The Rock Garden. 6–7 The Piazza, Covent Garden, WC2. ☎ **020/7836-4052**. Cover £5–£10 ($8.25–$16.50); diners enter free. Mon–Thurs 5pm–3am, Fri and Sat 5pm–4am, Sun 7pm–midnight. Bus: Any of the night buses that depart from Trafalgar Square. Tube: Covent Garden.

A long-established performance site, The Rock Garden maintains a bar and a stage in the cellar, and a restaurant on the street level. The cellar, known as The Venue, has hosted such acts as Dire Straits, Police, and U2 before their rises to stardom. Today bands vary widely, from promising up-and-comers to some who'll never be heard from again. Simple American-style fare is served in the restaurant.

Wag Club. 35 Wardour St., W1. ☎ **020/7437-5534.** Cover £5–£10 ($8.25–$16.50). Tues–Thurs 10pm–3am, Fri 10pm–4am, Sat 10pm–5am, Sun closed. No credit cards. Tube: Leicester Sq. or Piccadilly Circus.

The split-level Wag Club is one of the more stylish live-music places in town. The downstairs stage usually attracts newly signed, cutting-edge rock bands, while a DJ spins dance records upstairs. Door policy can be selective.

JAZZ & BLUES

Ain't Nothing But Blues Bar. 20 Kingly St., W1. ☎ **020/7287-0514.** Cover Fri £3–£5 ($4.95–$8.25); Sat £3–£5 ($5–$8); free before 9:30pm. Mon–Thurs 5:30–1am, Fri–Sat 6pm–3am, Sun 6pm–midnight. Tube: Oxford Circus or Piccadilly Circus.

The club, which bills itself as the only true blues venue in town, features local acts and occasional touring American bands. On weekends prepare to queue. From the Oxford Circus Tube stop, walk south on Regent Street, turn left on Great Marlborough Street, and then make a quick right on Kingly Street.

100 Club. 100 Oxford St., W1. ☎ **020/7636-0933.** Cover Fri £8 ($13.20) members and non-members, Sat £8 ($13.20) members, £9 ($14.85) non-members, Sun £6 ($9.90) members and non-members. Mon–Fri 8:30pm–3am, Sat 7:30pm–1am, Sun 7:30–11:30pm. Tube: Tottenham Court Rd. or Oxford Circus.

Although less plush and expensive than some jazz clubs, 100 Club is a serious contender. Its cavalcade of bands includes the best British jazz musicians and some of their Yankee brethren. Rock, R&B, and blues are also on tap.

✪ **Pizza Express.** 10 Dean St., W1. ☎ **020/7439-8722.** Cover £8.50–£20 ($14–$33). Daily 7:45pm–midnight. Tube: Tottenham Court Rd.

Don't let the name fool you: This restaurant-bar serves up some of the best jazz in London by mainstream artists. While enjoying a thin-crust Italian pizza, check out a local band or a visiting group, often from the United States. Although the club has been enlarged, it's important to reserve ahead of time.

✪ **Ronnie Scott's Club.** 47 Frith St., W1. ☎ **020/7439-0747.** Cover non-member £15–£20 ($24.75–$33), member £4–£8 ($6.60–$13.20). Mon–Sat 8:30pm–3am. Tube: Leicester Sq. or Piccadilly Circus.

Inquire about jazz in London and people immediately think of Ronnie Scott's, long the European vanguard for modern jazz. Only the best English and American combos, often fronted by a top-notch vocalist, are booked here. The programs inevitably make for an entire evening of cool jazz. In the heart of Soho, Ronnie Scott's is a 10-minute walk from Piccadilly Circus along Shaftesbury Avenue.

DANCE, DISCO & ECLECTIC

Bar Rumba. 26 Shaftesbury Ave., W1. ☎ **020/7287-2715.** Cover £3–£12 ($4.95–$19.80). Mon–Thurs 5pm–3:30am, Fri 5pm–4am, Sat 6pm–6am, Sun 8pm–1:30am. Tube: Piccadilly Circus.

Despite its location on Shaftesbury Avenue, this Latin bar and club could be featured in a book of "Underground London." A hush-hush address, it leans toward radical jazz fusion on some nights, phat funk on other occasions. Boasting two full bars and a different musical theme every night, Tuesday and Wednesday are the only nights you probably won't have to queue at the door. Monday's "That's How It Is" showcase features jazz, hip hop, and drum and bass; Friday's "KAT Klub" grooves with soul, R&B, and swing; and Saturday's "Garage City" buzzes with house and garage. On weeknights you have to be 18 and up; the age limit is 21 on Saturday and Sunday.

The Cross. The Arches, Kings Cross Goods Yard, York Way, N1. ☎ **020/7837-0828.** Cover £10–£15 ($16.50–$24.75). Fri 10pm–4:30am, Sat 10:30pm–6am. Tube: Kings Cross.

In the backwaters of Kings Cross, this club has stayed hot since 1993. London hipsters come here for private parties thrown by Rough Trade Records or Red Or Dead, or just to dance in the space's cozy brick-lined vaults. It's always party time here. Call to find out who's performing.

Diva. 43 Thurloe St., SW7. ☎ **020/7584-2000.** Cover £1.50 ($2.45). Mon–Sat 6pm–3am, July–Sept also Sun noon–3pm. Tube: South Kensington.

Diva combines a first-class Italian restaurant with a dance club. So get down with your manicotti! Meals, from £25 to £30 ($41.25 to $49.50) per head, are mostly Neapolitan-inspired. Only restaurant patrons are allowed into the disco (where recorded music is played).

Equinox. Leicester Sq., WC2. ☎ **020/7437-1446.** Cover £5–£12 ($8.25–$19.80), depending on the night of the week. Mon–Thurs 9pm–3am, Fri–Sat 9pm–4am. Tube: Leicester Sq.

The Equinox has established itself as a perennial favorite. It contains nine bars, the largest dance floor in London, and a restaurant modeled after a 1950s American diner. With the exception of rave, virtually every kind of dance music is featured here, including dance hall, pop, rock, and Latin. The setting is lavishly illuminated with one of Europe's largest lighting rigs, and the crowd is as varied as London itself. Equinox has been quite busy lately, hosting some of the U.K.'s hottest talents. Theme nights are geared to entertaining a worldwide audience, including a once a month "Ibiza" foam party—you'll actually boogie the night away on a foam covered floor. Happy hour drinks are £1.50 ($2.45) from 5 to 7pm.

Hippodrome. Corner of Cranbourn St. and Charing Cross Rd., WC2. ☎ **020/ 7437-4311.** Cover £4–£12 ($6.60–$19.80). Mon–Sat 9pm–3am. Tube: Leicester Sq.

Located near Leicester Square, the popular Hippodrome is London's grand old daddy of discos, a cavernous place with a great sound system and lights to match. It was Lady Di's favorite scene in her bar-hopping days. Tacky and touristy, the 'drome is packed on weekends.

Iceni. 11 White Horse St., W1. ☎ **020/7495-5333.** Cover Fri £12 ($19.80), Sat £10 ($16.50). Fri–Sat 10pm–3:30am. Tube: Queen's Park.

Attracting an older 20-something crowd on Fridays, and 18-to-25ers on Saturdays, this funky three-story nightclub features films, board games, tarot readings, and dancing to swing, soul, hip hop, and R&B. You can even get a manicure.

Limelight. 136 Shaftesbury Ave., WC2. ☎ **020/7434-0572.** Cover £6 ($9.90) before 10pm, £4–£12 ($6.60–$19.80) thereafter. Mon–Fri 10pm–3am (3:30am Fri); Sat 9pm–3:30am; Sun 6–11pm. Tube: Leicester Sq.

Although opened in 1985, this large dance club—located inside a former Welsh chapel that dates to 1754—has only recently come into its own. The dance floors and bars share space with plenty of cool Gothic nooks and crannies. DJs spin the latest house music.

✪ **Ministry of Sound.** 103 Gaunt St., SE1. ☎ **020/7378-6528.** Cover £12– £15 ($19.80–$24.75). Fri 10:30pm–6am, Sat midnight–9am. Tube: Elephant & Castle.

Removed from the city center, this club-of-the-hour is still going strong after all these years. It remains hot, hot, hot. With a large bar and an even bigger sound system, it blasts garage and house music to energetic crowds that pack the two dance floors. If the stimulants in the rest of the club have gone to your head, you can chill in the cinema room. Note: The club's cover charge is stiff, and bouncers decide who is cool enough to enter, so leave the sneakers and denim at home and slip into your grooviest and most glamorous club wear.

The Velvet Room (formerly The Velvet Underground). 143 Charing Cross Rd., WC2. ☎ **020/7734-4687.** Cover £6–£10 ($9.90–$16.50). Wed–Thurs 9pm–3am, Fri–Sat 9pm–4am. Tube: Tottenham Court Rd.

The Velvet Underground was a London staple for years. Times changed and the clientele grew up—hence The Velvet Room, a more mature setting that is luxurious but not stuffy. DJs Carl Cox and others spin favorite dance hits—more laid back to better represent the new theme. The Velvet Room hasn't sacrificed a shred of cool, and still sets a standard for the next generation of Soho bar life.

○ **Zoo Bar.** 13–18 Bear St., WC2. ☎ **020/7839-4188.** Cover £3–£5 ($4.95–$8.25) after 11pm. Mon–Sat 4pm–3:30am; Sun 4–10:30pm. Tube: Leicester Sq.

The owners spent millions of pounds outfitting this club in the slickest, flashiest, and most psychedelic decor in London. If you're looking for a true Euro nightlife experience replete with gorgeous *au pairs* and trendy Europeans, this is it. Zoo Bar upstairs is a menagerie of mosaic animals beneath a glassed-in ceiling dome. Downstairs, the music is intrusive enough to make conversation futile. Clients range from 18 to 35; androgyny is the look of choice.

LATIN RHYTHMS

Cuba. 11 Kensington High St., W8. ☎ **020/7938-4137.** Cover £2–£7 ($3.30–$11.55). Mon–Sat noon–2am, Sun 2–11pm. Tube: High St. Kensington.

This Spanish/Cuban–style bar-restaurant, which has a music club downstairs, features live music acts from Cuba, Brazil, Spain, and the rest of Latin America. Odd as it may seem, the crowd is equal parts restaurant diners, after-work drinkers, Latinophiles, and dancers. Salsa dance classes are offered Monday, Tuesday, and Wednesday from 8:30 to 9:30pm. Classes cost £4 ($6.60) Monday or £5 ($8.25) Tuesday and Wednesday. Happy hour is Monday to Saturday, noon to 8:30pm.

BARS

American Bar. In The Savoy, The Strand, WC2. ☎ **020/7836-4343.** Smart casual—no jeans, sneakers, T-shirts. Tube: Charing Cross, Covent Garden, or Embankment.

The bartender in this sophisticated gathering place is known for his special concoctions, "Savoy Affair" and "Prince of Wales," as well as what is reputedly the best martini in town. Monday to Saturday evenings, jazz piano is featured from 7 to 11pm. Near many West End theaters, the location is ideal for a pre- or post-theater drink.

Beach Blanket Babylon. 45 Ledbury Rd., W11. ☎ **020/7229-2907.** No cover. Tube: Notting Hill Gate.

Go here if you're looking for a hot singles bar that attracts a crowd in their 20s and 30s. This Portobello joint—named after a kitschy musical revue in San Francisco—is very cruisy. The decor is a bit wacky, no doubt designed by an aspiring Salvador Dalí, who decided to make it a fairy-tale grotto (or did he mean a medieval dungeon?). It's close to the Portobello Market. Saturday and Sunday nights are the hot, crowded times to show up for bacchanalian revelry.

The Library. In the Lanesborough Hotel, 1 Lanesborough Place, SW1. ☎ **020/7259-5599.** Tube: Hyde Park Corner.

For one of London's poshest drinking retreats, head for this deluxe hotel with its high ceilings, leather chesterfields, respectable oil paintings, and grand windows. Its collection of ancient cognacs is unparalleled in London.

4 The Gay & Lesbian Scene

The most reliable source of information on gay clubs and activities is the **Lesbian and Gay Switchboard** (☎ 020/7837-7324). The staff runs a 24-hour service for information on gay-friendly places and activities. *Time Out* also carries listings on such clubs. Also a good place for finding out what's hot and hip is **Prowler Soho,** 3–7 Brewer St. Soho W1 (☎ 020/7734-4031; Tube: Piccadilly Circus), the largest gay lifestyle store in London. (You can also buy anything from jewelry to CDs and books, fashion and sex toys.) It's open till midnight on Friday and Saturday.

The Box. 32–34 Monmouth St. (at Seven Dials), WC2. ☎ **020/7240-5828.** Daily 10am–11:30pm. Tube: Covent Garden.

Adjacent to one of Covent Garden's best-known junctions, Seven Dials, this sophisticated Mediterranean-style bar attracts more lesbians than many of its competitors. In the afternoon, it is primarily a restaurant, serving meal-size salads, club sandwiches, and soups. Food service ends abruptly at 5:30pm, after which the place reveals its core: a cheerful, popular place of rendezvous for London's gay and countercultural crowds. The Box considers itself a "summer bar," throwing open doors and windows to a cluster of outdoor tables that attracts a crowd at the slightest hint of sunshine.

Candy Bar. 4 Carlisle St., W1. ☎ **020/7494-4041.** Cover £2–£5 ($3.30–$8.25). Mon–Thurs 5pm–midnight, Fri 5pm–2am, Sat 2pm–2am, Sun 5pm–11pm. Tube: Tottenham Court Rd.

This is the most popular lesbian bar in London at the moment. It has an extremely mixed clientele from butch to fem and from young to old. There is a bar and a club downstairs. Design is simple with bright colors and lots of mirrors upstairs and darker and more flirtatious downstairs. Men are welcome as long as they are escorted by a woman.

The Complex. 1–5 Parkfield St., Islington, M1. ☎ **020/7738-2336.** Cover £8 ($13.20). Fri 10pm–4am. Tube: Angel.

On Fridays, this four-floor club is the site of Pop Starz, which has become one of the most popular nights in London. It offers a mix of indie, British pop, 1980s trash, and funk. Originally started as an alternative to the generic gay muscle boy dance parties, the once-weekly night has attracted a very mixed and loyal following.

Heaven. The Arches, Villiers and Craven Sts., WC2. ☎ **020/7930-2020.** Cover £3–£10 ($4.95–$16.50). Tube: Charing Cross or Embankment.

This club in the vaulted cellars of Charing Cross Railway Station is a London landmark. Owned by the same investors who brought the world Virgin Atlantic Airways, Heaven is one of the biggest and best-established gay venues in Britain. Painted black, and reminiscent of an air-raid shelter, the club is divided into at least four distinct areas connected by a labyrinth of catwalk stairs and hallways. Each area has a different activity going on. Heaven also has theme nights, which depending on the night are frequented by gays, lesbians, or a mostly heterosexual crowd. Thursday in particular seems open to anything, but on Saturday it's gay only. Call before you go.

Index

See also separate Accommodations, Restaurants, and Afternoon Tea indexes, below.

AFTERNOON TEA